TOUGH FRONTS

The *Critical Social Thought* Series
edited by Michael W. Apple, University of Wisconsin—Madison

TOUGH FRONTS

THE IMPACT OF STREET CULTURE ON SCHOOLING

L. Janelle Dance

ROUTLEDGEFALMER
New York and London

Published in 2002 by
RoutledgeFalmer
29 West 35th Street
New York, NY 10001

Published in Great Britain by
RoutledgeFalmer
11 New Fetter Lane
London EC4P 4EE

Routledge is an imprint of the Taylor & Francis Group.
Copyright © 2002 by RoutledgeFalmer
Design and typography: Jack Donner

Printed in the United States of America on acid-free paper.

Extracts from the essay, "Investing in Teaching and Learning: Dynamics of the Teacher–Student Relationship from Each Actor's Perspective," appear with the permission of Corwin Press, Inc. This essay, co-authored by L. Janelle Dance, Susan Roberta Katz, and Chandra Muller, originally appeared in *Urban Education*, 34 (4), pp. 292–337, ©1999 Corwin Press, Inc.

"Shadows, Mentors, and Surrogate Fathers" is reprinted with the permission of *Sociological Focus*, the journal in which it originally appeared (vol. 34, October/November 2001, pp. 399–415).

10 9 8 7 6 5 4 3 2 1

Library of Congress Cataloging-in-Publication Data

Dance, Lory Janelle.
   Tough Fronts : the impact of street culture on schooling / L. Janelle Dance.
       p.   cm. (Critical social thought)
   Includes bibliographical references and index.
   ISBN 0–415–93299–8 — ISBN 0–415–93300–5 (pbk.)
   1. Education, Urban—Social aspects—United States. 2. African Americans—Education—Social aspects. 3. Educational anthropology—United States. I. Title. II. Series.

LC5131 .D34 2002
306.43'2—dc21

                                                        2002024906

To my supportive uncle Bernard,
my "best good friend" Michele,
my "sister-cousin" Paula,
and my loving mother, Delma

Contents

Tables and Figures

Foreword

I begin one of my own books with a story of a boy who was constantly being blamed for discipline problems in the classroom and on the playground. It seemed that no matter what he did, he was singled out as likely to be a troublemaker, as someone who was probably involved in difficulties even when he wasn't. Given the unfortunate ways the politics of whiteness works, it shouldn't be a surprise that the child was African-American. The ways he sometimes dressed and held his body, his walk, his tastes in music—all of this brought forth particular forms of interpretation on the part of many of his teachers. For them, his manner signified *danger*. After years of being treated as if he was the "Other," it became harder and harder not to take on the identity that was being imposed on him.[1]

Stories of this kind are repeated thousands of times each day throughout our nation's schools. This particular one was more painful personally since it involved my own son. My own experiences and those of my son make L. Janelle Dance's *Tough Fronts* an even more powerful analysis for me about the realities of schooling for all too many children of color in the United States. But you don't need to have had such experiences to recognize the importance of what this author does here. Her book has the capacity to transform the fundamental ways educators look at children of color inside and outside of schools. In the process, it illuminates how popular culture such as music and dress helps create and sustain identities. And, just as important, it restores agency to Black youth by demonstrating the creative and strategic activity they engage in to make their ways in the unequal world they inhabit.[2]

Dance's book is one of those rare volumes that work on multiple levels. It both critiques and extends the previous research that has been done on African-American youth. It speaks to the entire tradition of explanation of how and why poor urban youth seem to do poorly in school and to what we might do about it. But it goes much further. It demonstrates with sensitivity and care the modes of interpretation, and the hopes and dreams, of these Black young men. In the process, Dance enables us to see the very real harm that can come from this society's prevalent assumptions about Black young men as always being anti-school, hard, and dangerous. The portraits of the young men collectively act, in essence, as a form of speaking truth to power.

Tough Fronts also gives us pictures of truly effective teachers, teachers who are able to connect with these very same youth and to keep their dreams alive. As such, it is a worthy successor to Gloria Ladson-Billings's justly well-known book, *The Dreamkeepers*.[3] Because of her detailing of both students and teachers, Dance is able to say some crucial things that have significant implications for the reform of urban education.

Unfortunately, all too many current school reform efforts are beside the point. They are often based on a fundamental misrecognition of the realities both of schools and teachers' lives, and even more damaging on an ignorance of the daily realities of the children who come to these schools. The emphasis on high-stakes testing, on reductive accountability schemes, on raising "standards," and so on may have rhetorical force in the public arena, but these emphases may also be based on quite flawed assumptions. As many researchers have shown, such "reforms" may not help but may actually do quite a bit of damage if they are not based on a more detailed understanding of these realities.[4] I can't imagine anyone involved in urban school reform—or any school reform for that matter—who wouldn't be chastened by the voices of the young men that come through so powerfully in this book. The kinds of reforms the youths call for, and they do so in quite an articulate manner, speak not to efficiency and testing, but to the creation of caring communities. Teachers who understand the lives and cultures in which these youth are immersed, teachers who constantly show a combination of respect, high expectations, and a willingness to listen and learn from their students' lives—these are the characteristics that these young men identify in the teachers who made a difference in their lives. Dance's analysis, as well, of the relations that these young men have with deeply committed Black men within the community provides evidence of the very possibility of difference in the current and future lives of children for whom many powerful sectors of this society have basically given up hope.

We should not be romantic here. In order to create the lasting conditions that might enable such teaching to go on in this society's schools, we would also need to alter the political economy of the city. We would have to challenge the politics of whiteness that is still such a powerful force in "our" politics and culture. And, we would have to recognize the dangers in continuing to *not* listen to the voices of those whom this society seems to delight in creating as the "Other."

All of these transformations will take time and immense collective effort, and there is no guarantee that they will actually happen. However, L. Janelle Dance shows that it is possible to begin now. A first step on what Raymond Williams so elegantly called our journey of hope[5] is to listen to the voices of urban youth and to recognize the complexity and ingenuity in their lives and dreams. Dance helps us take that first step and more. Because of this, her book is essential reading for anyone who cares about the lives of students in schools. But it is also of considerable importance to those people interested in youth culture, in critical theory in education, in the ways in which gender is constructed and lived out, and in the politics of identity. One last thing: I will ask my son to read it.

Michael W. Apple
John Bascom Professor of Curriculum and Instruction
and Educational Policy Studies,
University of Wisconsin, Madison

Acknowledgments

"Props"

Where shall I begin? There are *so many* people to thank. And, since this book grew out of dissertation research that began during the 1991/1992 school year, there is a decade's worth of acquaintances, friends, family members, students (respondents), and colleagues to whom I am indebted.

I begin with the subjects of my research, the students living in Cambridge and Boston, Massachusetts, who shared their opinions, experiences, and life stories. Your lived experiences provide this book, a primarily intellectual undertaking, with vitality, with heart, with *soul*. So I give "props," that is, thanks, to the "boyz," and girls, from The Port, The Coast, N.C., Roxbury, Dorchester, and the other "hoods" of Cambridge and Boston. I give "mad props," that is, many thanks, to the students and teachers of the Paul Robeson Institute for Positive Self-Development. Thanks to the Institute and Concerned Black Men of Massachusetts, Incorporated, especially Keith Motley and Richard O'Bryant, for allowing me to "hang around" and conduct research at the Institute. I also give much thanks and much love to Richie Cabral, Roberta Exilus, and Anthony Schofield, my research assistants. The interviews you conducted were "all that!" I acknowledge Ms. Roberta Cohen: Ms. Cohen, I appreciate the access you allowed me to the theory and practice of your pedagogy. Last, but not least, I thank "Malcolm Winfield": "Malcolm," thanks for sharing your life story with me.

To my academic mentors and colleagues. (Wow, this is one long list of people!) Sara Lawrence-Lightfoot, you helped me to find and sustain *my* vision and version of this book from among a clutter of notes, memos to file, and early drafts of book chapters. You also defended me when I was too fatigued and disoriented to defend myself. Sara, your accomplishments remain a constant source of inspiration. Mary Waters, your practical advice dissolved writing blocks and facilitated the writing and publishing process. Thanks for your candid advice, constructive critiques, and, especially, your compliments on my qualitative endeavors. Toni Turano, whenever we get together the magic that began at North House continues; your friendship, votes of confidence, and constructive critiques remain priceless. Pedro Noguera, I still cannot believe that you read *every page* of my dissertation to provide early feedback for this book! There are dissertation committee members who have not accomplished such a feat. Pedro, your comments, which are informed by scholarship, experience, and activism with urban students and schools, keep me grounded. Stanley Presser, thanks for reading early and later versions of the chapters and for providing practical advice about the next steps in the publishing process. Joe Feagin, the advice you gave on an early version of chapter 7 was reassuring; but more important, I really appreciate that whenever I call or see you at conferences, you take a moment from a hectic schedule to ask me how *I'm* doing. James Loewen and Steven Selden, thanks for agreeing to read the manuscript and for treating me to coffee and lunch to provide comments. Elijah Anderson, your encouragement that I keep this book unapologetically qualitative inspired me to drop one chapter, add another, and come to peace with the depth of my findings. Mary Hermes, Rochelle Gutierrez, and Paula Frederick, your feedback was brief but priceless; Paula, thanks for your detailed feedback on chapter 1.

Keisha Jones, one of my early undergraduates at the University of Maryland, I appreciate all the office-hour visits. I got more from those visits than you realize; thanks for your feedback on a different version of the introduction. Nicole Green, another bright undergraduate at the University of Maryland, thanks for reading and providing feedback on the same chapter. Thanks to many other colleagues who took time to read early pieces of this work. These godsends include Rhonda Williams, Katheryn Russell, Bonnie Thornton Dill, Linda Moghadam, and Frank Furstenberg. Additional godsends include Philly public schoolteachers and friends Lou Austin, Lisa McClendon, and Lydia Gonzales. Also, because every little bit helps, I thank my research assistants Marla Kohlman, Laurie Bates, Tallese Johnson, Kishi Animashaun; my students from SOCY 699Q (especially Stephani Hatch and Tim Recuber), Fall 1999 and Honors 288K, Fall 1999; and last-minute assistance provided by Jose A. Irizarry, Emmanuel (E. C.) Ejiogu, and Thomas Bern.

I am grateful to my friends who continue to believe in me, tolerate me when I babble on about details that are boring and minute, and encourage me during my most deflated moments. Thank you, Crystal Byndloss, Allen LeBlanc, Roberta Udoh, Dayle Delancey, and all others who have been a constant source of moral support. Moreover, among my innermost group of friends, there are those of you who have clearly soared above and beyond the call of duty: Michele Lugiai ("Miche!"), Mark R. Warren, and Toni "Emma" Thomas, your efforts and support have been invaluable.

Discipline, perseverance, indomitable spirit, self-control, and integrity are the tenets of Tae Kwon Do. My passion for and training in the martial arts, especially in Tae Kwon Do, keep me centered and relatively stress-free. My instructors and fellow practitioners, especially T. J., Calvin, John, and Ric, encourage a healthy balance between mind and body. Without this mind-body link, I may have completed this book at the expense of my spiritual, physical, and emotional health. First, I pay gratitude to my instructors. Thank you Grand Master Jun Saeng Yoo and Mrs. Hyung O. Yoo, thank you Mr. Jae H. Kim and Mr. Michael O'Malley, thank you Masters John Holloway and Chun Jae Park. Thank you Wayne Dean and Ronnie Vaughn. (Thank you Joel G. Howard and Bruce Lee, for inspiring me to become a martial artist in the first place!) Second, I pay thanks to my fellow practitioners who have never allowed me to use this book or the research that preceded it as an excuse to neglect my martial arts training or dreams of Olympic competition. Thanks to T. J. Desch-Obi, David Dance, Calvin Côté White, John Fields, Major Battle, Ricardo Wong, Kaminapata Dabinga, Eric Nisenzon, Gordon White, Gayle Lassen, Collette Chambers, Jason Yoo, and Mark Cheng.

Special appreciation, love, and thanks to my family. Paula (Paula Setzer-Storrs), our ongoing conversations continue to guide my path. Uncle Al (Alfred Greene

Dance), your recent death has left me devastated, but your legacy of love and support continues to compel me. Uncle Bernard (Bernard Clark Duse Jr.), without your provision of support and writing space, this book would not have been possible. Linda (Linda Duse), thank you for helping me get away from it all; I am blessed to have you as my sister. "Jr." (Phillip M. Duse Jr.) thanks for providing the incentive that compelled me to finish the second draft of this book; I am blessed to have you as my brother. David (David "Dunga" Dance), having a cousin who is both a martial artist and a scholar has meant so much to me. Mom (Delma M. Dance), you are so precious to me; thank you for your everlasting patience, love, devotion, and support. Most important, thank you for all the sacrifices you have made so that your only child has all the opportunities that you dreamed she would have.

Preface

It is the dawn of the third millennium, and the American Sociological Association holds its ninety-fourth annual meeting.[1] The title for this year's conference is "Transitions in World Society: At Century's End." The conference program lists hundreds of workshops, meetings, and sessions; I am particularly drawn to a special session titled "The Progress and Status of Black Americans at the Coming Millennium."[2] According to two of the panelists at this session, Stephan and Abigail Thernstrom, Blacks suffered as members of an American caste group for over three hundred years, endured the harsh racism and discrimination of Jim Crow segregation, migrated to northern industrial cities, and eventually won many battles fought during the civil rights movement. But such group oppression belongs to the past. At present, at the "coming millennium," African Americans are substantially well-off. In fact, proclaim the Thernstroms, African-American progress has been so substantial that Blacks should no longer be the beneficiaries of race-specific social welfare policies.

I sit and listen to the Thernstroms' Eurocentric points of view. Their rosy picture of racial progress, stance against affirmative action, and call for race-neutral policies remind me of Charles Murray and Dinesh D'Souza's calls for the same. The Thernstroms' presentation echos sentiments like those voiced by Allan Bloom and Arthur Schlesinger, who romanticize and overstate the progress and accomplishments of Western civilization and of America "the beautiful." Neo-conservatives like the Thernstroms suggest that most Black Americans should bring in the new millennium singing Katharine Lee Bates's famous anthem, "America the Beautiful." I will not be surprised if the Thernstroms end their presentation by exclaiming, "America! America! God shed his grace on thee. And crown thy good with brotherhood, from sea to shining sea!" The Thernstroms have definitely overlooked an important segment of the African-American population: urban and inner city students from low-income communities. These American students are the subjects of *Tough Fronts: The Impact of Street Culture on Schooling*.

The ideologies of the Thernstroms, Murrays, D'Souzas, and other spokes-scholars of the American Right are resurgent at the dawn of the third millennium. Neo-conservative ideologies are often hidden "under the guise of antistatism, of keeping government 'off the backs of the people,' and 'free enterprise.'"[3] The American Right does not limit these ideologies to economic and political arenas, but extends them to the arena of schooling as well. Michael Apple stresses this point:

> The sphere of education has been one of the most successful areas in which the Right has been ascendant. The social democratic goal of expanding equality of oppor-

tunity ... has lost much of its political potency and its ability to mobilize people. The "panic" over failing standards and illiteracy, the fears of violence in schools, the concern with the destruction of family values and religiosity, all have had an effect. These fears are exacerbated and used [manipulated], by dominant groups within politics and the economy who have been able to move the debate on education (and all things social) onto their own terrain, the terrain of "tradition," standardization, productivity, and industrial needs.[4]

The Thernstroms, other neo-conservatives, and some old-line liberals would have us believe that the social ills of racism, discrimination, and other forms of group oppression no longer present formidable obstacles for Black Americans. Hence, in the educational arena, Black student failure no longer results from inadequate schooling, mainstream policies, and discriminatory practices but from individual shortcomings, a lack of the right values—pun intended—and these students' failure to embrace the great Western traditions and ideals of America "the beautiful."

Return with me to the American Sociological Association's ninety-fourth annual meeting. The Thernstroms' presentation is not well received at this session on "The Progress and Status of Black Americans at the Coming Millennium." Critics of the Thernstroms on the panel and within the audience acknowledge pockets of Black progress, but they elaborate the stubborn racist realities of America "the beautiful" that remain unchanged and difficult to overcome. For example, Joe Feagin, a European-American sociologist, offers overwhelming evidence of anti-black racism at the coming millennium. As I continue to sit and listen to the debate, I agree with Feagin, the audience, and other panelists about the stubborn racist realities that persist at the century's end. I breathe out a sigh of relief: within the confines of this American Sociological Association conference, neo-conservative ideologies have been successfully challenged, critiqued, and deconstructed. However, I breathe in a sigh of despair: neo-conservative sentiments thrive elsewhere in America "the beautiful." The urban students from low-income communities, the subjects of *Tough Fronts*, live beyond the confines of academic conferences about the progress of Black Americans. These students live within the social structural confines of America "the inner city." Even more, if inner-city students were to walk into this academic session, I *seriously* doubt that they would be welcomed by the Thernstroms. I even ponder the degree to which these students would be welcomed by the more liberal and progressive scholars in attendance.

Now I think of inner-city students as I look around the conference room and scrutinize the mannerisms, demeanors, and apparel of the audience and panelists. I listen to the tone, cadence, and dialect of standard English they use to air the academic discourse. Suddenly these diverse individuals—women and men who are Black, White, Latino, and Asian, but mostly Black and White—in this room appear monolithic. As members of the audience walk up to the podium to ask questions of panelists, I notice that we academics all dress alike, gesture alike, talk alike, and so on. As this session ends, there is time for one last question. I raise my hand. Clad in apparel and mannerisms similar to all others attending this session, I walk to the front of the conference room. Once at the podium, I look out at the audience and assume a more urban hip-hop posture. I relax over the podium, grasp and bring the microphone close to my mouth, and speak in an urban, black English dialect, "Yo . . . Whatz up? Check this out, youknowwhatI'msayin'. Y'all be dissin' my boyz and girls in the hood, youknowwhatI'msayin'. But then, I peep the tv, and y'all be rockin' our gear, youknowwhatI'msayin'. How ya gonna dis us and then rock our gear? Whatz up with dat?"[5]

There is complete silence in the conference room for about five seconds. My dialect and demeanor disrupt the academic discourse. From my vantage point at the podium, Whites in the audience appear confused, Blacks appear embarrassed or ashamed, everyone appears speechless. Only a Black male member of the audience and Joe Feagin on the panel smile as though they grasp the point I am about to make. I stand erect, assume a more academic posture and speak in a standard, mainstream English dialect, "I don't talk like that most of the time, but the urban Black students with whom I hang out while conducting research do. My question to the audience and panelists: 'For those of us who are not [from the American mainstream], who do we become when we join the academy, what do we give up [from our own cultures], what language [or dialect] do we speak? And for the Thernstroms, which Black Americans do you accept? Those who dress, speak, and behave like you? If so, what does that say about racism [and progress at the coming millennium]?"[6]

The looks of confusion, embarrassment, and shame on the faces of the audience dissolve into looks of relief and understanding. The audience and panelists, the Thernstroms excepted, applaud as I walk back to my seat. My point appears well received and concludes this session on "The Progress and Status of Black Americans at the Coming Millennium." Likewise, *Tough Fronts* points out that the problem for urban and inner-city students is not that they fail to embrace America "the beautiful," but that America "the mainstream" refuses to embrace them.

As the third millennium dawns, Black and Latino-American students who reside in low-income urban neighborhoods find themselves between a rock and a hard place. These students find themselves between the rock of Rightist American mainstream ideologies and the hard place of America's inner-city streets. They find themselves between the rock of an American mainstream that views them as thugs and villains and the hard place of urban streets that often require these students to don hard postures to survive. *Tough Fronts: The Impact of Street Culture on Schooling* contributes the voices and experiences of urban students to scholarly debates about schooling, progress, and the status of Black Americans at the dawn of the new millennium.

A Study of Street-Savvy Students

JASON:	Yeah man, John is really hard! That nigga be walkin' 'round wit a nine. He showed it to me the other day.
SHANE, KENNETH, MALIK:	Word!
KENNETH:	Yep, that mothafucka's ill, yo.
ME (L. J. DANCE):	Wait a minute! Wait a minute! Who y'all talkin' bout?
MALIK:	This student at our school who always be carryin' a gun and he's ill enough to use it. He's hard, yo. People be givin' him mad respect.
ME:	He's "hard" because he carries a gun? He ain't "hard." The gun's "hard."
KENNETH:	Tomni [referring to me by my nickname], you might be able to do karate, but you can't stop no bullets. Talkin' 'bout some "Heeeeyah!!! . . . Oh shit, I've been shot!"
JASON, SHANE, MALIK:	[Laughter]
ME:	Y'all ain't funny. I ain't tryin' to block nobody's bullets. All I'm sayin' is, if your friend John stepped to me without his gun, I'd whip his ass. How "hard" can he be if an almost thirty-year-old woman can whip his ass. He's not hard, the gun is hard.

My first attempt to write this introduction left me somewhat speechless. I am many things, but speechless is rarely one of them. So, I decided to share the inspiration for *Tough Fronts*, the moment quoted above, which occurred several years ago. This introductory chapter also covers the research methods employed; the scholars and others sources of inspiration for this book; the role of race, gender, class, and region in this study; the sociological frame, or glue, that holds this book together; and a constructive critique of scientific objectivity. This introductory chapter ends with a summary of chapters to come and a glossary of street-savvy terms.

The initial research for this book began while I was in graduate school. Prior to conducting my dissertation research, I worked as a volunteer teacher in a Cambridge, Massachusetts after-school program for students at risk of failing. Some days there were moments between program activities when students sat around classroom tables in gender and ethnic specific cliques, discussing a variety of topics. I would wander from table to table, but found myself most at home with the clique of Black and Latino boys. I have always been a tomboy at heart who feels quite comfortable as "one of the boys." It was during one of these hanging-out-with-the-boys moments that a student in the Cambridge program began to describe one of his peers as "hard," that is, tough or ruthless like a gangster. This particular conversation occurred before I had chosen my research topic. Therefore, I had no fieldnotes from which to reproduce this conversation verbatim and I may have placed the words of one student in the mouth of another. But, if my memory serves me correctly, the gist of the conversation was basically that quoted at the beginning of this introduction.

During this conversation, we continued to debate whether or not John would be "hard" if he was butt-naked and without his gun. I commented that Bruce Lee would be "hard" or tough butt-naked, and one of the students joked, "That moth-afucka's dead. He ain't hard at all, no more." If my memory serves me correctly, this group of students concluded that John would not be so tough without his gun, then they turned their analyses to another student they knew who would be tough "even without a gun." As we continued to debate, I realized that they heard me and that, more importantly, I heard them. I had asked them to consider whether certain students were really hard, and they pushed me to understand the practicality of presenting oneself as hard within street cultural contexts.

The conversation that opens this chapter was one of the first I had with urban students about street culture and being "hard." During my first year of volunteer teaching at the Cambridge program, this concept popped up so frequently that I decided to stop debating with and begin listening to students in Cambridge, and, eventually, students in Boston. I asked these students to share their expert, street-based experiences about what it means to be or pose as "hard." Hence, this book presents *postures* of toughness. This study of tough postures derives from more than seventy interviews and almost four years of ethnographic observations with middle and junior high school students, roughly twelve to sixteen years old, from urban and inner-city neighborhoods. As mentioned above, one group of students attended a supplemental, after-school program for at-risk youths in the Cambridge public school system; the other group of students attended a supplemental school program for at-risk youths in the Boston public school system.[1] With rare exceptions, students in both of these programs reside in urban neighborhoods that are economically impoverished. Most of these street-savvy students are male and most of the males are Americans of African, Afro-Caribbean, or Latino-Caribbean descent. Only a handful of female and non-Black male experiences grace the pages that follow; therefore, unless otherwise indicated, the masculine forms of pronouns signify Black or Latino (Brown) males. The students are real but all names are pseudonyms. My main research objectives are threefold: (1) to better understand the experiences of street-savvy students who act "hard" like a "gangsta"; (2) to explore the implications of gangsterlike posturing on schooling; and (3) to breathe students' lives into scholarly debates about the state of (urban) public education in the United States.

By "street-savvy," I mean urban youths who are not sheltered from the criminal aspects of street culture (for example, drug trafficking and gang violence). Because they are not sheltered, these students have acquired a practical understanding or savoir-faire about navigating urban streets. I prefer the term "street savvy" over the term "streetwise" because "wise," when applied to urban youths from low-income communities, may conjure images of students who are "wise guys" or "wise" in the pejorative sense. "Savvy" calls forth images of students who employ a sophisticated know-how about street cultural contexts.

During the early days of my research, before I asked the first formal interview question or took the first fieldnote, I spent one year hanging out with urban students in the school-based settings mentioned above. Then after this initial year, by research design, I allowed my desire for a deeper, closer, more subjective and ethnographic understanding of urban students to eclipse a broader, distant, and more objective quantitative understanding. Hence, from the start of my research to the writing of this book, my quest for subjective understanding remained empirically grounded and guided by facts derived from observations and interviews. From the start, I made a commitment to street-savvy students like that poignantly described by John Lofland in *Analyzing Social Settings*.[2]

> The commitment to get close, to be factual, descriptive, and quotive, constitutes a significant commitment to represent the participants *in their own terms*. This does not mean that one becomes an apologist for them, but rather that one faithfully depicts what goes on in their lives and what life is like for them.... There is a conveyance of their prides, their shames, their secrets, their fellowships, their boredoms, their happinesses, their despairs [emphasis in original].

In making this commitment, I honored a long-standing precedent set by qualitative researchers.[3] In the pages that follow, I represent street-savvy students in their own terms to ensure that this book contains social scientific facts complicated by hopes, despairs, follies, insights, passions, and other unquantifiable yet socially meaningful human qualities. The terms of teachers and other school officials are equally important, but in this book, I have given street-savvy students my undivided, scholarly attention.

INSPIRATIONS AND MOTIVATIONS

There are several sources of inspiration for my work with urban students from marginalized, low-income communities. First, I am persuaded by the works of social scientists who argue that, contrary to popular belief, (American) schools are not great equalizers of inequality. From Pitrim Sorokin (in 1927) to James Coleman, Pierre Bourdieu, Michael Apple, Samuel Bowles and Herbert Gintis, Eleanor Leacock, John Ogbu, Henry Giroux, Shirley Brice Heath, Lisa Delpit, Gloria Ladson-Billings, and Ann Ferguson (in 2000), an assortment of sociologists, economists, anthropologists, psychologists, and education theorists have identified a variety of mechanisms associated with schooling that reproduce, instead of alleviate, social inequality.[4] Following the lead of these scholars, in the chapters that follow, I scrape beneath the surface of "hard" or tough student postures to uncover their valuable implications for social inequality. Beneath the surface of tough postures lie student critiques of the schooling mechanisms that facilitate inequality.

Critical theorists and effective schools researchers provide a second source of inspiration. Critical theorists clarify the subtle collaborations between schools and mainstream power structures that function to re-create the inequality preexisting in wider societal arrangements. (By "mainstream," I refer to middle- and upper-class social structures and practices that are Eurocentric.) More specifically, critical theorists identify economic, cultural, and political arrangements between schools and society that replicate social inequality.[5] In contrast, effective schools researchers restore faith in public schools as great equalizers of inequality. Instead of identifying the mechanisms associated with schooling that reproduce inequality, these researchers identify the factors that allow schools to reduce inequality. Those who crave a brief literature review of critical theories and effective schools findings are welcome to peruse the appendix. However, suffice it to say in this introduction that the critical theories and notions most instrumental to this study are those expounded by Pierre Bourdieu, Michael Apple, and Henry Giroux. In addition to critical theories, I also eventually weave James Coleman's notion of social capital into my analyses of the schooling mechanisms that re-create inequality.

The lectures and writings of Sara Lawrence-Lightfoot provide a third basis of inspiration. In lectures, Professor Lawrence-Lightfoot frequently lamented the absence of students' voices from scholarly deliberations on schooling. With respect to this noticeable absence of the student perspective, the words of Jonathan Kozol echo my—and I dare say, Lawrence-Lightfoot's—convictions: "It occurred to me that we had not been listening much to children in these recent years of 'summit conferences' on education, of severe reports and ominous prescriptions. *The voices of children frankly had been missing from the whole discussion*" [emphasis added].[6] In writings, Lawrence-Lightfoot calls attention to the role of teacher empathy in schooling and researcher subjectivity (or artistry) in the social scientific process of data collection. Her example, teachings, and writings have a profound impact upon the manner in which I conduct and reflect upon the research process.

Finally, as an African-American woman raised in (and by) a Black, working-class community, I am inspired by my hometown acquaintances, friends, and family members. Like many Americans of color and residents of lower-income communities in the United States, they struggle to maintain dignity and respect in a country that has historically (and often contemporarily) labeled them as lazy, unintelligent, and destined to fail. My social origins provide access, insight, empathy, and experiential data that are often lacking—or conveniently dismissed as insider bias—in social scientific studies of ethnic minority communities.

THE INTERSECTIONS OF RACE, CLASS, GENDER, AND REGION IN THIS STUDY

Race, gender, class, and region (spatial situation) figure prominently in this book. To borrow the theoretical framework of Black women sociologists like Bonnie Thornton Dill and Patricia Hill Collins, race, gender, class, and region are major, mutually constructing features of social organization that shape Black and Latino students' experiences. Collins argues, and I agree, "Collectively, the work of … African American women sociologists suggests that not race nor gender nor economic class alone could adequately explain Black women's experiences."[7] The same intersectional paradigm applies to the experiences of Black and Latino students.

Being "hard" like a "gangsta" is viewed by several youths in my study as inextricably linked to being Black—or Latino (non-white)—male, low-income, and from a tough urban neighborhood. This social profile of the Black, urban, low-income male as gangster emanates from both mainstream society and the streets. Students who are Black, urban, low-income, and male frequently find themselves wedged between a mainstream rock and a street cultural hard place, regardless of the degree to which they personally identify with the urban gangster. These students are constantly bombarded with social stereotypes that proclaim that real Black men are hard or tough like a gangster. Hence, students who find themselves at the intersections of race (African- or Latino-American), gender (male), class (economically impoverished), region or geographic location (urban/inner-city), and educational status (at risk of failing) constantly confront oppressive stereotypes that distort who they are. Some students exist with stereotypes at these intersections, some subsist, some succumb, and some resist the stereotypes. All students are maintained at risk of failing in school.

Furthermore, these students are not disproportionately represented in school failure statistics because there is something innately wrong with being low-income, from a tough urban neighborhood, Black or Brown, or male. Contrary to popular stereotypes, the low-income, male students in this study have American mainstream dreams and aspirations. It is just that these mainstream dreams are sometimes juxtaposed or fused with anti-mainstream, survivalistic sentiments. My findings suggest that this juxtaposition of mainstream dreams and anti-mainstream sentiments is not a chicken or egg tautology. Which came first? The mainstream dreams. Which came second? Rejection by the mainstream. That is to say, because they resemble the popular social construct of the urban gangster, Black and Brown males from low-income neighborhoods are more likely than their peers to be rejected by representatives of American mainstream institutions. As observed by Douglas Glasgow, and substantiated by William Julius Wilson and Elijah Anderson, Black males from low-income urban communities tend to be "rejected and labeled as social problems by the police, the schools, employment and welfare agencies; they [are] the victims of the new camouflaged racism."[8] This mainstream rejection eventually takes its toll with some students: it deflates and levels aspirations, creates a fertile ground for survivalistic, anti-mainstream sentiments, and renders individuals who are Black, Brown, male, urban, and low-income more vulnerable to involvement in illicit street cultural activities. During their middle and junior high school years, the vast majority of students in my study hold fast to their dreams despite this rejection. But as they mature into their late teens and early twenties, the constant mainstream rejection begins to weaken their resolve.

Similarly, in my study other urban students—female or non-Black, or non-low-income students—also exhibited vulnerability to involvement in illicit street cultural activities. Some of these students experienced this vulnerability because they too, albeit to a lesser degree, were victims of mainstream rejection and street cultural pressures. They met three out of the four characteristics of the social profile (for example, low-income, Black, and urban but female; or low-income, urban, and male but non-Black). But others coveted or feigned Blackness, maleness, and even low-incomeness because they associated these attributes with the urban "gangsta." As will be discussed in chapter 3, this urban gangster has a certain charismatic appeal which seems to transcend boundaries of race, class, tough neighborhoods, and—albeit to a lesser extent—gender to influence many urban youths to act "hard."

As claimed and reiterated throughout this book, only a small minority of urban youths are actually involved in hardcore criminal activities despite the fact that many urban youths don gangster mannerisms, language, and dispositions. However, the social construct of low-income Black urban male as gangster tends to obscure the statistical reality that the average urban Black or Brown youth is not hard at all, and this is especially true of students in their middle to junior high school years.

A SOCIOLOGICAL FRAMEWORK

My quest for understanding the lives of the students in this study has led me to the works of an eclectic group of experts, a group that includes individuals who have survived the streets as well as an assortment of scholars. All of these sources provide pieces to a complex jigsaw puzzle of factors; these pieces yield an evolving yet incomplete picture. However, the piece of understanding contained in this book is essentially sociological: dynamics between social structure and social actors animate the researched story that unfolds. In other words, this story situates the narratives and lived experiences of individual students (called "social agents" or "social actors" in sociological terms) within the context of street culture (considered a social structure or institution by sociological standards). As you read the pages that follow, you will encounter several individual students like Malik, Shane, Kenneth, and Robbie, but the star of this story is an African-American ninth grader named Malcolm (Malcolm's life story traverses chapters 4, 5 and 6).[9]

I argue that the seemingly personal problems and individual choices of street-savvy students like Malcolm are influenced by street cultural dictates and customs. I use the phrase "influenced by" with discretion: the codes and dictates of street culture influence, but do not determine, the lives of street-savvy students. Elijah Anderson describes these customs and dictates in more popular terms as "the code of the street," that is, "a set of informal rules governing interpersonal behavior [and prescribing] both a proper comportment and proper way to respond if challenged."[10]

I delve beneath the surface of postures that are hard and gangsterlike to uncover what these postures mean to street-savvy students; I also aim to demonstrate students' power, albeit limited, to defy, resist, or, at least, redefine social structural impositions. Given the imposing nature of the code of the streets, if students were *completely* powerless, they would not merely don gangsterlike demeanors, they would all become gangsters. And, while a few students in my study do participate in violent and criminal street cultural activities, *the vast majority do not.* For example, of the seventy students interviewed and nearly two hundred students observed for this study, far less than ten percent presented evidence of involvement in street cultural activities that were violent and gangsterlike.

By focusing upon the prerogative that social actors have to interpret and reappropriate social structural influences, I join those social scientists who assert that human beings are not merely puppets on the strings of social structure.[11] A gangsterlike posture is usually a temporary disposition that urban students strategically adopt to navigate the streets instead of a foregone conclusion, permanent mind-set, or career orientation. I am not suggesting that there are no pawns of street culture and extreme social marginalization who aspire to be gangsters. Nor, on the contrary, am I arguing that social structural barriers are easily overcome. I am merely asserting that for most street-savvy students in this study, gangsterlike posturing is a comportment that is temporary, strategic, and survivalistic. However, as illustrated by Malik's story in chapter 2, the mainstream biases of schooling can change temporary, survivalistic attitudes into firm political convictions. Under these circumstances, a gangsterlike pose or tough front can become an act of rebellion or resistance.

SCIENTIFIC OBJECTIVITY AND "KEEPING IT REAL"

There is one last research card that I must lay on the table of this introductory section: my approach to the scholarly pursuit of scientific objectivity. During the first year or so of my graduate student training, a friend and colleague shared a prophetic warning that, to this day, shapes the scholar that I aspire to become. He cautioned in a mentoring tone, "Many scholars, especially scholars of color, undergo a process where, in the name of 'scientific objectivity,' they are stripped of their heart and soul and left confined to the dispassionate, one-dimensional perspective of their intellect." These were not his exact words, but these words convey the essence of his exhortation. When I hung out with urban students, I did so with my heart, soul, and intellect intact. By this I mean, without being imposing and when appropriate, I revealed my feelings, moral core, and intellectual as well as political motives. The students in this study refer to this holistic comportment as "keeping it real." Had I approached the students in the study with objective intellect alone and not allowed them access to my emotional and moral fiber, I would have never gained their trust or convinced these students of my genuine interest in their lives.

In reviewing fieldnotes, interview transcripts, and dissertation chapters to write this book, there have been times when I have tuned out my heart and soul to obtain abstract, conceptual, and more objective clarity on the lives of urban students. The reader may even notice fluid shifts in perspective between heart, soul, and intellect in my writing; indeed, there have been occasions when the latter waxed and the former two perspectives waned. But when appropriate and possible, I have allowed my data to sift through all three perspectives. I would rather acknowledge and embrace my biases and multiple frames of reference than have delusions of grandeur about the bias-free power of my intellect. I believe that the quest for scientific objectivity looms as a worthwhile, though unattainable, destination. The road toward objectivity only adds clarity to social scientific findings when researchers ponder and acknowledge the biased stops that they make along the way; that is, if researchers "keep it real."

In this introductory chapter, I have divulged the inspirations, motivations, sociological frame, and research methods that lay the foundation for this study of urban students who assume hard, gangsterlike postures.

In chapter 1, I review scholarly depictions of Black Americans. I revisit what the experts have to say about Blacks in general and urban Black males in particular. (I provide no review of scholarly depictions of Latinos, because the Latino males in this study viewed themselves as both Black and Latino. These males were also frequently seen by onlookers as Black.) Many of these depictions obscure agency and thereby portray Blacks as listless, faceless objects or cultural automatons. Despite scholarly depictions, once you meet these so-called objects face to face, see them eye to eye, and become acquainted with them person to person, they become agents of history, or at least agents of their story. Then in chapter 2, as well as the chapters that follow, I allow the experiences of the real experts of this study, that is, the students, to speak for themselves. These student experiences provide valuable insights into how gangsterlike posturing can be a form of resistance and why urban streets facilitate hard postures or tough fronts. In short, this chapter sheds new light on the social forces that conspire to forge hard postures.

In chapter 3, I draw upon field observations, students' narratives, and illustrative events to elaborate three variations of a gangsterlike pose, that is, three conceptual constructs: hardcore, hardcore wannabe, and hardcore enough. The labels "hardcore" and "hardcore wannabe" were actual terms used by urban students to describe their peers who appropriate postures and attitudes that are gangsterlike. I devised the label "hardcore enough" (or "hard enough") to designate a third category of students who assume hard postures. All three of these categories are ideal generalizations. With the understanding that real urban students are not confined to ideal categories, these conceptual constructs become useful sociological generalizations that capture essential elements of gangsterlike posturing.

Integrating interviews with street-savvy students and a case study of a maverick teacher, chapter 4 examines the role of social capital and cultural capital in the teacher-student relationship. Social capital can be briefly defined as resources derived from social networks and relationships among two or more individuals. Cultural capital, briefly defined, refers to the linguistic codes, dispositions, tastes, and other cultural practices of middle- and upper-class Americans that are necessary for successful social interactions within American mainstream settings and institutions. Interview data and field observations reveal that teacher caring as well as viable teacher advice about avoiding the illicit activities of street culture are particularly valuable social capital resources in successful relationships between teachers and street-savvy students. However, because these students are usually deficient in mainstream cultural capital, they are less likely to encounter caring teachers and less likely to have adequate access to other forms of social capital in the teacher-student relationship.

Chapter 5 gives urban youths complex, multi-dimensional, visual form through a qualitative technique called portraiture, created by Sara Lawrence-Lightfoot.[12] This chapter chronicles the dynamic life story of Malcolm, an African-American male student from Dorchester, Massachusetts. Thanks to an influential mentor, Malcolm has become hard enough to avoid being seduced by the dark side of the streets, but *most of the time*, he does not act tough at all. In other words, this chapter provides stark contrasts to the popular image of inner-city males as gangsters; it demonstrates that inner-city students like Malcolm are not confined to the gangsterlike postures that they must assume from time to time.

In chapter 6, I present the supplemental school program, the Paul Robeson Institute, that helped to guide Malcolm's life. The Paul Robeson Institute for Positive Self-Development is an example of a school-based environment sensitive to the unique needs of street-savvy Black American male students like Malcolm. In addition to academic classes like science and black history, the institute provides its students with mentors and role models to whom inner-city youths can relate. This analysis is the culmination of over two years of ethnographic research involving field observations, interviews, group discussions, journals, and surveys at this supplemental, after-school program. I demonstrate how the mentors and teachers at this institute facilitate academic success. They do so by understanding the origins of gangsterlike posturing and valuing and reinforcing the culture that street-savvy students bring to the classroom.

In chapter 7, I shed light upon the age-old myths (and stereotypes) of Black men as villains or deviants and how myths embodied in racialized metaphors, symbols, and stereotypes impose themselves as real. While offering my expert opinion, I draw heavily upon the scholarly works of Joe Feagin, Katheryn Russell, and Toni Morrison to characterize the American predisposition to fear Black males. This predisposition exemplifies symbolic violence and manifests in racial alibis, political strategies, news media accounts, and even the supposedly creative imaginations of science fiction writers. Unlike individuals who engage in blatantly racist acts of violence, those who engage in symbolic violence may not be aware that their actions are racist.

In chapter 8, the concluding chapter, I discuss the new light that my study sheds upon claims, theoretical and descriptive, about why some public schools re-create, whereas others level, inequality. Effective schools research figures prominently in this discussion. I also offer evolving policy considerations about how schools can deal with attitudes and mannerisms born out of street culture, without losing street-savvy students.

This book is inspired by and part of a critical discourse on schooling. Henry Giroux and Peter McLaren caution, "One major problem facing the recent outpouring of critical discourse on schooling is that over the years it has become largely academicized."[13] In an attempt to avoid this problem, I have written this book for a broad audience that includes academics, as well as teachers, youth workers, policy makers, college and high school students, and all others who have an interest in the experiences of street-savvy students. Some members of this broad audience may be unfamiliar with certain sociological terms and concepts. With that in mind, I define key concepts within chapters, include a glossary of social scientific terms at the back of the book, and reiterate key points that readers who are social scientists may take for granted. Some chapters may be of particular interest to teachers and youth workers, others may be of particular interest to scholars, and others to policy makers and innovators of school reforms. Those who prefer to delve immediately into the experiences of students may want first to read chapters 2, 3, and 5, and then read the rest of the book. Those who prefer first to read about effective teachers and mentors may want to read chapters 4, 5, and 6, and then the rest of the book. Those who prefer to start with the social scientific backdrop of this study should first read chapters 1 and 7; and those who seek policy or school reform recommendations should start with chapter 8. This book reads best, however, from start to finish.

Some of the terms and concepts used in this book, though not progressive, are standard to social scientific and popular writings. For example, "race" is a standard concept, even though "racial-ethnic group" or "ethnic group" are more appropriate and accurate terms. Likewise, "ethnic minorities" is a standard concept though "people(s) of color" is more accurate. The standard term "inner city" is sometimes misleading because not all impoverished urban communities are geographically located in the center of metropolitan areas. And "underclass" and "at-risk student" are pejorative and monolithic terms used to describe groups of individuals who are diverse. I considered replacing these terms with more appropriate concepts. Though inadequate, these are the terms most commonly used by scholars, teachers, youth workers, policy makers, and the like. Therefore, I use them in this book.

In closing this introductory chapter, I reiterate my political agenda for writing this book: to contribute the voices and experiences of street-savvy students to debates about schooling. Urban schools must acquire an empathetic understanding of what life is like for the students they serve. Otherwise, combating the negative aspects of street culture without an adequate and realistic understanding of how students relate to this culture and survive this culture is a losing battle: the casualties are reflected in high suspension, expulsion, and dropout rates for inner-city youth, especially Black and Brown males.

GLOSSARY OF STREET-SAVVY TERMS

This glossary contributes to an understanding of the terms—pun intended—of street-savvy students. (The glossary at the end of this book contains the terms of social scientists.) Therefore, I have purposefully placed this glossary in the introduction of this book instead of relegating it to the appendix. In order to interview and observe street-savvy students on their own terms, I often switched from standard English to my native black English vernacular and employed many of the terms below. Many of these terms were familiar to me, but a few were new to me and I acquired them in the course of conducting research. Several of these terms reappear throughout this book in students' quotes, vignettes, and narratives.

to be "all that"—to be important; to be attractive; to be special

bad—a mistake

to beat someone down—to fight someone; to assault someone

booty—nasty; disgusting

boyz (or boy)—neighborhood friends (or friend) who constitute a loosely knit gang or support system

buggin' out—to go crazy or lose control

bum rush—to move quickly and aggressively toward someone or something

can't get with—unable to understand or espouse or relate to

to chill (or to chill out)—to relax; to calm down

crazy—a lot; a large amount

crew—a small group of neighborhood friends who hang together and look out for or protect each other.

deep—insightful; profound; thought-provoking

diss—to disrespect or dismiss someone

to be down—to be hip or cool; to be included or a part of something; to understand someone or something; to be respected or accepted by someone or some group

a fade—a hairstyle, popular in the late 1980s and early 1990s, in which the hair is worn about one-half inch or more long on the top of the head and cut close to the scalp or bald on the sides and back of the head

five (or 5–0)—the police

frontin—to fake something or lie about something in order to impress one's peers

gangsta—gangster

to get rolled on—*see to roll on someone*

going for mine—to look out for number one, that is, oneself

to hang—to cope with or meet the challenge of a confrontation

to have someone's back—to support or look out for someone

hard (or hardcore)—the state of being a street-savvy and tough gangster who would actually commit criminal, violent, or ruthless acts

hardcore wannabe—the state of acting hard because it is fashionable or prestigious, for example, a means of gaining social esteem in urban youth culture

herb (or erb)—marijuana

to hit the skins—to have sexual intercourse

hood—neighborhood

to hook someone up—to assist or look out for someone; to provide someone with needed resources

ill—crazy or demented; messed up

kickin' it—to pal around; to accompany a friend during fun activities; to hang out with a friend or friends

to kick to the curb—to throw away; to get rid of; to dismiss or treat someone unfairly

knot—a bundle of money

"Later!"—"See you later"

"Let's be out."—"Let's leave or depart."

a little somethin'-somethin'—something; something special; something extra; or something of substance

to mack (or to go mackin' or on the mack)—to look for girls to date; to date more than one girl at a time

mad—*see crazy*

nine—a semi-automatic handgun that holds a round the size of which is nine millimeters (9 mm)

"Peace!"—"Good-bye"

phat—cool; impressive; awesome; nice

to play someone—to fool or tease someone; to disrespect someone

props—short for propers; giving someone or something the proper acknowledgment; showing proper appreciation

to punk someone—to treat someone with blatant disrespect; to treat a man as less than a man.

to rock—to wear or don something, for example, to wear clothes, accessories, styles, and the like

to roll on someone—to do something before someone else; to take advantage of an opportunity that someone else overlooked or that someone else moved too slowly to act upon; to out-maneuver or to overpower; to beat someone up.

to shoot hoops—to play basketball

somethin'-somethin'—*see a little somethin'-somethin'*

to step off—to walk away; to back down

to step to—to approach and confront or challenge someone or something

the streets—the rough or infamous neighborhoods or sections in urban areas that have the highest rates of poverty, joblessness, unemployment, illicit activities, welfare recipiency, physically violent confrontations, and so on

to sweat someone or something—to admire someone; to admire with an intent to possess; to hound; to pursue; to pressure; to worry about something

to talk smack—to make empty claims, statements, or threats

to throw down—to fight

24/7/365—all day, all week, all year, that is, all the time

Word—"That's true."; "That's correct."; "I agree."

part I

"Expert" Points of View

ONE

There Are No Agents Here

Scholarly Depictions of Black Americans

MURALS IN THE CITY

In urban and inner-city neighborhoods, where ethnic minorities subsist at or below the poverty line, you often come upon beautifully painted murals. These murals often burst with color and activity: children are playing, residents are lending one another a helping hand, flowers are growing, adults are mentoring and nurturing, or heroes like Malcolm X, Martin Luther King, or César Chávez are reincarnated in larger-than-life portraits as guardians of the neighborhood. Sometimes urban murals are somber memorials to lives lost to homicide, but more often they are full of life, activity, and agency. The artists who create these murals often move beyond stereotypes to capture real, dynamic, fully human characteristics of individual residents, popular heroes, and community activities. These characterizations contrast sharply with the depictions of ethnic minorities in social scientific writings. Social *scientists* often shun *artistic* license like that taken by the painters of urban murals, that is, subjective license to vitalize and portray residents in vibrant colors. Social scientists filter urban residents through screens that are objective and analytical, sieves designed to yield empirically sound depictions. Social scientists paint dispassionate portrayals that are supposedly undistorted by researcher subjectivity and bias. Yet the scholar's pen may yield more distorting portrayals than the mural painter's brush: social scientists often inscribe ethnic minorities in books, articles, and other texts as abnormal, monolithic, static, faceless, listless objects.

Sucheng Chan observes that scholars have portrayed ethnic minorities in the United States in four contrasting perspectives: ethnic minorities as deviant or deficient; ethnic minorities as valuable contributors to the American cultural mosaic; ethnic minorities as exploited victims relegated to the lowest social status positions within the institutional structure of the United States; and finally, ethnic minorities as "agents of history—men and women who make choices that shape their lives, even when these may be severely limited by conditions beyond their control."[1] Of these four perspectives, extreme characterizations of deficiency and victimization prevail as the most problematic when they eclipse individual agency. Although Chan's research focuses upon Asian Americans, these four perspectives apply to other ethnic minorities, including White ethnic Americans, Hispanic Americans, Native Americans, and African Americans.[2] With respect to the latter two groups, for example, scholarly portrayals swing between extreme characterizations of deficiency and victimization.

The pendulum of depictions for Native Americans (the Indigenous peoples of the Americas) swings between deficient, lazy red savages and victimized conquered people or vanishing people relegated to the past.[3] For African Americans, the pendulum sways between deficient, genetically inferior welfare recipients and hapless descendants of American slavery and apartheid.[4] These depictions stereotype Indigenous peoples and African Americans as beings without *human* agency, as pawns of biologically determined, primitive instinct or puppets on the strings of macro-structural forces, strings that control their every action, motivation, and aspiration. The historical episodes and legacies of inhumane government-sanctioned policies of conquest, land dispossession, and genocide, in the case of Indigenous peoples or Native Americans, or chattel slavery and apartheid, in the case of Blacks or African Americans, may be the most severe macro-structural predicaments imposed upon Americans of color within the borders of what has become the United States of America.[5] Indigenous Americans and African Americans, as well as Mexican Americans, have been described as castelike or involuntary minorities. Unlike those ethnic groups who immigrated to the United States by choice, the ancestors of Indigenous, African, and Mexican Americans were dehumanized, colonized, and subsequently Americanized by forceful and often violent means.[6] Hence, today, many Indigenous, African, and Mexican Americans, as well as other Americans of color, remain to be fully accepted as "real" Americans; they remain excluded from the fold of the American social fabric. Asian Americans have also experienced caste or apartheidlike treatment within the borders of the United States, treatment that ranges from laws barring Asian immigrants from entering the United States, to laws barring their acquisition of U.S. citizenship, to internment within concentration camps.[7] Despite scholarly portrayals to the contrary, however, Americans of color have confronted, survived, succumbed to, overcome, or resisted devastating historical events and other social structural constraints not as passive pawns or puppets, but as dynamic agents of history.

Even when scholars leave human agency intact, however, Americans of color are often cast in images that are monolithic or undifferentiated. For example, Indigenous Americans are often portrayed as noble savages or children of nature who subsist within the spatial constraints of reservations, and African Americans have been cast as soulful and cool ghetto dwellers who subsist within the spatial constraints of inner-city neighborhoods.[8] Monolithic images like the noble savage or the cool ghetto dweller transform the members of ethnic groups into an undifferentiated mass of cultural automatons. In these cases, scholars delimit the agency of Indigenous and Black Americans to a set of predictable responses, to an Indian way or Black way of doing things.[9] To the contrary, Indigenous Americans and Black Americans exhibit group solidarity as well as intragroup conflict and individual dissent. It should go without saying that they exhibit a wide variety of responses, practices, and roles that range from the culturally unique to the ethnically hybrid, from the conventional to the innovative. Without a doubt, the well-being of many Americans of color continues to be severely constrained by forces beyond their control. The point I make here is not that social structural forces should be ignored or minimized. I emphasize that those Americans of color constrained are a vital segment of humanity, not lazy red savages, criminals, deviants, noble savages, or cool ghetto dwellers.

This chapter reviews scholarly depictions unique to Black Americans. Given the focus of *Tough Fronts* on Black male students from urban neighborhoods that are economically impoverished, my review of literature is skewed toward accounts of urban Black males in particular. The inclusion of studies on the Black middle class and Black women would yield a more comprehensive review of the literature. Yet, for the sake of drawing more attention to scholarship that applies to Black males from impoverished urban neighborhoods, studies limited to the Black middle class and Black women are not included.[10] Among other things, this chapter revisits theories about the culture of poverty, the growth of the urban underclass, and oppositional culture, and then concludes with a constructive critique of these theories and notions. The remainder of this chapter focuses exclusively upon Black Americans. However, the previous paragraphs reveal that there are some striking similarities (or stubborn consistencies) in the manner that scholars characterize Americans of color in general, and Blacks and Indigenous peoples in particular. Unlike the artists who paint urban murals, scholars seem to have difficulty with moving beyond stereotypes to capture the real, dynamic, human agency of Americans of color.

THE SCHOLARLY GAZE UPON BLACK AMERICANS

Scholars often occupy positions of relative privilege within society. It is from such elite and lofty points of view that scholars have gazed upon Blacks in general and *urban* Black Americans in particular. This gaze has often degraded; other times it has flattered. But most of the time, it has been an essentialist gaze. I deliberately choose the words "essentialist" and "gaze" to characterize the academic enterprise of studying urban Black Americans. Disregarding contradictions and hybridity, as well as eclectic and syncretic practices, scholars have taken a long, fixed stare and found urban Blacks essentially inferior, or mainstream, or victims, or virtuous, or oppositional. A vast majority of academic accounts fall into three of these categories: Blacks as inferior, Blacks as mainstream, or Blacks as pawns or victims. There is a shortage of long, fixed stares that regard urban Blacks as individuals with human agency and diverse cultural practices. In *Yo' Mama's DisFUNKtional: Fighting the Culture Wars in Urban America*, Robin Kelley applauds *Drylongso: A Self-Portrait of Black America*, by John Langston Gwaltney, as a noteworthy exception to the vast majority of scholarly accounts:

> Few ghetto ethnographers have understood or developed Gwaltney's insights into African American urban culture. Whereas Gwaltney's notion of core [black] culture incorporates a diverse and contradictory range of practices, attitudes, and relationships that are dynamic, historically situated, and ethnically hybrid, social scientists of his generation and after—especially those at the forefront of poverty studies—treat culture as if it were a set of behaviors. They assume that there is one identifiable ghetto culture and what they observed was it.[11]

While reading in *Drylongso* the "personal narratives ... offered [to Gwaltney] in contexts of amity, security and hospitality,"[12] one encounters the agency, range of practices, and diversity of attitudes voiced by Gwaltney's respondents. Instead of the usual depiction of static, monolithic objects, Gwaltney's respondents are subjects; they figure prominently as vibrant, dynamic, opinionated individuals.

Broadly speaking, then, this chapter reviews five scholarly portrayals of Black Americans: (1) Blacks as essentially inferior, deviant, or dysfunctional; (2) Blacks as essentially mainstream or decent; (3) Blacks as essentially virtuous and central; (4) Blacks as essentially victims of historical and social-structural forces; (5) Blacks as essentially oppositional or antagonistic. *Tough Fronts* falls into a sixth and underdeveloped perspective: urban Black youths, to recall the words of Sucheng Chan, as "agents of history—[adolescents] who make choices that shape their lives, even when these may be severely limited by conditions beyond their control."[13] As I move from scholarly accounts of deviancy toward this book's view of agency, I do not attempt to include every single study ever documented. Instead, I review works that are exemplars of these five perspectives. Furthermore, instead of summarizing each work in exacting detail, I discuss the dominant characterizations of Blacks conveyed.

Blacks as Inferior, Deviant, Dysfunctional

> Enlightenment philosophy was instrumental in codifying and institutionalizing both the scientific and popular European perceptions of the human race. The numerous writings on race by Hume, Kant, and Hegel played a strong role in articulating Europe's sense not only of its cultural but also racial superiority. In their writings ... "reason" and "civilization" became almost synonymous with "white" people and northern Europe, while unreason and savagery were conveniently located among non-whites, the "black," the "red," the "yellow," outside Europe.
>
> —Emmanuel Chukwudi Eze, *Race and the Enlightenment*[14]

As far back as the 1700s, western European scholars argued that Negroes were inferior to Whites. In the 1800s, Social Darwinists and eugenics scholars like Francis Galton would add their findings to claims about the inferiority of non-whites. Among other things, Galton once asserted that "the Negro has strong impulsive passions, and neither patience, reticence, nor dignity."[15] Like the twentieth-century eugenicists and Social Darwinists who followed, Galton called for social policies to control human breeding by discouraging breeding among groups deemed "inferior" and encouraging members of the "superior" groups to marry and procreate.[16] Other eugenic policies pursued in the early 1900s included immigration restrictions, residential segregation, and school reforms.[17]

Some may argue that these claims about Blacks as inferior are passé. Enlightenment scholarship is three hundred years old; eugenic theories and policies that were popular in the United States during the 1930s have been debunked as pseudo-scientific babble. But Enlightenment scholarship influenced the founding patriots of the United States of America; Enlightenment scholars inspired the men of conviction and vision who framed the Declaration of Independence and the Constitution. Thomas Jefferson, for example, authored essays "in support of what [he] believed to be the innate or 'natural' inferiority of the Negro (and superiority of the white) in the areas of physical beauty and mental and intellectual capacity."[18] Over two hundred years later, theories of intellectual inferiority remain popular among a segment of the educated elite. At the dawn of the twenty-first century, social scientists from distinguished institutions like the University of California and Harvard continue to endorse Enlightenment and eugenic-like theories about the inherent inferiority of Black people.[19]

Genetic Explanations of Black Inferiority

The works of Arthur R. Jensen, Richard Herrnstein, and Charles Murray exemplify more recent scholarship about Blacks as inferior. These scholars espouse theories of biological determinism. In the late 1960s and early 1970s, University of California psychologist Arthur R. Jensen authored "How Much Can We Boost IQ and Scholastic Achievement," and held fast to claims that Blacks were, based upon genetics, inherently less intelligent than whites. In Jensen's defense, Harvard psychologist Richard Herrnstein concludes:

> Jensen answered the title's rhetorical question about IQ with a scholarly and circumspect form of "not very much." The article is cautious and detailed, far from extreme in position or tone. Not only its facts but even most of its conclusions are familiar to experts. The failure of compensatory education was the occasion for the article, which served especially well in assembling many scattered but pertinent items. Jensen echoes most experts on the subject of the IQ by concluding substantially more can be ascribed to inheritance than environment.[20]

In the 1980s, Charles Murray wrote *Losing Ground: American Social Policy 1950–1980*. Murray argues that governmental welfare policies and practices caused an increase in poverty. He resurrects eugenic-like sentiments by suggesting that poor Blacks are impervious to government welfare policies. He contends that the vast majority of *poor people* (Murray's code words for urban Blacks), the vast majority of *hardcore unemployed* (code words for urban Black males), the vast majority of *AFDC recipients* (code words for Black women), and the vast majority of *poor and disadvantaged students* (code words for inner-city Black students) are an undeserving poor who have failed to pull themselves up by their bootstraps.[21] Murray makes several assumptions reminiscent of eugenics movement theories. Just to list a couple, he hypothesizes that poor Blacks would not thrive in an education system that was tuition-free through graduate school because they do not succeed in the current education system that is free through the twelfth grade. He further suggests that a few hard-working Black parents should be provided with educational vouchers for their children, but the vast majority of poor Black students should be herded into a special bootcamplike school system.[22]

Finally, in 1994, Murray and Herrnstein co-authored *The Bell Curve: Intelligence and Class Structure in American Life*, which continued and expanded upon Jensen's and Herrnstein's earlier arguments about race and intelligence.[23] In these works, Blacks and other ethnic minorities (Asians excepted) are not merely depicted as inferior and dysfunctional; these social scientists go on to conclude that very little can be done to ameliorate poverty in urban ghettos or to change the low educational achievement outcomes of ethnic minorities. According to scholars like Jensen, Herrnstein, and Murray, social programs targeting poverty and educational achievement have failed because these programs "misinterpreted genetic differences as environmental."[24]

Culture of Poverty Explanations of Black Inferiority

In contrast to claims that the inferiority of Blacks is biological or genetic, some researchers categorize Black inferiority as a cultural phenomenon. Actually, in lieu of the term "inferior," cultural explanations employ terms like "deviant" or "dysfunctional" or "pathological." Social researchers like Oscar Lewis, Daniel Moynihan, and Kenneth Clark argue that minorities from urban ghettos are entrapped in a "culture of poverty."[25] In anthropological terms, Lewis defines the culture of poverty as a "culture that provides human beings with a design for living, with a ready-made set of solutions for human problems."[26] Once the culture of poverty comes into existence, it becomes self-sustaining; after this transformation, the acculturation of children begins at an early age. Lewis continues, "By the time slum children are 6 or 7 they have usually absorbed the basic attitudes and values of their subculture. Thereafter they are psychologically unready to take full advantage of changing conditions or improving opportunities that may develop in their lifetime."[27]

Moynihan explicitly describes this cultural entrapment as a "tangle of pathology."[28] Moynihan acknowledges that many Black families have escaped the grips of the tangle of pathology; he points out, however, that even these stable families remain at risk of being drawn back into it. This risk, according to Moynihan, is especially high for Black youths. Similar to Lewis's view of slum children, Moynihan notes, "In a word, most Negro youth are in danger of being caught up in the tangle of pathology that affects their world, and probably a majority are so entrapped. Many of those who escape do so for one generation only: as things now are, their children may have to run the gauntlet all over again."[29] Both Lewis and Moynihan acknowledge that the culture of poverty initially results from wider structural forces like poverty, discrimination, and residential segregation. Yet they both dwell on the fact that this tangled, dysfunctional culture eventually perpetuates itself. Hence, according to scholars like Lewis and Moynihan, social pathologies within Black communities have little to do with genetics; they are created by structural forces and then maintained by a self-perpetuating subculture. Though Lewis, Moynihan, and Clark expressed these views in the 1960s, this line of thinking is far from passé. For example, Stephan Thernstrom, a Harvard University historian, and Abigail Thernstrom, a senior fellow at the Manhattan Institute, include family disorganization as well as cultural and social values as reasons for "the serious inequality that remains [between Black and White Americans]." Their book *American in Black and White: One Nation, Indivisible* was published in 1997.

Blacks as Mainstream or Decent

Many researchers write against theories that cast Blacks in inferior and dysfunctional images. They portray urban Blacks as integral to and in intimate contact with the

American mainstream. Exemplars of this perspective include ethnographers like Elliot Liebow, Ulf Hannerz, and Elijah Anderson.[30] In *Tally's Corner: A Study of Negro Streetcorner Men*, Elliot Liebow conducts ethnographic observations in Washington, D.C., and affirms that black culture is not a self-perpetuating tangle of pathology. He finds the culture of Black men from a low-income urban neighborhood strongly linked to the American mainstream. Liebow contends, "This inside world does not appear as a self-contained, self-generating, self-sustaining system or even subsystem with clear boundaries marking it off from the larger world around it. It is in continuous, intimate contact with the larger society—indeed, it is an integral part of it."[31]

In *Soulside: Inquiries into Ghetto Culture and Community*, Ulf Hannerz differentiates urban Blacks into four main lifestyles or ideal types—"mainstreamers, swingers, street families, and streetcorner men"—but acknowledges that "there are many individuals who are less clearly oriented towards any one of [these life styles].[32] Overall, Hannerz endorses Liebow's sentiments and finds that "poor [urban Black] people share the aspirations of those with more adequate incomes and would soon approach these in their way of life, were their own economic opportunities improved." Hannerz, whose ethnographic research was also based in Washington, D.C., argues, "[M]ore attention should be paid to the fact that poor people share mainstream ideals."[33]

In *A Place on the Corner*, similar to the urban ethnographies of Liebow and Hannerz, Elijah Anderson conducts research among poor Black men who reside in Chicago's South Side. In contrast, Anderson does not directly argue against culture-of-poverty characterizations of urban Blacks. While Liebow and Hannerz state and reiterate that urban Blacks are not "carrier[s] of an independent cultural tradition,"[34] Anderson's study implicitly corroborates this finding. He spends more time delineating the status hierarchy and values among a group of poor Black men who are viewed by more mainstream Americans as a monolithic group of "lowlifes."[35] However, like Liebow and Hannerz, Anderson illuminates the degree to which the aspirations of the men in his study overlap with those of the American mainstream, the degree to which these men adhere to a code of "decency."[36] Anderson concludes:

> Within the extended primary group at Jelly's [bar and liquor store], a "visible means of support" and "decency" appear to be the primary values, while "toughness" "gettin' big money," "gettin' some wine" and "havin' some fun" are residual values, or values group members adopt after the "props" supporting decency have for some reason been judged unviable, unavailable, or unattainable.[37]

In *Code of the Street*, Anderson's most recent ethnography conducted in the 1990s, he renews these claims about decency. He maintains that the majority of Black residents from inner cities "are decent or trying to be," and they "share many of the middle class values of the wider white society."[38] In short, social scientists such as Liebow, Hannerz, and Anderson argue that although macro-structural constraints like poverty, segregation, and discrimination may necessitate circumstantial variations and strategic adaptations, urban Blacks espouse mainstream ideals. Those residents from inner-city communities who fail to live up to mainstream values are precluded by social structural constraints. That is to say, "the pervasiveness of poverty, unemployment, and dependency in [inner cities makes] it nearly impossible for them to live up to ideals they in fact [espouse]."[39]

Blacks as Virtuous and Central

In addition to academic depictions of Blacks as mainstream are those of Blacks as virtuous, central, and, in a few cases, superior. The Afrocentric works of Maulana Karenga and Molefi Kete Asante exemplify this view. While Liebow, Hannerz, and Anderson argue against theories of Blacks as inferior by accentuating the overlap of values and aspirations between urban Blacks and mainstream Whites, Afrocentric scholars argue against inferiorizing narratives by critiquing and deconstructing Eurocentric schools of thought. A central thesis and critique of Afrocentric works is that Eurocentric biases, prejudices, preferences, ideologies, theories, and so on masquerade as universal truths in the humanities and social sciences.[40] Asante affirms and elaborates this "radical" critique in the opening pages of *The Afrocentric Idea*:

> My work has increasingly constituted a radical critique of the Eurocentric ideology that masquerades as a universal view in the fields of intercultural communication, rhetoric, philosophy, linguistics, psychology, education, anthropology, and history. Yet the critique is radical only in the sense that it suggests a turnabout, an alternative perspective on phenomena. It is about taking the globe and turning it over so that we see all possibilities of a world where Africa, for example, is subject and not object. Such a posture is necessary and rewarding for both Africans and Europeans. The inability to "see" from several angles is perhaps the one common weakness in provincial scholarship. Those who have delighted us most thoroughly and advanced thought most significantly have been those thinkers who explored different views and brought new perspectives.[41]

In addition to promoting false claims about universality, according to Afrocentric scholars, the vast majority of Eurocentric social scientists have been far less than objective when depicting Blacks. Asante contends that these scholars have confused objectivity with "a kind of collective subjectivity of European culture."[42] Hence, scholars like Asante and Karenga seek to restore African (and Black American) virtue, dignity, and centrality by halting and reversing the "progressive Europeanization of human consciousness."[43]

African-centered critiques of Eurocentric "truths" had been offered by several Black writers and scholars who were born in the late 1800s—for example, Ida B. Wells-Barnett (born in 1862), W. E. B. DuBois (born in 1868), Zora Neale Hurston (born in 1891), and Paul Robeson (born in 1898)—several decades prior to the civil rights movement. However, it was from the crucible of debates, tribulations, challenges, and achievements of 1960s black cultural nationalism and the civil rights movement that African-centered studies crystallized into an academic discipline.[44] Melba Joyce Boyd, the current chair of the Department of African Studies at Wayne State University, recalls the exact birth date of black studies:

On April 4, 1968, Dr. Martin Luther King was assassinated in Memphis, Tennessee. On April 5, 1968, in Kalamazoo, Michigan, the black students at Western Michigan University occupied the Student Center Building and demanded a black studies curriculum and a scholarship fund in the face of a heavily armed National Guard. This occurrence was characteristic of sixties radicalism on college campuses and, for the most part, was responsible for the establishment of black studies on predominantly white campuses.[45]

Thus, from the start African-centered scholars in the United States have explicitly advanced political agendas, academic progress, and social justice. As explained by Karenga, "Black studies evolved in the midst of the emancipatory struggle of the sixties that linked intellectual emancipation with political emancipation, campus with community, intellectuals and students with the masses, and knowledge in the academy with power in society." "Afrocentricity," defined as "placing African ideals at the center of any analysis that involves African culture and behavior,"[46] emerged as a critical theory in the late 1970s.[47]

As mentioned above, Afrocentric works are directly opposed or antithetical to Eurocentric portrayals like those that characterize Blacks as inferior. These scholars remove Blacks from the periphery of the "white" academic universe, relocate them to the center of black or Afrocentric studies, and resuscitate African agency. In lieu of singing the praises of ancient Greek and Roman contributions to humanity, Afrocentric scholars extol the virtues and contributions of ancient Egypt and other African civilizations. As a critique of Eurocentric materialism, they offer Afrocentric personalism. Likewise, Euro-linear analyses and dichotomies are juxtaposed with Afro-circular approaches.[48] And a few Afrocentric scholars who espouse extreme beliefs move beyond depictions of Blacks as virtuous and central to assertions of Blacks as superior. These claims of black superiority are not nearly as pervasive as accounts of black inferiority espoused by the European Enlightenment, American eugenics movement, and biological determinists. And most Afrocentric scholars condemn pro–black claims of genetic superiority.[49] But similar to Arthur Jensen and Richard Herrnstein, Afrocentric extremists link intelligence to genetics. These scholars provide an antithesis to Jensen, Herrnstein, and Murray's IQ thesis: Whites are inferior and black genetic superiority derives from a link between melanin and intelligence.[50]

Similar to ethnographers and other social scientists who view social structural factors like poverty, unemployment, and discrimination as primary impediments to the progress of urban Blacks, Asante implicates Eurocentric technologies, theories, practices, and values that have been mobilized to "dislocate and disorient African people."[51] Hence, in recasting Blacks as virtuous and as central, Afrocentric scholars do not seek to replace white domination with black domination. Instead they seek to facilitate black progress by correcting Eurocentric distortions and thereby contribute to a more multicultural understanding of humanity. Asante concludes that to do otherwise and "allow the definitions of Africans as marginal and as fringe people in the historical processes of the world is to abandon all hope of reversing the degradation of the oppressed."[52]

Blacks as Victims

Similar to Afrocentric scholars, some social scientists focus upon the wider structures and macro contexts in which Black Americans are situated or dislocated. Afrocentrics focus primarily—though not exclusively—upon intellectual spatial situations (institutions of higher learning) and academic constraints. Sociologists like William Julius Wilson or Douglas Massey and Nancy Denton focus upon geographical spatial situations (the inner city) and structural constraints. In contrast to depictions of Blacks as inferior or mainstream or virtuous, these sociologists highlight the wider structural factors that exist "beyond the ability of any individual to change; [forces like residential segregation that constrain] black life chances irrespective of personal traits, individual motivations or private achievements."[53] William Julius Wilson's works are most exemplary of this approach. Social scientific research on inner cities provides the social structural context for *Tough Fronts*. I will, therefore, elaborate findings like Wilson's in greater detail than the other works included in this review of the literature.

Blacks as Victims of Social Structural Forces

The focus upon the structural configuration of cities and the impact of this structure on individuals within cities is a long-standing sociological preoccupation. In classic essays on city life, German and Chicago School sociologists describe an ideal-typical city that consists of economic, cultural, individual, and ecological domains.[54] Economically, this city is a fortress, colony, or settlement—or a conglomeration of settlements or neighborhoods—with a money-based instead of an agriculturally based means of subsistence. Culturally, the ideal-typical city provides a center of intellectualism that fosters mainstream beliefs, norms, and values. With respect to the individual, the city generates and sustains a moral climate in which innate individual dispositions may evolve to full and free expression.[55] And ecologically, the city consists of a complex habitat with a human community of man-made values, norms, laws, formal social organization, and institutions and structures. When applied to contemporary research on inner cities like that of William Julius Wilson, these four domains provide qualitative criteria for assessing spheres of social interaction unique to inner cities.

In *The Truly Disadvantaged: The Inner City, the Underclass, and Public Policy*, Wilson argues that social-structural factors (for example, historic discrimination, the decline of low-skilled occupations, and the exodus of middle-class Blacks) caused a transformation of inner-city neighborhoods in major metropolitan areas. He holds that this transformation left inner-city areas in a state of isolation and dislocation characterized by illegitimate births, female-headed households, high rates of crime, joblessness, and poverty. Basically, Wilson's argument can be represented by the model in Table 1.1.

This model describes the transformation of inner cities that occurred *after* the 1960s. According to Wilson, prior to the 1960s and shortly after World War II, inner-city communities "exhibited the features of social organization—including a sense of community, positive neighborhood identification, and explicit norms and sanctions against aberrant behavior."[56] Underlying this social organization of the

TABLE 1.1. WILSON'S MODEL EXPLAINING THE GROWTH OF THE UNDERCLASS

I	II	III
Structural Factors →	Transformation →	Dislocation
Historic Discrimination (Slavery, Jim Crow segregation, pre-1950s labor market discrimination, etc.)	**Transformation of the Urban Class Structure** (Concentration of extremely poor Blacks and absence of social buffer previously provided by working- and middle-class Blacks)	**Crime**
		Concentrated Poverty
Migration North and South		**Joblessness**
		Shortage of Marriageable Men
Age Structure (Youth) of Migrants		**Female Householders**
		Out-of-Wedlock Births
Changing Economic Structure ■ Shift from goods-producing to service-producing industries ■ Labor market polarization into low vs. high-wage sectors ■ Technological advances ■ Relocation of manufacturing industries out of inner cities		
Labor Surplus (Entry of women and baby boomers into the labor market)		
Exodus of Working- and Middle-Class Blacks		

mid-twentieth-century inner-city were the four domains of social interaction enumerated by German and Chicago School sociologists. That is to say, during this period, the inner city was racially segregated, but the presence of manufacturing jobs as well as working- and middle-class families provided the urban poor with a link to the economic, cultural, individual, and ecological spheres of the wider metropolitan area of the city. First of all, racial discrimination precluded many Blacks from certain activities within the formal economy—namely private sector white-collar positions—but at least the urban poor had access to manufacturing and other low-skill occupations. Second, Black working- and middle-class families linked the urban poor to the city culture of intellectualism and mainstream values. For example, Wilson argues that the very presence of working- and middle-class families provided the more economically disadvantaged inner-city families with "mainstream role models that help keep alive the perception that education is meaningful."[57] Third, Black working- and middle-class families provided the urban poor with more varied and mainstream possibilities for individual expression. Again, due to racial discrimination, Black Americans were denied the range of full expression or the amount of personal freedom described in German and Chicago School sociological writings on city life. Nevertheless, the urban poor of the mid-twentieth century had fewer constraints upon personal freedom and individual expression than the urban poor of today. At the very least, the urban poor were exposed to a balance between the social forces of organization and those of dislocation. Wilson explains:

[A] perceptive ghetto youngster in a neighborhood that includes a good number of working and professional families may observe increasing joblessness and idleness, but he will also witness many individuals regularly going to and from work; he may sense an increase in school dropouts but he can also see a connection between education and meaningful employment; he may detect a growth in single-parent families, but he will also be aware of the presence of many married-couple families; he may notice an increase in welfare dependency, but he can also see a significant number of families that are not on welfare; and he may be cognizant of an increase in crime, but he can also recognize that many residents in his neighborhood are not involved in criminal activity.[58]

Finally, because urban poor working- and middle-class families shared the same neighborhood or habitat, the inner city of the mid-twentieth century was racially segregated but ecologically more stratified and reflective of the class structure, social organization, human community, and so on of the wider metropolitan area.

Unlike this mid-twentieth-century inner city, today's inner cities are both radically segregated and socially isolated from the economic, cultural, individual, and ecological domains of the wider metropolitan area. Where there was once a stable degree of connectedness to the wider metropolitan area of the city, two essential features are missing: namely, economic structural access to the formal economy and representatives of mainstream cultural values. In more specific terms, the loss of manufacturing and low-skill occupations as well as the ensuing exodus of Black working- and middle-class families had economic, cultural, individual, and ecological consequences. Economically, the urban poor have declining access to formal economic opportunity. Culturally, the urban poor, especially young males, eschew mainstream values for values more applicable to their immediate social situation.[59] Ecologically, the inner city becomes socially isolated such that "a disproportionate concentration of the most disadvantaged segments of the urban population" interact mostly with others who are similarly situated and less representative of the wider metropolitan area.[60] Individually, one has less direct exposure to different possibilities for personal growth. The perceptive youngster described above is no longer exposed to a balance between social organization and dislocation. Instead, social dislocation becomes the norm.

Other sociologists complement, critique, and build upon Wilson's basic argument about the structural causes of the urban underclass. A recurrent critique of *The Truly Disadvantaged* is that Wilson inadequately assesses present-day anti-black racism and discrimination. For example, Massey and Denton agree with Wilson's basic argument but contend that were it not for severe residential segregation, the structural factors enumerated by Wilson "would not have produced the disastrous social and economic outcomes observed in inner cities [during the 1970s and 1980s]."[61] Massey and Denton assert that the residential segregation experienced by Black Americans is far more extreme than the transient segregation experienced by other ethnic minorities.

No group in the history of the United States has ever experienced the sustained high level of residential segregation that has been imposed on blacks in large American cities

for the past fifty years. This extreme racial isolation did not just happen; it was manufactured by whites through a series of self-conscious actions and purposeful
institutional arrangements that continue today. Not only is the depth of black segregation unprecedented and utterly unique compared with that of other groups, but it
shows little sign of change with the passage of time or improvement in socioeconomic
status.[62]

Hence Massey and Denton contend that historic discrimination is not the only form
of discrimination that contributed to the growth of the urban underclass; historic
and contemporary residential discrimination prevail as key factors.

Michael Omi and Howard Winant constructively critique Wilson. They acknowledge the importance of Wilson's policy perceptions but assert that "the racial
discrimination which civil rights era legislation was designed to outlaw remains ubiq-
uitous." Joe Feagin and Hernán Vera, whose findings are elaborated in chapter 7 of
this book, supplement Wilson's model with episodes of white racism that are blatant,
symbolic, *and contemporary;* Sut Jhally and Justin Lewis add subtle yet pervasive
forms of enlightened racism.[63] By "enlightened racism," Jhally and Lewis mean the
tendency among members of the white American mainstream to ignore or deny class
barriers and believe that all Blacks can succeed like the Huxtables from *The Cosby
Show* if they work hard and embrace white cultural values.[64] Last but not least,
Wilson supplements his own model. In his more recent book *When Work Disappears: The World of the New Urban Poor,* in addition to the disappearance of work,
Wilson adds statistical discrimination—that is, prejudice toward an individual based
upon presumptions about that individual's ethnic or social group—and American
ideals of rugged individualism as factors that sustain and perpetuate the urban underclass.[65] Hence a new and critiqued version of Wilson's model (see table 1.2)
explaining the growth and continuation of the urban underclass includes additional
structural factors, namely contemporary forms of racism and discrimination.

As enumerated in this model, the findings of Wilson, Massey and Denton, and
other sociologists provide analyses of urban Black Americans and inner cities that are
brilliantly detailed, comprehensive, and extensive. However, in clarifying the
structural factors that lie beyond the control of individual Black Americans, these
sociologists unwittingly suggest that urban Blacks are *controlled by* these forces, when
in fact they mean to convey that Blacks are *constrained,* sometimes severely, by structural forces. The exclusive focus upon structure overshadows agency to the point of
depicting Blacks as hapless victims of social structure. Born out of this view of
Blacks as hapless victims is another characterization that particularly applies to Black
youths from inner cities: the monolithic, angry Black male opposed to the American
mainstream.

Blacks as Oppositional: The Case of Inner-City Youths

Massey and Denton reason that "[i]n response to the harsh and isolated conditions
of ghetto life, a segment of the urban black population has evolved a set of behav-
iors, attitudes, and values that are increasingly at variance with those held in the
wider society."[66] Almost three decades prior to Massey and Denton, Kenneth Clark
made similar assertions in *Dark Ghetto*: "Because the larger society has clearly rejected

TABLE 1.2. WILSON'S MODEL EXPLAINING THE GROWTH OF THE UNDERCLASS
(The critiqued version.)

I Structural Factors →	II Transformation →	III Perpetuation →	IV Dislocation
Historic Discrimination	Transformation of the Urban Class Structure (Concentration and Social Buffer effects)	Statistical Discrimination	Crime
Migration North and South		Disappearance of Work	Concentrated Poverty
Age Structure (Youth) of Migrants		American Belief in Rugged Individualism	Joblessness
Changing Economic Structure			Shortage of Marriageable Men
Labor Surplus			Female Householders
Exodus of Working- and Middle-Class Blacks			Out-of-Wedlock Births
Residential Segregation (resulting from racist housing market practices and policies)			
Blatant and Enlightened Forms of White Racism			

[the black ghetto dweller], he rejects ... the values, the aspirations, and techniques of that society."[67] However, one of the most renowned proponents of the oppositional culture thesis is anthropologist John Ogbu.

Ogbu defines oppositional culture as an antithetical system of values and beliefs that shapes the attitudes and aspirations of Black Americans in general, not just residents of inner-city communities. In more comparative terms, oppositional cultures exist in other societies where ethnic minorities have a castelike relationship to the dominant group. Like Black Americans in the United States, the Buraku outcasts in Japan and the Maoris in New Zealand have generated oppositional cultures that are antithetical to dominant group cultures in their countries.[68] The oppositional system of values results from cultural inversion, "the tendency for members of one population, in this case a minority group, to regard certain forms of behavior, events, symbols, and meanings as inappropriate, precisely because they are characteristic of members of another population, [for example,] white Americans."[69] Black Americans employ cultural inversion strategies to oppose derogatory stereotypes attributed to them by White Americans and to "turn the table against whites." The oppositional culture of a minority group is a direct consequence of the racist and discriminatory practices of the dominant group. Ogbu concludes, "Because secondary cultural differences are developed in opposition to and in response to perceived unjustified treatment by the dominant group, such cultural differences are intimately tied to the minorities' sense of group identity."[70] In the educational arena, for example, black group identity and solidarity lead inner-city students to link academic success to "acting white." Hence, "many black students who are academically able do not put forth the necessary effort and perseverance in their schoolwork and, consequently, do poorly in school."[71]

To the extent that oppositional culture explanations adequately capture minority group responses to dominant group oppression, the acculturation of urban youths occurs within four domains of group affiliation: (1) as members of a castelike or involuntary minority group within the United States; (2) as *urban* Black Americans socially isolated within inner-city communities; (3) as Black students who "cope with the burden of 'acting white'" in schools that favor mainstream (Eurocentric) culture[72]; and (4) as Black youths initiated into inner-city street culture via adherence to a code of the street.[73] The first three group affiliations have been addressed above in my reviews of Wilson's, Massey and Denton's, and Ogbu's findings. Elijah Anderson's most recent work tells the researched tale of the fourth domain.

In *Code of the Street: Decency, Violence, and the Moral Life of the Inner City*, Anderson delineates the complexities of the code of the street. He defines this code as "a set of informal rules governing interpersonal public behavior, particularly violence" that prescribe "both proper comportment and the proper way to respond if challenged" or confronted within street cultural contexts.[74] Anderson explains that the norms of this code "are often consciously opposed to those of mainstream society."[75]

> For those living according to the rules of that culture, it becomes important to be tough, to act as though one is beyond the reach of lawful authority—to go for bad. In this scenario, anything associated with conventional white society is seen as square; the hip things are at odds with it. The untied sneakers, the pants worn well below the waist, the hat turned backward—all have become a style. These unconventional symbols have been taken over by people who have made them into status symbols, but they are status symbols to the extent that they go against what is conventional.[76]

As mentioned in an earlier section of this chapter, Anderson acknowledges that the majority of Black residents from inner cities "share many of the middle class values of the wider white society."[77] Yet a major contribution of Anderson's revealing ethnography is his careful explanation of the norms and informal rules unique to street cultural settings.

To sum up the findings of Massey and Denton, Ogbu, and Anderson, Black urban youths find themselves in the quadruple oppositional predicament of (1) being members of an American caste, who are (2) racially segregated and socially dislocated in inner-city communities, (3) averse to "acting white" in public schools, and (4) constantly exposed to the code of the street. The works of Massey and Denton, Ogbu, and Anderson, though they thoughtfully and accurately capture the social, spatial, and cultural dynamics of inner-city life, yield a composite portrayal of Black youths as oppositional or antagonistic.

A Constructive Critique of Scholarly Depictions of Black Americans

Of all the depictions of Blacks reviewed in this chapter, those that cast Blacks as genetically and culturally inferior prompt deconstructive and scathing critique. Culture-of-poverty explanations blame the victim without adequately linking the tribulations of urban Blacks to social-structural factors. Genetic explanations like those of Jensen, Herrnstein, and Murray are empirically unfounded, rely heavily upon sources that can be traced to white supremacist factions of the eugenics move-ment,[78] and overlook a host of social environmental factors that must be considered when comparing Blacks to Whites. The remaining depictions of Blacks as main-stream, virtuous, victims of social structures, and oppositional lend themselves to compliments as well as constructive critiques.

Strengths of Scholarly Depictions

Accounts of Blacks as mainstream, virtuous, and central are necessary correctives to the persistent portrayal of Blacks as inferior. Depictions of Blacks as pawns or vic-tims of social-structural constraints are necessary correctives to explanations of poverty that blame the victim or implicate individual shortcomings. The view of Blacks as oppositional is a productive alternative to theories that suggest that the low educational achievement of Black students results from an inability to learn. That is, the claim that Black students are averse to learning due to group solidarities and affil-iations challenges claims that Black students are incapable of learning.

As I have stated and reiterated throughout this chapter, urban Black Americans are a diverse group of individuals. It consequently takes a combination of scholarly angles and social scientific findings before we even begin to approach adequate char-acterizations of the varied and similar ways these individuals respond to structural and cultural constraints. With the exception of the inferiorizing narratives, an overall strength of the theses and theories reviewed in this chapter is their collective findings. These findings, when weighed cumulatively, converse, critique, supplement, and build one upon the other. Blacks are not either essentially mainstream or essentially virtuous or essentially victims or essentially oppositional or, to critique *Tough Fronts*, essentially agents. The only thing essential about Black Americans and all Ameri-cans of color is their humanity. Blacks possess all these attributes and many more that remain uncovered by social scientific research.

Shortcomings of Scholarly Depictions

Scholarly depictions of Blacks as mainstream (or sharing mainstream aspirations) suggest that if it were not for exposure to and contact with the White American mainstream, Black Americans would not come to espouse so-called "mainstream" ideals on their own. Afrocentric scholars provide ample evidence that African culture contains many virtues identified in the United States as European or American in origin. However, Black Americans have come to espouse so-called mainstream values as well as other ideals through a process that is more eclectic and syncretic than black (Afrocentric) or white (Eurocentric). Melba Joyce Boyd eloquently describes this process.

> Afro-Americans are not simply Americans of African descent. We are a multicultural people whose expressions and experiences have evolved from Africa, Asia, Europe, and, most specifically, the Americas. This fusion has created an eclectic culture, a jazz ide-ology. It is not a linear extension of Africa or simply the sum of its parts. Through its dissidence, invention, and reinvention, new imaginings thrive. To ignore the diversity that resides within us is to deny the very essence that signatures our humanity.[79]

This quote by Boyd takes issue with the essentialist stance conveyed in Afrocentric works, Eurocentric works, and all academic accounts of the experiences of Black Americans. Patricia Hill Collins offers a constructive critique of Afrocentric scholarship in particular: "Despite its trenchant critique of scientific racism, Afrocentrism turns a blind eye toward the sexist bias of that same science."[80] Although Afrocentric scholarship restores the human dignity of Black Americans, this restoration of dignity does not include gender equality.

Wilson, Massey and Denton, Ogbu, and Anderson make contributions to social science that are exceptional and indispensable; they reveal the social and cultural structures, often taken for granted, that undermine the commonwealth of Black Americans, especially those from urban communities. This focus upon structure unintentionally paints Blacks as pawns or puppets fatalistically fixed to the strings of social structures or cultural sentiments. In characterizing the transformation, isolation, and dislocation of inner cities, structural explanations tend to overstate the change in the realm of cultural values and the resulting impact upon individual aspirations. Wilson corroborates this point in *When Work Disappears*. In this followup to his theses in *The Truly Disadvantaged*, Wilson employs qualitative interviews and quantitative data sets (namely, the Urban Poverty and Family Life Study) to reveal that a substantial majority of poor Blacks ascribe not to oppositional cultural ideals, but to more mainstream values like the work ethic. For example, Wilson reports, "[F]ewer than 3 percent of the black respondents from ghetto poverty census tracts denied the importance of plain hard work for getting ahead in society, and sixty-six percent expressed the view that it is very important."[81]

Wilson takes greater care in *When Work Disappears* than he did in *The Truly Disadvantaged* to leave inner-city residents with a modicum of agency. Anderson takes even greater care to accentuate agency in *Code of the Street*. Both would probably agree with the following assertion voiced by Wilson:

> The social action—including behavior, habits, skills, styles, orientations, attitudes—
> [discussed in *When Work Disappears*] ought not to be analyzed as if it were unrelated
> to the broader structure of opportunities and constraints that have evolved over time.
> *This is not to argue that individuals and groups lack the freedom to make their own choices,*
> *engage in certain conduct, and develop certain styles and orientations, but it is to say that*
> *these decisions and actions occur within a context of constraints and opportunities that are*
> *drastically different from those present in middle-class society.* [emphasis added][82]

Nonetheless, even when individual researchers take care to elucidate the agency of urban Blacks, we remain drawn to notions, theses, and theories about pathology. Social scientists and the general public tend to, in Sara Lawrence-Lightfoot's words, "[F]ocus on what is wrong rather than search for what is right."[83] I suggest that the centuries old scholarly tradition of casting Blacks as inferior combines with the contemporary social scientific practice of obscuring agency to steer our attention toward pathology. It is easy to focus upon the pathologies of faceless, agencyless, monolithic beings. *Tough Fronts*, while borrowing the backdrop of social structural accounts, places urban students in the foreground. Once you meet these students face to face, see them eye to eye, and become acquainted with them person to person, they become agents of history, or at least agents of their story. Their problems and pathologies may not diminish, but these may be seen as the problems of humanity, instead of the pathologies, dysfunctions, and abnormalities of inner-city Blacks.

Philippe Bourgois, author of *In Search of Respect: Selling Crack in El Barrio,* suggests that the shortage of face-to-face accounts of inner-city residents results from researchers being either "too elitist or too frightened" too encounter these individuals in person.[84] Instead of being either too elitist or too frightened, some scholars may simply seek to reveal broader social forces often overlooked or taken for granted. Works such as these make meaningful contributions to social science. But Bourgois's point is well taken and worth pondering. Social scientists cannot conduct research that is empirically whole and socially useful if they are "too elitist or too frightened" or if they are too preoccupied with structure, or too distant and too objective to see inner-city residents in living color. With regard to this last point, social scientists could learn a lot from the artists who paint inner-city murals.

TWO

Postures Forged
by Social Marginalization

[T]o be hardcore to me it's just ... like a killer mentality or something. I don't care about the police. I'm going for mine [looking out for number one] or whatever, carrying guns or whatever.

—Interview with student from the Boston metropolitan area

In *Cool Pose: The Dilemmas of Black Manhood in America,* Richard Majors and Janet Mancini Billson sketch postures of "poise under pressure" or "cool masculinity" assumed by American males of African descent.[1] By "cool pose," Majors and Billson refer to the "presentation of self many black males use to establish their male identity" against a social and historical backdrop of marginalization and racial oppression in the United States.[2] The authors conceptualize "cool pose" in ambitious terms as creative and adaptive, as expressive of both pride and bitterness:

> The purpose of posing and posturing—being cool—is to enhance social competence, pride, dignity, self-esteem, and respect.... Being cool also expresses bitterness, anger, and distrust toward the dominant society for many years of hostile mistreatment and discrimination.... It is in this context that we define cool pose as a creative strategy devised by African-American males to counter the negative forces in their lives.[3]

In an attempt to capture every possible manifestation of cool posturing, Majors and Billson's analyses span history and geography. They speculate that Afro-masculine displays of coolness range as far back as civilizations of Africa during 2000 to 3000 B.C. and to subcultures as recent as inner cities in the present-day United States. Majors and Billson have, without question, identified a captivating social phenomenon worthy of their scholarly investigation. However, they overextend the concept "cool pose" to include Black male postures that are hardy or strong as well as comportments that are hardened or "hoodlummed"; they mix presentations of self that project confidence with those that mask insecurities. Coolness applies to the regal and majestic pride of West African kings and the tough, hypermasculine attitudes of African-American gang members. As a result, "cool pose" becomes an intriguing but rather amorphous and elusive concept, a concept that may generate more questions than answers and policy implications. Nearly two decades prior to Majors and

Billson's study, sociologists and ethnographers sought to define "soul" and this concept was equally elusive. Majors and Billson, nonetheless, provide a noteworthy exploration of the "historical, social, and cultural significance of cool in the lives of black males and [outline] the dilemmas facing them" toward the end of the twentieth century.[4]

Similar to the authors of *Cool Pose*, I present postures or fronts frequently assumed by urban teens who are usually, though not exclusively, American males of African ancestry. Instead of coolness, this posturing allows an urban teen to project a "hard" or gangsterlike image that facilitates survival on tough urban streets. However, my study does not span centuries or civilizations; it derives historically from the 1990s and is geographically situated in the Boston and Cambridge, Massachusetts, metropolitan areas of the United States. Also in contrast to the authors of *Cool Pose*, I sculpt postures of toughness that have more precise conceptual form. I hope these concepts will provide relatively definitive answers about why some urban students assume gangsterlike poses; I hope these answers will inspire school reforms and hypotheses for future studies that are both qualitative and quantitative in scope.

In *The Presentation of Self in Everyday Life*, Erving Goffman distinguishes between the front, expression, or presentation that one "gives" and the expression that one "gives-off." The first type of expression is communication in the narrow sense and "involves symbols and their substitutes" used to "convey the information that [the individual presenter or actor] and others are known to attach to these symbols."[5] The second type of expression, communication in the broad sense, "involves a wide range of action that others can treat as symptomatic of the actor, the expectation being that the action was performed for reasons other than the information conveyed in this way."[6] Goffman goes on to point out that "the individual does of course intentionally convey misinformation by means of both of these types of communication, the first involving deceit, the second feigning."[7] The point I make here is that Goffman suggests that the age-old Shakespearean adage "All the world's a stage" applies to the way individuals behave every day. As explained by James Henslin:

> People in everyday life are actors on a stage, the audience consists of those persons who observe what others are doing, the parts are the roles that people play (whether occupational, familial, friendship roles, or whatever), the dialogue consists of ritualized conversational exchanges ("Hi, How ya doin?"; Hey, bro', wha's hapnin'?; How's it goin'?; the hellos, the goodbyes, and the in-betweens), while the costuming consists of whatever clothing happens to be in style.[8]

The students in my study are simply everyday (young) people who realize that the impression they give or give-off on the streets must be good enough to secure safe passage, or, at least, to reduce their chances of inviting disrespectful or violent encounters. Instead of "intentionally conveying misinformation" through deceit, students who "play the role" of the urban gangster intend to survive the streets through donning gangsterlike mannerisms; that is, the ultimate goal is not to misinform but to move about the streets unscathed.

In the pages that remain in this chapter, the experiences of Malik, in particular, and other street-savvy students, in general, will shed light upon the origins of gang-sterlike posturing. After defining the streets from the perspectives of students, I end this chapter by presenting a critique voiced repeatedly by students in this study: "Teachers just don't understand the streets"; teachers just do not understand the origins (or purpose) of gangsterlike postures.

MALIK'S RESOLVE[9]

My earliest memory of Malik (also known as Maka) dates back to my first year as a volunteer teacher in the Cambridge after-school program. At that time, Malik was a seventh grader whose tough posture was often interrupted by a great sense of humor and a contagious pearly white smile. Shortly before coming to the Cambridge program, Malik had lived in Boston. He had been rendered homeless after his Boston residence was sprayed and defaced by machine-gun fire. As a result, for most of his seventh grade year, Malik had stayed in a Cambridge homeless shelter with his maternal aunt. By the start of his eighth grade year, Malik moved with his aunt to a working-class community near Cambridge.

Malik's new residence placed him beyond the bussing jurisdiction of the Cambridge after-school program, so I volunteered to provide him with transportation. During our bi-weekly commutes to and from the program, Malik began to confide in me; he shared his insights, aspirations, regrets, and despairs with me. He eventually came to regard me as a mentor and "big sister." One of Malik's most frequent laments was that his teachers at his middle school did not believe in his ability to excel in school, and they expressed no sensitivity to the dangerous aspects of street culture with which he had to contend. According to Malik, these teachers and other school officials could not care less that, as the new kid on the block, he was frequently attacked by neighborhood toughs and, in order to discourage future attacks, he had to retaliate with gangsterlike resolve. Even worse, these teachers viewed Malik as the troublemaker when, in actuality, he was merely defending himself. As the fall semester progressed, Malik found it increasingly difficult to prevail against his teachers' consensus that he was a special education student destined to become a street thug. He began to lose all motivation to invest in the learning process with teachers who held him in such low academic regard.

I distinctly remember one conversation Malik and I had during the spring semester of his eighth grade year. Actually, Malik did most of the talking and I did most of the listening. In a whispered yet sincere tone, Malik thanked me for "being down" and "having his back." In other words, Malik was grateful to have a "big sister" who understood his street-based struggles and supported his efforts to excel in school. He exclaimed, "If my [public school teachers] had my back like you, I'd be busting A's in all my classes!" Malik voiced a particular regret that his science teacher, Ms. Johnson, did not have his back.[10] He lamented that she viewed him as a little thug, and that she was convinced that he would fail her class. Ms. Johnson expressed little faith that he could successfully design, complete, and receive an A on his science project, a feat that he had to accomplish to pass her class.

Malik did not want to fail but refused to invest fully in the learning process with an unsupportive teacher. He went through the motions of going to school and attending Ms. Johnson's class, but because she expected him to fail despite his efforts, Malik boycotted her assignments. Malik did not oppose or boycott Ms. Johnson for the sake of being oppositional; Malik did so because he was not convinced that she believed in his academic abilities. Upon discovering that failure was imminent, I volunteered to assist Malik.

The very next day, Malik went to school and did something he had not done all semester: he bragged about his science project. Just one day before, Malik had been apathetic; now he was eager to design a science project involving hydrochloric acid (HCl). He had clearly and emphatically informed me that he loathed the thought of "doing a boring project with Venus flytraps" like the rest of his classmates. I carefully advised Malik about other options, and he expressed the most interest in a project that would examined the effects of hydrochloric acid on paramecia (one-celled organisms). Malik eagerly researched, conducted the experiment, videotaped, and typed the results of his project. At the end of the semester, he enthusiastically presented his project to Ms. Johnson and his science class and earned an A. However, from the moment that I intervened to facilitate his project until the day of his presentation, Ms. Johnson doubted Malik's ability and repeatedly voiced suspicions that I "would do the project for him." Below is an excerpt from a letter that I forwarded to Ms. Johnson in response to her low expectations of Malik and unfounded suspicions of me. Instead of writing an angry letter that countered Ms. Johnson's accusations with criticisms, I overlooked her suspicions and focused on the positive:

Dear Ms. [Johnson]:

I appreciate you taking time from your class . . . to share your concerns about [Malik] with me. . . . I wanted to take this opportunity to reassure you that my goal is to work with [Malik] on his science project, not to do his project or any other assignment for him.

    From the concerns that you voiced . . . I gather that you and I have the same goals for [Malik]: to nurture his interest in science and improve his performance. Please let me know if you feel there are particular areas in which Malik could use additional help with Science, and I will be happy to pass your advice on to his Tutor.[11]

I advised Malik, tutored him, arranged for him to videotape his project in a Harvard science laboratory, and relentlessly believed in his ability to excel, but I did not do the project for him.

Ms. Johnson persisted in her view of Malik as a special education student incapable of completing a science project. She embraced this view until the end of the school year when, to her surprise, Malik passed the scrutiny of the in-class presentation with extraordinary results. A day after his presentation, Malik was genuinely excited about Ms. Johnson's revised opinion of his academic abilities. He proclaimed with a prideful smile, "Ever since my science project, Ms. Johnson has been in my corner. She's really proud of me!" Albeit at the end of the school year, Malik was elated that, finally, one of his teachers "had his back."

When Malik graduated to the ninth grade—and from the Cambridge after-school program—he encountered new teachers who revived the old self-fulfilling prophecy that he was a special education student destined for school failure. Again, as had been the case with his eighth grade teachers, none of his ninth grade teachers showed sensitivity for Malik's street-based struggles. At the start of the semester, Malik had been physically assaulted by working-class White students who were members of an anti-black gang. In addition to being bombarded by the normal amount of disrespect allocated to high school freshmen, Malik could not tolerate being "dissed" on the streets. In self-defense, he brutally assaulted the students who attacked him and formed a gang of his own to discourage future conflicts. As the fall semester progressed, Malik became increasingly annoyed with school officials' reprimands for his resolve to defend himself; he became more and more committed to his gangsterlike comportment.

I learned from Malik's aunt the exact moment when he became irrevocably indignant with school officials' biased regard for his struggles. In December of his ninth grade year, Malik and his aunt were summoned to meet with the school psychologist and his school-based social worker. Although these school officials made a few positive comments, a bleak consensus was clearly communicated to Malik: "If you don't get your act together, you will end up in a gang." His aunt recalled that as she listened to the psychologist's characterization of Malik, she thought to herself, "None of the negative stuff this psychologist is saying fits who Malik is." His aunt continued, "But I looked in Malik's eyes and I saw him give up. It was as if he said, 'You guys aren't going to give me a fair chance. I give up!'" This time Malik boycotted the school officials' and teachers' unanimous consensus by dropping out of school.[12]

Like Malik, some street-savvy students eventually refuse to have anything to do with mainstream teachers and other school officials who lack empathy for student travails beyond the walls of the school. In cases like these, I agree with Henry Giroux's assertion that student resistance "has little to do with the logic of deviance ... pathology, learned helplessness ... and a great deal to do ... with the logic of moral and political indignation."[13] So, to reiterate, some students will assume a gangsterlike posture as a form of political resistance. These students resist the Euro-assimilationist expectations of mainstream teachers that all students conform to a white, middle-class standard.[14] Student interviews and field observations suggest that mainstream school officials are likely to view boycotting students as troublemakers instead of political activists; mainstream school officials are more likely to suspend, expel, or—as illustrated by Malik's story—push resistant students out of school than to embrace and understand them. In response to such marginalization, students like Malik harden in their resistance. It is at this point that gangsterlike postures may begin to evolve into deeply held convictions.

STUDENT DEFINITIONS OF "THE STREETS"

As illustrated by Malik's story above, life beyond school walls, life on the streets presents challenges with which urban students must contend. The streets are full of trials and tribulation, challenges of which school officials are unaware, or realities in which school officials have little interest. How do urban students define "the streets"? In the literal sense of the word, a "street" is "a thoroughfare, especially in a city, town, or village, that is wider than an alley or lane and that usually includes sidewalks."[15]

Students in my study rarely give a literal definition of "the streets"; instead, they define the streets in more idiomatic terms. According to these youths, "the streets" are the infamously tough areas in urban neighborhoods where illicit and dangerous activities take place. Hence, the streets could be a park, or an alley, or a street, or a street corner, or a playground, or another publicly accessible outdoors area. Both Boston and Cambridge students affirm that *most* of the time, even the infamous streets are not anti-mainstream sites of criminal activity or violence. *Most* of the time, the streets are sites where urban teens socialize with their friends and are involved in activities like "chillin," joking, or playing basketball. Students in Cambridge and Boston agree that as long as you are not in the wrong place at the wrong time, the streets are a popular social gathering place.

> The streets? Places that I chill, that's the streets. It's where I go after work, to chill. (Interview with Karl, Cambridge)

> [The streets are] a place where kids go. They chill . . . they can do whatever they want on the streets. Its the opposite from the house actually. You know, you have fun on the streets, but most of the time you just sit in the house doing nothing. You can do a lot of things and stuff; [the streets] are a good place. (Interview with Malcolm, Boston)

> [The streets are] where everybody hangs out, where you talk to your friends, where everyday life is happening in front of you. (Interview with Cher, Cambridge)

> Well, streets mean to me somewhere where I can talk, be myself, just hang out with my friends. (Interview with Kadeem, Cambridge)

> It's [that is, the streets] like a good place to go and find lots of friends and stuff like that. (Interview with Henri, Boston)

Although I researched the pathological aspects of street culture, sentiments like those expressed above served as constant reminders about the positive aspects of street culture. According to these definitions, the streets often serve as a place for positive social support and interactions. As a result, by "street culture," I refer to the full range of patterned, recurrent social interactions typical to urban and inner-city streets, from hanging out with one's peers or shooting hoops to joining gangs or crews, dealing or using drugs, and engaging in other violent, mobsterlike activities. Nevertheless, as embodied in Malik's story, the ultimate goal of my research was to understand the dissonance between the violent and criminal demands of street culture and the more mainstream, Eurocentric expectations of schools. Toward that end, the remainder of this chapter, as well as the chapters that follow, focuses more upon student experiences of illicit and dangerous activities than their experiences of the positive aspects of street culture.

THE SINISTER SIDE OF "THE STREETS"

> The streets, for me, they can be dangerous, they can be good, bad, all depends on the type of person you are and who you hang with. . . . When the streets are bad, it's like, there's a lot

of violence, a lot of fights and most of those fights are in between groups, so therefore, that's why I said the people you hang with.

—Interview with Kirkland, Cambridge

Sometimes [the streets are] a bad place, like at nighttime [when you] chill with your friends, it can be drive-bys and stuff like that.

—Interview with Henri, Boston

Students from Cambridge and Boston have anecdotes about the illicit and dangerous aspects of street culture. However, Boston students perceive themselves as more likely than Cambridge students to find themselves "in the wrong place at the wrong time." And the consequences of this circumstance are more likely to be life-threatening. Boston youths perceive themselves as more likely to be around others who are using or selling drugs, to encounter others involved in gangs, to be caught in the crossfire of violent confrontations or retaliations, and the like. When defining "the streets," Boston students describe the illicit aspects of street culture in more blatant and fatalistic terms than students from Cambridge.

In my neighborhood people make drug deals right in front of your eyes. (Journal entry by Jamie, Boston)

L. J. DANCE (L.J.D.):   What advice would you have for kids about violence?
RONELL: Just try to avoid, you know, hanging with gang members. Try to stay away from the corners. Try to stay away from that [the violence].
L.J.D.:   What kind of stuff goes down on the streets you would want to avoid?
RONELL: Shootouts, you know, robberies, stuff like that. (Interview with Ronell, Boston)

[The] streets is just, it's a place that, it's like, if you're in the wrong place at the wrong time, then . . . you gonna die or you gonna get blamed if your boy does something but you didn't do it. (Interview with Jakes, Boston)

In a nutshell, for Cambridge students, the recurring pattern of illicit street cultural activities includes drug deals, crew affiliations and retaliations, violent fights, and the possibility of someone pulling out a gun or a knife.[16] For Boston students, the streets possess all of the illicit activities found in Cambridge, plus gang affiliations and retaliations, and a higher probability that someone would stab someone with a knife or shoot someone with a gun. It is important to note that despite the more blatant depictions of Boston's street culture, students in Boston *and* Cambridge portray the illicit activities as more structured than random, more patterned than unsystematic. Like public schools, the streets are a social institution that lay a unique set of cultural norms and expectations upon students. In schools, cultural etiquette often requires "good" students to dress, talk, and comport themselves in ways consistent with the American mainstream. On the streets, cultural etiquette often requires "down" students to don hip-hop fashions, profane and derisive language, and physically aggressive comportment.

During field observations and interviews, I found quotes like those above from Boston students dismaying, but not surprising. Out of America's hundred largest cities, Boston ranks thirty-sixth for its number of extreme poverty tracts, four-teenth for its poverty tracts, thirty-fifth for its distressed tracts, and forty-ninth for its severely distressed tracts.[17] Boston is America's forty-sixth largest central city, and ranked eighteenth out of one hundred for the degree of black-white segregation.[18] In other words, although Boston is a moderate-sized city, it scores 74.0 on the Index of Dissimilarity. This score would be 0 if Boston neighborhoods were totally integrated and 100 if neighborhoods were totally segregated. A score of 74.0 means that 74 percent of Boston's Black residents would have to move to achieve residential patterns throughout Boston in which neighborhoods were totally integrated.[19] In short, Boston, unlike Cambridge, has neighborhoods that suffer from extreme social dislocation and isolation typical of inner-city areas (see figures 2.1 through 2.3).[20]

According to sociologists who study urban areas, as discussed in chapter 1, social dislocation indicators include disproportionately high rates of crime, poverty, job-lessness, single-parent households, and welfare recipiency. The effects of this dislocation are exacerbated by social isolation from mainstream representatives and institutions.[21] Implicit in Cambridge students' definitions of street culture are the effects of indicators like relative poverty and (perceptions of) an increasing crime rate, but not the exacerbating effect of social isolation. Implicit in Boston students' definitions and descriptions of street culture, as illustrated by Malcolm's quote below, are the exacerbating and compound effects of social dislocation and social isolation.

L.J.D.: Do you think [teachers at your Boston public school] understand what kids have to deal with on the streets today?

MALCOLM: No. None of them. Cause, my teachers . . . none of them live in Boston. They live out in Newton and Cambridge and Framingham and stuff where there's not a lot of violence at. You don't have to grow up living tough cause it's kind of, it's kind of rich out there. And around here, it's all messed up. Like Blue Hill Ave., man, I work on Blue Hill Ave. I have to clean up the street. I be seeing all types of stuff, man. People, crack heads walking up and down the street asking you for a quarter, man. The streets, the pavement is all messed up cause nobody's gonna fix it. It's like, it look like a mountain. It's terrible.

L.J.D.: How does it make you feel when you see that?

MALCOLM: I mean, it makes me feel like nobody care about the city, cause if they did, they would have done something about it.

L.J.D.: They wouldn't just let it rot away like that?

MALCOLM: Yeah, it's pretty much gone. There used to be . . . oh, I have one teacher in my school named Mr. P. He's kinda cool. Mr. P. told me he used to live on Blue Hill Ave. and he's pretty old, too. And, when he used to live there, every street, all those abandoned buildings, had stores. He said it was a pretty rich street, like Newbury Street is. But it just, it just, somehow it got violent and then everybody moved out. And all the abandons are, all the buildings are, condemned, and, it's a wasteland. If you walk down that street, I bet if there were twenty houses on that street, eighteen of them are condemned. (Interview with Malcolm)

FIGURE 2.1. NEIGHBORHOODS OF BOSTON

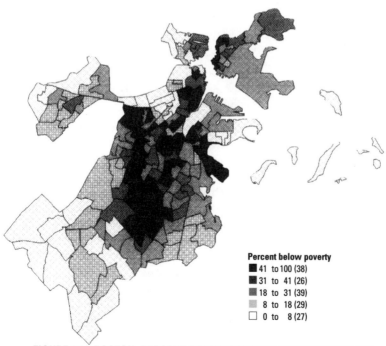

Percent below poverty
■ 41 to 100 (38)
■ 31 to 41 (26)
▨ 18 to 31 (39)
▫ 8 to 18 (29)
□ 0 to   8 (27)

FIGURE 2.2. BOSTON: PERCENT BELOW POVERTY, 1990 CENSUS DATA

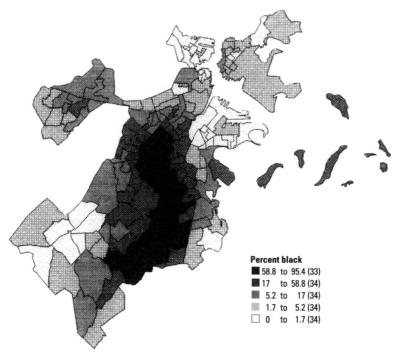

Percent black
- 58.8 to 95.4 (33)
- 17 to 58.8 (34)
- 5.2 to 17 (34)
- 1.7 to 5.2 (34)
- 0 to 1.7 (34)

FIGURE 2.3. BOSTON: PERCENT BLACK, 1990 CENSUS DATA

Unlike Malcolm, none of the students from Cambridge have a "Blue Hill Ave." experience to recount. Cambridge has no rows of desolate or abandoned buildings that students could characterize as a wasteland or neighborhoods like those described in Jonathan Kozol's *Savage Inequalities* as "death zones."

> In Boston, the press referred to areas like these as "death zones"—a specific reference to the rate of infant death in ghetto neighborhoods—but the feeling of the "death zone" often seemed to permeate the schools themselves.[22]

The relatively poorer neighborhoods of Cambridge are pockets of poverty that are a hop, skip, and a jump away from residential affluence, Harvard University, and the Massachusetts Institute of Technology (MIT). At the very least, these neighborhoods include stable working-class families. Instead of "death zones," affluent zones permeate the boundaries of most Cambridge public schools.

Scholars who study poverty maintain that when ethnic minorities are restricted by structural disadvantages like job and housing discrimination, inadequate educational opportunities, and low incomes, and are spatially confined to desolate inner-city neighborhoods, they survive by means of an "underground economy, composed of drug trade, prostitution, theft, and other illicit activities."[23] Since Cambridge has no desolate neighborhoods with concentrated poverty comparable to Boston, I was puzzled by the frequency with which students described illegal street cultural activities existing in Cambridge. However, further investigation of this phenomenon resolved this Cambridge street cultural enigma.

As indicated above, Cambridge students typically consider "the streets" of Cambridge to be located in "the rough neighborhoods" in Cambridge; these "rough neighborhoods" suffer from relatively higher degrees of social dislocation—or lower degrees of social organization—than other Cambridge neighborhoods. More specifically, students identify parts of North Cambridge (NC), Central Square (Neighborhood 4/Area Four), and Cambridgeport (the Port) as the most dangerous areas of Cambridge (see figure 2.4). As indicated by table 2.1, from 1992 to 1996, on average these neighborhoods had the highest arrest rates for attempted homicides, drug arrests, and street robberies.[24] Cambridge students from rough neighborhoods depict their situation as comparable to that of inner-city students in the concentrated poverty areas of Boston and other larger cities.

As mentioned above, interviews and field observations suggest that Cambridge youths do not find themselves in the predicament of "being in the wrong place at the wrong time" with the frequency of their Boston peers. However, this predicament is recurrent. Consequently, students who reside in the tough neighborhoods of Cambridge, as well as those who reside in the tougher neighborhoods of Boston, are

TABLE 2.1. GEOGRAPHIC BREAKDOWN OF ATTEMPTED HOMICIDES, STREET ROBBERIES, AND DRUG ARRESTS, CAMBRIDGE, MASSACHUSETTS, 1992–1996[a]

	Attempted Homicides					Drug Arrests					Street Robberies				
	92	93	94	95	96	92	93	94	95	96	92	93	94	95	96
#1 East Cambridge	NA[b]	3	4	NA	4	12	16	9	20	9	21	25	11	25	22
#2 Neighborhood 2 (MIT Area)	"	0	0	"	0	1	1	2	3	1	10	7	9	6	7
#3 Neighborhood 3 (Inman/Harrington)	"	5	0	"	2	23	12	9	13	23	14	6	15	16	15
#4 Neighborhood (Area 4)	"	5	8	"	5	84	76	78	75	76	48	48	65	54	45
#5 Cambridgeport	"	1	7	"	3	22	22	34	20	21	37	35	31	31	31
#6 Mid-Cambridge	"	0	0	"	0	12	11	17	24	14	14	14	17	22	24
#7 Riverside	"	0	0	"	3	13	13	21	23	15	20	7	13	28	12
#8 Agassiz	"	1	1	"	0	1	2	0	2	1	4	3	8	7	11
#9 Neighborhood 9 (Peabody)	"	1	0	"	0	9	0	7	8	5	20	3	22	20	11
#10 Neighborhood 10 (West Cambridge)	"	2	2	"	1	15	7	5	3	6	15	13	12	13	5
#11 North Cambridge	"	6	8	"	2	8	41	11	21	17	21	36	24	34	17
#12 Highlands	"	0	0	"	0	0	1	1	1	2	0	7	8	0	0
#13 Strawberry Hill	"	0	0	"	0	0	1	1	0	1	8	4	4	0	0

a. Cambridge Police Department, "Part One Crime Reports and Neighborhood Crime Reports," January 1992–December 1992, January 1993, January 1994–December 1994. Cambridge Police Department, "Annual Crime Report, 1996: Neighborhood and Business District Crime Profiles."
b. NA means "Not Available." Although the geographic breakdown for attempted homicides was not listed in the 1992 Crime Report, fifteen attempted homicide arrests were reported.

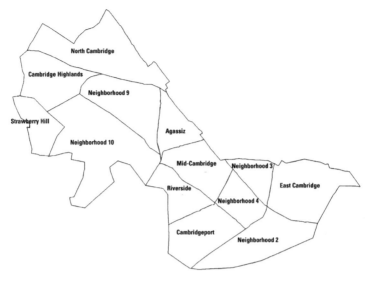

FIGURE 2.4: NEIGHBORHOODS OF CAMBRIDGE

exposed to persistent patterns of illicit street cultural activities. Most have acquired informal, commonsense knowledge of the cultural codes and dictates by which they must abide to navigate the streets. As explained by Elijah Anderson:

> By the time they are teenagers, most youths have either internalized the code of the streets or at least learned the need to comport themselves in accordance with its rules. . . . The code revolves around the presentation of self. Its basic requirement is the display of a certain predisposition to violence. Accordingly, one's bearing must send the unmistakable if sometimes subtle message to "the next person" in public that one is capable of violence and mayhem when the situation requires it, that one can take care of oneself.[25]

To Boston and Cambridge students, the urban gangster epitomizes the tough persona with "a certain predisposition to violence," who is "capable of violence and mayhem when the situation requires it." As illustrated in chapter 3 below, the "gangsta" persona has both survivalistic and charismatic appeal to street-savvy students who seek to send the message "I can take care of myself!" Before elaborating student definitions about the urban gangster, I present the recurrent student sentiment previously mentioned: "Teachers just don't understand the streets!"

"Teachers Just Don't Understand the Streets"

During field observations in Boston and Cambridge, students exclaimed that some staff members did not and could not understand their situation. Due to the ethnic diversity of the teachers and staff, this exclamation was more frequent in the Cambridge program than in the Boston program. Those students who felt misunderstood were quick to dismiss, disobey, and sometimes confront the staff members whom they (the students) perceived to be representatives of mainstream culture, staff members who "weren't down." At the Boston program, the Paul Robeson Institute, where the staff and students were all African-American males, the students were more likely to assume that staff members were aware of the demands of the streets. Nevertheless, at both programs, students with actual or fashionable ties to street culture tended to gravitate toward, have more respect for, and pay more attention to teachers who had at least established a reputation for being caring, or, at most, earned the label of being "down." Consequently, becoming schoolwise—that is, acquiring the instructional material, mannerisms, and habits necessary for academic success—was often more a function of student willingness to cooperate with a teacher than with student aptitude or ability.

More specifically, for some students the willingness to obey a teacher was sometimes dependent upon whether a student feels pressure to act "hardcore" and whether a teacher was aware and sensitive to this pressure. This does not mean, however, that the teacher had to tolerate hardcore behavior. Instead, it means that a teacher whose attitude or mannerisms or language conveyed sensitivity to the pressures of the streets was more likely to elicit student cooperation. The fieldnotes below document an instance when being "down" resulted in student cooperation.

[During a Cambridge program session] right before a [group activity] started, Stefan and Mark arrived late . . . . I asked them to join us and Stefan said, "I'm tired of doing that stupid stuff." I said [in a persuasive tone devoid of any trace of slang or urban youth cultural reference], "Well sometimes you have to do 'stupid stuff' so you can appreciate the fun stuff. . . . And if you really think this game is stupid, give it a try first and then tell us [the teachers and staff] what's stupid about it." So much for my [mainstream-dialect] pep talk because Mark and Stefan joined Shane, who was already sitting on the sideline of the gym and [boldly] refused to participate. Another teacher went over to talk them into playing, but still they refused to participate. The director had decided to start the game without them when Rick (a teacher) made one last [successful] attempt to talk them into playing. Later, I asked Rick what he said to the boys, and he responded, "I said, 'Yo, you guys can play or not play. I'd really like to work with you, we'd really like to work with you, but we will also tell you good-bye, there's the door. . . . You can git wit this [the activity] or you can git wit that [the door]."[26]

Rick succeeded where I and the other staff members failed for several reasons: I forgot that I was talking to urban teens and used a dialect more appropriate for Harvard students, I failed to give the boys an ultimatum, and there was nothing remotely "down" about my whole approach. Was Rick's success due to his gender? Not necessarily, because I typically had success with acquiring student cooperation at the Cambridge program when I left my mainstream dialect on the doorstep and reclaimed my more street-savvy dialect. Rick, I, and a few other teachers typically had success with acquiring student cooperation. What did we have in common that differed from the teachers who had difficulty with eliciting student cooperation? At the very least, the students considered us to be caring; at the very best, the students considered us "down."

Rick's success was not merely the result of what he said (that is, the ultimatum) but of how he said it. He used a street-savvy dialect and rapperlike hand gestures when he addressed the boys, and he made reference to a rap that was popular at the time, "The Choice is Yours," saying "you can git wit this or you can git wit that."[27] The differences between my approach to the above incident and Rick's may seem subtle, but field observations suggest that these subtle differences are important.

Hence, a teacher can demonstrate sensitivity (or insensitivity) through the manner she or he addresses a disruptive or uncooperative student. Instead of conveying a mainstream sentiment like "Come on Johnny, why don't you behave like a good little boy and cooperate and enhance our community spirit?", a "down" teacher might say (or, at least, convey), "Yo J., I know this is how you act when you're with your boyz, but don't play me like that. I'd appreciate a little cooperation right now."[28] My field observations and interviews suggest that "down" teachers have the most success with motivating and eliciting support from students who are (becoming) hard and students who are hardcore wannabes.

A Typology of Students and Teachers

From student interviews and field observations, I developed a typology of three types of teachers encountered by the students in my study: (1) uncaring/unempathetic teachers, the teachers who seem not to care about students in general and who do not understand the streets in particular; (2) caring/unempathetic teachers, who care about students in general, but do not understand the streets in particular; (3) caring/empathetic teachers, who care about students in general and understand— or care enough to learn about—the streets in particular, that is, teachers who are considered "down" by street-savvy youth. My observations about student-teacher cooperation indicate that when you match a student who acts or postures as "hard" with an uncaring and unempathetic teacher, an impasse in student-teacher cooperation is probable. At the other extreme, when you match a student who acts "hard" with a teacher who cares and can empathize (or, at least, sympathize) with the demands of the streets—that is, a "down" teacher—student-teacher cooperation is probable. Below, in table 2.2, is "A Typology of Students and Teachers" that cross-tabulates the ideal-types of students (hard, hardcore wannabe, and hard enough)

TABLE 2.2. A TYPOLOGY OF STUDENTS AND TEACHERS

	Hard	Hardcore Wannabe	Hard Enough
Uncaring/ Unempathetic Teacher	No Cooperation	Whimsical Cooperation	Moderate Cooperation
Caring/Unempathetic Teacher	Marginal Cooperation	Whimsical Cooperation	Moderate to Adequate Cooperation
Caring/Empathetic Teacher (A "Down" Teacher)	Moderate To Adequate Cooperation	Moderate To Adequate Cooperation	Adequate Cooperation

No Cooperation—Student refuses to cooperate with the teacher.
Whimsical Cooperation—Student will cooperate with teacher if his/her peers will cooperate.
Marginal Cooperation—Student will cooperate with minimal effort or enthusiasm.
Moderate Cooperation—Student will cooperate with minimal to average effort or enthusiasm.
Adequate Cooperation—Student will cooperate with average to maximum effort or enthusiasm.

with the three ideal-types of teachers to illustrate the consequences for student-teacher cooperation. This table is an abstraction of teacher-student interactions that occurred at the Cambridge and Boston supplemental school programs. (For the most part, the Boston program, described in detail in chapter 6, had more "down" teachers than the Cambridge program.)

As this typology suggests, to facilitate student-teacher cooperation street-savvy youths need more "down" teachers. However, these "down" teachers must also be competent teachers who are able to teach their subject matter. Interview data suggest that between "down" teachers and street-savvy students there is a mutual under-standing of the code of the streets. "Down" teachers are not quick to suspend so-called disruptive students. Instead, they are likely to call the bluff on tough, gang-sterlike behavior. "Down" teachers are not just teachers, they are also mentors and friends. Most important, "down" teachers take the time to get to know and under-stand their students. When I asked students if there was anything they would change about school, implicit in many of their responses was a call for more teachers who are "down."

> L.J.D.: Okay, if you were principal [of your school], would you give teachers any kind of advice about how to deal with students?
> KEENAN: Be their friend.
> L.J.D.: Be their friend? Now you're the principal, I mean, I'll give you even more power. You're the superintendent . . .
> KEENAN: Try to be their friend.
> L.J.D.: Anything else?
> KEENAN: And be there for them.
> L.J.D.: Be there for the students?
> KEENAN: Yeah.
> L.J.D.: To be their friends. Does that mean, like be there so students can talk to you?
> KEENAN: Yeah, until they (students) feel comfortable with you and the learning. So if you get along with the teacher, then you really be interested in what you're learning cause it makes it easier. If you don't like the teacher, you don't really care. Like, I know a few kids, they're like, "Oh I don't like the teacher, I ain't going to class. I'm cutting." The whole reason is because they don't like the teacher. I think that's important. (Interview with Keenan)

CONCLUDING REMARKS ABOUT (UN)EMPATHETIC TEACHERS

"Teachers just don't understand." This sounds like the age-old whine of the teenager. What is the difference? My data strongly suggests that the difference is that street-savvy students who are misunderstood may end up in expulsion, suspension, and dropout statistics. Field observations and interviews suggest that unempathetic teachers mislabel street-savvy students as irrationally disruptive and uneducable. Street-savvy students who feel misunderstood are unlikely to cooperate with unem-pathetic teachers. Without student-teacher cooperation, there can be no transfer of the skills and competencies necessary for movement into the American mainstream. This vicious cycle places street-savvy youths at risk of failing in school.

Just because a teacher exudes empathy and understanding, this does not mean his or her classroom will be hardcore incident free. In other words, sometimes the most caring and empathetic teacher is no match for peer pressure and student desire to gain peer respect. But field research and interviews suggest that for empathetic teachers, in-class hardcore incidents seem more the exception than the rule. Unfortunately, if the student claims in this study are reliable and the sample generally representative, urban students from low-income neighborhoods in Cambridge and Boston have substantially less than a fifty-fifty chance of encountering an empathetic teacher during any given school year. This point is elaborated in chapter 4. If empathy is a key determinant of student-teacher cooperation, then a lack of empathy has negative consequences for the educational performance of students who cannot (or will not) leave their "hard" attitudes and mannerisms at the school doorstep.

In the next chapter, I present student perspectives on what it means to be or to act "hard."

part II

The Perspectives of Street-Savvy Students

THREE

On Being "Hardcore," a "Hardcore Wannabe," or "Hardcore Enough"

ASSUMING A "HARD" POSTURE

While sequestered in graduate school, I served over six years as a resident assistant and tutor in an undergraduate residence house. Given the academic duties of resident tutors and graduate students, I attended more than my fair share of academic forums, often referred to as "teas." In addition to the delicious teas and cookies that were served, these forums often featured a scholar who would give a talk or presentation about her or his most recent research project, article, or book manuscript. Career success in academia required that I become adept at putting on my best intellectual face and endure these events: I would attend these events appropriately dressed in somber grays, blues, blacks, or beiges and join my colleagues in the intellectual small talk that preceded the scholarly presentation. We would stand around with folded arms; our faces were accessorized with pensive and discerning gazes. We would converse in academese and obey other rules of intellectual etiquette. I, like my colleagues, adhered to an informal "code of the teas."

On a few occasions, I broke the rules by ignoring the dress code and wearing bright yellows or powerful reds. Once I even attended a scholarly event wearing one white shoe and one black shoe—but an otherwise matching pair—to complement my white stretch pants and black leotard top. Sometimes during intellectual conversation, I would switch from academese to my native black English vernacular. I would utter observations replete with black linguistic idioms and colloquialisms. This linguistic switch made my comments less accessible to my colleagues, yet they rarely asked me to translate my statements into mainstream English. Instead, as required by the code of the teas, they nodded their heads and smiled as though they understood.

This occasional disregard for the code was my way of engaging in subtle resistance by selectively boycotting rules of this informal code. But my ultimate goal was to survive, maybe even thrive, in academic circles. Hence, I never mounted a full revolt. Although I was rarely the first in line for these scholarly events, once present, I donned most of the mannerisms that distinguish one as an intellectual. To this day, I still don the erudite mannerisms that broadcast to my colleagues and students that I *am* an academic. In reality, the *who* that I am extends well beyond my academic comportment.

Some urban students must attend the school of the streets. Many in this study have had to master the art of projecting gangsterlike presentations of self, when, in reality, the *who* that they are extends far beyond their gangsterlike demeanors, mannerisms, and attitudes. During the years from 1991 to at least 2001, a gangsterlike demeanor included blousy and baggy hip-hop modes of dressing, a physically aggressive posture, profane and derisive language, and a ruthless outlook on involvement in violent and criminal activities. To the undiscerning eye, these students might appear reducible or confined to the tough postures they assume. A few of the students I interviewed and observed seemed well on their way to becoming gangsters through extensive involvement in the drug trade and other illicit activities. However, for the vast majority of students, assuming a hard or gangsterlike posture was merely a means to impress their peers; or, striking a "hard" pose was a means of conveying (or reiterating) the sentiment that "I do not want to be a gangster, but I can behave like one if the situation demands!" Just as academics range from those whose intellectual postures reflect definitive aspects of their personalities to those who only assume these postures to survive academia, street-savvy students range from the few whose gangsterlike postures reveal definitive characteristics to the many who only strike hard poses to survive the streets.

"IDEAL" VARIATIONS OF THE URBAN GANGSTER THEME

In this chapter, I will introduce three variations of an urban gangster theme—that is, three different labels used to describe street-savvy students who appropriate gangsterlike postures: hard, hardcore wannabe, and hardcore enough. "Hard" (or "hardcore") refers to the state of being a street-savvy and tough gangster who has actually committed criminal, violent, and ruthless acts. A so-called hard student is typically involved in the illicit aspects of street culture. As defined in chapter 2, by "street culture" I mean recurrent, patterned social interactions and practices typical of urban and inner-city streets that range from hanging out with one's peers or shooting hoops, to joining gangs or crews, dealing or using drugs, and engaging in violent gangsterlike activities. "Hardcore wannabe" names the state of acting hard because it is fashionable or prestigious—that is to say, a superficial means of gaining social esteem in urban youth culture. A student labeled as a "hardcore wannabe" has either no involvement or sporadic, peer-pressured involvement in the negative aspects of street culture. Finally, "hardcore enough" (or "hard-enough") denotes the state of being street-savvy and tough enough to convince one's peers that you could be ruthless if you had to be but that you choose not to be. A student considered "hard-enough" usually avoids participation in the negative aspects of street culture but lives in neighborhoods where illicit activities take place.

These three terms are more fully conceptualized in the pages that follow. However, the reader should keep in mind that the terms "hardcore," "hardcore wannabe," and "hardcore enough" refer more to static or fixed ideals than to dynamic, real-life street-savvy students. These labels represent abstract snapshots uncomplicated by the human capacity for flux and change. Therefore, the definitions of "hardcore," "hardcore wannabe," and "hardcore enough," signify the ideal hardcore student, or the ideal hardcore wannabe student, and so on. Ideal-types derive from empirical observation and delineate essential and reliable characteristics of real phenomena; as a result, they are instrumental for designating a precise meaning of terms. "Ideal-types" are not to be confused with stereotypes, which are generalizations of real phenomena that are unreliable, unfounded, and exaggerated.

The term "ideal-type" was coined by Max Weber, one of the founding theorists of sociology, and viewed by Weber as a useful sociological tool. But Weber acknowledged, and I agree, that an ideal-type's shortcoming is also its strength. Because ideal-types are constructed for the sake of conceptual clarity and precision, "it is probably seldom if ever that a real [urban student] can be found [who] corresponds exactly to one of the ideally constructed pure types."[1] Weber goes on to elaborate:

> The more sharply and precisely the ideal-type has been constructed, thus the more abstract and unrealistic in this sense it is, the better it is able to perform its function in formulating terminology, classifications, and hypotheses.[2]

In other words, the more precise my definitions of "hardcore," "hardcore wannabe," and "hardcore enough," the less these concepts exactly correspond to real-life, dynamic, individually unique urban students, and thus, the better these concepts function as precise sociological definitions. Ideal-types allow social scientists to simplify reality for the sake of intellectual understanding.

"HARDCORE" URBAN TEENS: FACTS AND FICTIONS

Newspaper Account #1 Two black teenage males, Kevin "O-dog" Jones and Caine Woods, are prime suspects in the armed robbery of a Korean convenience store and the murder of the store owners. Allegedly, the two suspects had entered the store to buy beer. But [the district attorney alleged] that when the grocer commented to Jones that he felt sorry for the youth's mother, the angered teen shot the grocer in the head, demanded the security videotape from the grocer's wife, and fatally shot her. Woods claims he had nothing to do with either murder. Both youths have been arraigned on murder in the first degree, and two counts of armed robbery.

According to [residents from the suspects' neighborhood], Jones watched the videotape of the incident repeatedly and bragged about the murders *without remorse*. . . .[3]

Newspaper Account #2 Four black Brooklyn youths were indicted on armed robbery and murder charges. [According to police reports,] three nights ago four black males entered Quiles' Convenience store. Allegedly, they were only planning to rob the store, but one of the teens, Roland Bishop, shot the store owner, known to Harlem residents as "Ole man Quiles," in cold blood. Less than a quarter mile from the initial crime scene, one of the teens, Raheem Porter, was found murdered. [Police later learned] that Bishop had shot both Quiles and Porter. Allegedly, after fleeing the scene of the crime, the four teens had regrouped and, when Porter admonished Bishop for shooting the grocer, Bishop shot Porter. The three teens decided to cover up the incident and . . . the [other two teens] involved in the double murder did not identify Bishop as the murderer.

The news that it was Bishop who murdered Porter came as a surprise. Porter's sister commented, "He [Bishop] attended my brother's funeral and consoled me as if he had nothing to do with the murder. He promised me that they would find the murderer. He was Raheem's best friend, but *has no remorse about the murder*. I still can't believe Bishop murdered Raheem in cold blood."

The other two teens indicted on murder and armed robbery charges decided to reveal Bishop's involvement in the double murder only after a remorseless Bishop made attempts on their lives. [One of these teens] exclaimed [in court], "I think Bishop's lost it man. I mean, seriously man, he was talkin' some way-out shit last night about how he got more "juice" than everybody else on the streets; that everybody better learn not to fuck with him unless they want to end up like Porter and Quiles. . . ."[4]

Newspaper Account #3 Teenagers call it "knockout," and it's a modern-day version of survival of the fittest, where young toughs, often fortified with lots of beer, try to floor a stranger with one punch in a "game" for kicks and to earn a twisted kind of respect.

"Everyone wants to be tough, everyone wants a name for themselves," said one [high school] student yesterday as he talked about his former "punk" days when he and his friends would get drunk and randomly assault people on Boston streets, much like the "wilding" episodes that so terrorized citizens in New York in 1989.

But yesterday, the assistant district attorney had two old-fashioned names for the alleged actions of three [local] teen-agers that, he charged, resulted in the death of Bjorn Persson, a [Scandinavian] student at [a local university]: armed robbery and murder.

"They went to the . . . campus for the expressed purpose of stealing money from [university] students," prosecutor Murray said during separate arraignments, first for James O'Sullivan, 17, and Alejandro Valdez, 18, and then for Ron McHale, 15, who was arraigned separately because he is a juvenile.

When the attack on Persson and his companion was over, Murray said, the three [teens] crossed over the Main Avenue bridge, tossing their victims' wallets into the river.

Their next stop was a convenience store . . . where they split their $33 booty three ways, got napkins to wipe off the knife, and regrouped for what they thought would be the next round of a game they called "knockout," Murray said.

Even after Persson was fatally stabbed, Murray suggested in court, *there was no remorse expressed by Ron McHale*, who allegedly plunged the five-inch knife into Persson's heart.

"When he stabbed Mr. Persson, he bragged about how the knife had gone all the way through Mr. Persson's body," Murray told the court.[5]

One of the above newspaper accounts is journalistic fact, and the others are motion picture fiction. Yet all three articles paint nightmarish images of hard urban youths. The hard or hardcore urban youth is often depicted in motion picture and journalistic media as a ruthless, brutal gangster without remorse. Unless you are familiar with the plot summaries of the two feature films presented above, it may be difficult (without reading the endnotes) to determine the real journalistic account from its fictional, motion picture counterparts.

The third newspaper account describes real events; the first two accounts are fictitious. Ron McHale is a real person; Kevin "O-dog" Jones and Roland Bishop are fictional characters.[6] Yet each teen characterized in these newspaper accounts is more caricature than fully human, more monster than complex individual. Student interviews suggest, and I concur, that in real life, hard youths are not as one-dimensional as feature films and newspaper articles suggest.

O-dog, Bishop, and Ron McHale are stereotypical depictions. The stereotypical hardcore inner-city youth is a ruthless gangsterlike Black (or other ethnic minority) male from a desolate, low-income urban area who carries a gun and participates in drive-by shootings and other senseless acts of violence *without fear or remorse.*

A variety of media, including the film industry, nightly news, and newspaper articles, present the "urban gangsta" as the prevailing stereotype of urban and inner-city youths in America. This characterization thrives because many individuals' only exposure to urban youths comes from the nightly news or feature films. Feature films, in particular, sculpt these youths in vivid, captivating, menacing images and derisive words. For example, the character O-dog, from *Menace II Society,* is described and portrayed as "the craziest niggah alive, America's nightmare: young, black and didn't give a fuck."[7] Over the years of conducting research and writing a book about urban youths, I have frequently found myself in disagreement with a variety of individuals who insist that *most* urban youths are, at worst, ruthless, murderous gangsters like O-dog, or, at best, petty thugs and criminals. These individuals have come from all walks of life, but few have literally walked on inner-city streets. My critics have included friends, family members, casual acquaintances, professors, graduate students, college students, secondary school teachers, politicians, and social workers, just to name a few. Although a couple of these critics had social origins in inner-city communities of the 1950s, none of these individuals had walked in low-income urban communities of the 1980s or 1990s.

During the spring semester of 1998, one of my colleagues invited me to lecture about my qualitative research in her undergraduate course on research methods. Despite my empirically based claims to the contrary, the students in the lecture hall remained haunted by nightmarish specters of the urban gangster. One of the students insisted, as several others nodded in agreement, "But [urban students] *are* dangerous, so shouldn't [public school] teachers be scared?" I responded in a tone that acknowledged his concern yet critiqued his generalization: "If teachers are scared, it is probably because they focus on the few students who are violent. A few urban students may be dangerous, but the popular view that the vast majority of urban students are gangsters is based more upon fiction than fact. If teachers became better acquainted with more inner-city students, they would not project the violent actions of the few onto the nonviolent many." As I lectured, I hoped the voice of reason and weight of empirical findings would exorcise gangster images from popular nightmares. But I sensed, based upon past experiences, that the nightmares of these students would probably continue and I would eventually encounter many more individuals who held similar misconceptions.

The stereotypical hard teen looms in popular images as thoughtless, remorseless, fearless, and fully seduced by the illicit aspects of street culture. In contrast, the ideal-typical hard teen harbors insights, remorse, fears, concerns, and the like; he endeavors to reconcile the mainstream ideals of schooling with the illicit and violent realities of street culture. The stereotypical hard teen has no feelings all of the time, but the ideal-typical teen hides his (or her) feelings most of the time. Some street-savvy students in my study claim to know teenagers who act like the fictional character

O-dog; most students seriously doubt that real-life hard students possess O-dog's ruthless psyche. Unlike the stereotype, the ideal hard student has vulnerabilities and frailties. As explained by a one student:

> To me, to be hard means to be hardcore. . . . It would mean that you'd always have to, you know, act like you're tough all the time. Even if . . . you really get hurt physically or emotionally, you know, whatever . . . you wouldn't show your feelings. . . . In other words, when people look at you, they would think that you like have no heart or something. . . . But deep down inside, umm, you know, [the hard person] will just be holding it inside, and just playing a role. . . . (Interview with Timmy, Cambridge)

Though there were no remorseless O-dogs, in my study, there were a few students designated as hard by their peers. These students earned their hard reputations either from participation in drug-trafficking, ganglike activities, or from being prone to fits of extreme rage and physical aggression. Most important, these students were viewed by their peers as having a legitimate basis for being (or becoming) hard because they were (or had previously been) residents of tough neighborhoods. For the ideal-typical hard student, gangsterlike mannerisms are deemed necessary for survival on tough urban streets. As explained earlier in this chapter, these mannerisms include hip-hop modes of dressing, a tough attitude and posture, profane and derisive language, and violent and criminal behavior.

At the time of my first round of interviews and field observations, most of these so-called hard students were middle school age (between eleven and fourteen years old); they had yet to make career commitments to life on the streets. A more appropriate label for these youths would be "students in the process of becoming hard." Becoming hard is a process facilitated by student experiences of social marginalization within and beyond the walls of school. These experiences include ethnic cultural devaluation, low educational expectations, race- and class-based discrimination, residential segregation, urban poverty and deterioration, and pessimistic forecasts about the declining viability of legal means of employment.[8] As students become hard, they convince themselves that they cannot care about others because others, including mainstream teachers, have demonstrated a lack of caring toward them. Yet, even in the process of becoming hard, these students inadvertently exposed their altruistic cares and concerns.

For example, when I volunteered as a teacher for the Cambridge program, a hard student, Jason, often expressed concern that other students in the program were "heading down the wrong road." During one of these conversations with Jason, I challenged, "The other day, you said you didn't care about anything, but you do care; here you are worried about Linda." Jason then paused, resumed a hard posture, and responded, "I'm not worried about her, I just think somebody should talk to her." This conversations transpired away from public scrutiny in the shadows and corners of the classroom. Jason did care, and, before he dropped out of the Cambridge program, we had other moments when he would inadvertently reveal his concerns and show his vulnerabilities. But at the age of thirteen, Jason was selling drugs and in the process of convincing himself that in his socially marginalized world caring about others was a liability.

Like Jason, Malik (introduced in chapter 2) was another so-called hard student involved in both the drug trade and gang-related activities. Malik constantly threatened to drop out of the Cambridge program and he frequently feigned insensitivity to everyone and everything. Yet Malik labored to return to the program after he moved to a different school district. The fieldnote excerpt below documents Malik's efforts.

> During snack time,[Malik] arrived with a friend. . . . This year, he's no longer in the Cambridge school system, but [he] really wanted to continue coming to the [Cambridge program]. . . . Last year, [Malik] frequently "dissed" the program, at least when he was around other [Cambridge program] kids. . . . This year, he walked more than half the distance from his school . . . [approximately two miles] . . . to the [Cambridge program]. He brought his friend with him because there were some boys in his new neighborhood who wanted to fight him.[9]

Like Jason, Malik believed that, regardless of his personal preference and individual capacity for compassion, his social circumstances demanded that he develop a ruthless disregard for others. This have-to-be-hard outlook was the main sentiment that distinguished the hard students in my study from students who were hardcore wannabes or hard-enough.

In addition to convincing themselves that they could not care about the lives of others, these students viewed themselves as having few viable options except eventually to become gangsters. In their neighborhood, you had to be involved in the drug trade or ganglike activities to get respect and earn a living. Furthermore, these students, once optimists, were becoming more and more discouraged by their experiences within mainstream settings, especially school-based settings. As evidenced by the interview excerpt below, Malik found his eighth grade schooling experiences particularly discouraging.

> MALIK: [A couple of my teachers at my old school] use to push me to work.
> L.J.D.: They don't push you to work at [your new school]?
> MALIK: They don't show no support. If nobody's gonna show no support at a school . . . why would you wanna work? (Interview with Malik)

Despite this lack of support, Malik and other hard students tentatively held on to crumbling ideals about schooling. These students still had moments when they dared to dream that through education they could move into the American mainstream, or at least acquire the stuff (income, wealth, material goods, and the like) of which the American dream was made. Malik remained vulnerable to this ideal of schooling throughout his middle school years:

> L.J.D.: Do you think going to school is important?
> MALIK: Yeah . . . because I don't want to be a dropout. That's why I try my hardest. You see, I'm not gonna give up and then pay for it like Malcolm X did—gave up school and went to nightclubs and all that. I'm not like that. I'm going to try my hardest. Before [school] use to get me so pissed off [I'd just say], "Fuck that shit, forget about it [school]." Now, I got "crazy" [a lot of] books on Malcolm X. . . . (Interview with Malik).

As elaborated in chapter 2, less than one year after this interview, Malik dropped out or, more appropriately, was pushed out of school in the ninth grade. Jason was also pushed out of school. I adopt the concept "pushed out" because I agree with scholars who argue that students from marginalized, low-income communities do not simply drop out of school.

> "Drop out" implies a conscious choice on the part of the students, as if all options were open to them. However, students of color leave school largely because they feel discriminated against, stereotyped, or excluded.... The term "push out" puts the responsibility on where it should appropriately fall: schools and schooling in the U.S.[10]

Malik became increasingly doubtful that he would ever receive a fair chance to succeed in school, increasingly doubtful that his teachers would "have his back," and increasingly more vulnerable to the streets. Once fully disillusioned with school, students like Malik cease to wish for acceptance within the school walls. It then becomes even more imperative that they acquire power and respect in their own neighborhoods. As one student put it:

> [S]ome kids wanna join gangs for respect, and some of them wanna just like, they just, some of them want to have respect for their own self, and some of them want to have respect for their own neighborhood. (Interview with TJ)

Hence, unlike the hard urban monster of fiction and news media accounts who arrives on the scene radically and completely opposed to everything mainstream, the hard urban teen feels alienated by the schooling process and suppresses his remorse and fear. This student wants to believe in mainstream ideals but is convincing himself that he has no viable alternative but to immerse himself in the illicit activities of street culture—that is, no viable alternative but to become a gangster.

Unlike their hard peers, hardcore wannabes lack legitimate claims to the drug trade and gangsterlike activities because they do not live in neighborhoods where criminal, street-based activities take place. The ideal typical hardcore wannabes dons gangsterlike mannerisms not because he has no other viable alternatives but because he (or sometimes she) lacks peer respect. The wannabe believes that a gangsterlike reputation will translate into social esteem. As elaborated in the next section, hardcore wannabes desire to be "down" with their hard peers who can "hang" in tough neighborhoods.

THE "HARDCORE WANNABE"

Shane is a seventh grade Afro-Caribbean student disdained as tall and goofy by his classmates. At thirteen years of age, Shane has not yet become fully acclimated to his lanky 6'2" man-size frame. Shane's body often betrays him during athletic activities like basketball: his best attempts to move with rhythm and poise end in clumsy and awkward presentations of self. Shane is also of Haitian descent, a characteristic that he actively hides from his peers by frequently reminding teachers not to say out loud his French-sounding last name. In the Cambridge program, Haitian students are often harassed and ridiculed by other students, especially by other Black students, as unattractive, undesirable, and undeserving of companionship.[11] Unlike Jason and Malik, Shane is not considered the least bit hard by his peers: he lacks legitimate claims to involvement in the illicit activities of street culture. Shane, nonetheless, masquerades as tough and has thereby been labeled as a "hardcore wannabe."

The Jacket Incident[12]

Shane wants to be, or at least appear to be, hard because he desires the esteem and respect of his classmates instead of their ridicule and irreverence. He frequently looks for opportunities to demonstrate that he is not the tall, goofy, hardcore wannabe that his classmates consider him to be. One late September afternoon at the Cambridge after-school program, the students were playing basketball in the gym, when the director announced that the buses had arrived to take the students home. As usual, the students gathered their coats, jackets, and book bags and bolted for the door. Shane lingered behind and frantically searched for his jacket. I urged Shane, "Hurry up before you miss the bus!" He responded, "I can't find my jacket.... Someone stole my jacket!" I asked if he had possibly left it in the classroom, and he insisted, "No, I left it right here on the floor!" He angrily mumbled something about "getting his boyz on someone if they had messed with his jacket" and, as I walked him to the bus, Shane continued to grumble about what he would do if someone had "fucked" with his jacket.

When we arrived outside at the front entrance of the school where the buses were waiting, Shane assumed a posture that was tough and gangsterlike, walked boldly out, and yelled to the other students, "Has anyone seen my jacket?" Kenneth, another student, held up Shane's jacket up and offered, "Here it is!" Shane rushed toward Kenneth, yelling threats and profanity. This unprovoked attack placed Kenneth on the defensive and then he, too, assumed a hard posture. Kenneth intentionally dropped the jacket on the ground and exclaimed, "Fuck you niggah!" The other kids laughed and urged Kenneth and Shane to fight. Jason stood in the background laughing as he joined the chorus of instigating students. Shane picked up his jacket in pursuit as Kenneth walked toward the bus. I rushed to stand between Kenneth and Shane. Shane yelled that he was going to get his "boyz" on Kenneth, and Kenneth responded, "This is what I think about your boyz." Kenneth bent over, pulled down his pants, and mooned Shane. Kenneth then pulled up his pants and boarded the bus. Shane tried to board the bus behind Kenneth, but I got on the bus before Shane and prevented him from boarding. One of the other teachers pulled Shane aside, and I got off the bus. The bus departed as Kenneth yelled at Shane from the window and Shane yelled back from the sidewalk. Later on at the staff meeting, I learned that Jason—one of Shane's so-called "boyz"—had taken the jacket. When Kenneth held up the jacket, he was just trying to give it back, until, of course, Shane threatened Kenneth.

At the next meeting of the Cambridge after-school program, Shane brought a miniature baseball bat (about fifteen inches long) with which he intended to threaten Kenneth. He and two other students started walking to a convenience store in blatant defiance of a rule to the contrary. After they ignored my and another teacher's admonition that they could not walk to the store during program hours, we decided to walk with them. Shane was boasting about what he was going to do to Kenneth. I explained to Shane that the whole incident was his "bad" (that Shane was in the wrong) because his "boy" Jason had taken his jacket, not Kenneth. Shane seemed momentarily startled by a nascent realization that he had falsely accused Kenneth, but he would not, could not back down from his original plan, and some of the other kids were encouraging him to fight. By confronting Kenneth, a student with a reputation for being tough, Shane hoped to prove once and for all that he, too, was hardcore.

We returned from the store and entered the classroom. Kenneth did not wait for Shane to "talk smack" and "step to" him. Kenneth immediately walked over to Shane and asserted, "You been doing all this talking about getting your boyz on me. You don't need no boyz. Let's you and me 'throw down' right here, right now!" Shane began to back away, but Kenneth, who was angry and serious, continued to advance. I stood between the two of them and then Shane began to "talk smack." In other words, Shane made empty threats. A couple of teachers took Shane out of the room, but Kenneth, who was responding to Shane's threats and was sincerely prepared to fight, followed them out of the room. I grabbed Kenneth around the waist from behind and gently, but firmly, restricted his movement. Another teacher stood in front of Kenneth, but Kenneth slowly dragged me down the hall in his effort to physically confront Shane. Instead of standing his ground, Shane backed away as he continued his verbal assault.

To Shane, this jacket incident was an opportunity to prove that he was hard. In the eyes of his peers, however, this incident reconfirmed that he was a hardcore wannabe; they noticed that Shane's verbal assault on Kenneth was unsubstantiated by his physical retreat. These students viewed Shane's unconvincing gangsterlike performance as an opportunistic attempt to gain social esteem for the sake of social esteem, not for the sake of surviving the streets. Neither Shane nor any of the students I interviewed considered themselves to be hardcore wannabes. But Shane, other students from Cambridge, and students from Boston assert that the majority of Cambridge students who act hard like a "gangsta" are actually hardcore wannabes performing for their peers.

The ideal typical hardcore wannabe does not reside in a neighborhood where illicit street cultural activities are commonplace. As a result, he lacks the street cultural experiences, exposures, social constraints, and limited employment prospects that forge a gangster identity and subsequent lifestyle. Furthermore, the typical wannabe, unlike the typical hard student, is not pushed out of school. As a result, he has no justifiable basis for involvement in drug trafficking or gang-related activities, and no practical use for a gangsterlike reputation other than impressing his peers. That is, while the typical hard student assumes gangsterlike mannerisms as a means of surviving and eventually thriving in the streets, the typical wannabe appropriates gangsterlike modes of dressing, language, and claims of ruthlessness as a sort or fashion statement or trend. As expressed by one student and corroborated by most:

[Sometimes black and white kids act hardcore because] it's kind of like a trend. It's like, like the baggy pants of whatever, walking with a limp, you know, just having . . . that rugged . . . look of whatever. You know, it's like, it's a label so everybody wants to follow that trend (Interview with Reni).

To the undiscerning eye of school officials unfamiliar with the streets, the typical wannabe may appear to be genuinely tough when he is merely making a fashion statement, merely putting on a gangsterlike poker face and praying no one will call his bluff. School officials may be convinced by a wannabe's performance, but other street-savvy students are rarely convinced. These students see through the gangster-like facade. The following sentiments were commonplace:

> Hardcore wannabes see the sort of glorification of the hardcore kids and they wanna associate with it. What it comes down [to] is [the wannabes] don't really have the state of mind to make them be tough, good fighters and be able to stand up for themselves and they just wanna [act tough] to sorta be down or to be associated with something. (Interview with Casper)

> Oh, a difference between a [wannabe and someone who is hard] is a wannabe will try to get to that hardcore [level], and the hardcore [student] is already at that level. [The hardcore student] can just go around, he can fuck with anybody he wants to. A wannabe will try to do what he does to follow in [the hardcore student's] footsteps. (Interview with Lewis)

To paraphrase the two students quoted above, the typical hard student is regarded as tough, a good fighter, and at a level within street cultural circles where he can "fuck with anybody he wants to." The typical hardcore wannabe feigns but does not genuinely possess these gangsterlike abilities. Furthermore, because the typical hardcore wannabe acts hard for fashion's sake, and not for the sake of surviving the streets, he incites disrespect. The following student expressed his disrespect of wannabes, a sentiment that surfaced frequently and passionately during interviews.

> Society nowadays, from the movies, shows kids how to be powerful and be in control and whatnot. So like kids nowadays are on a power trip. They wanna be powerful. They wanna be "all that" [i.e, be important], as they say.... I've seen [hardcore wannabes].... I don't hang around kids like that. I don't, you know, I don't find them particularly ... interesting or friendly.... I can't deal with that. I don't take garbage from anybody.... Someone comes up to me try to be hardcore, I'm gonna put them on their butt. So, you know ... people think I'm straight-up hardcore, you know. That's because I don't take the garbage that they give me. (Interview with Kwon)

In his quest for peer respect, Shane did not substantiate his verbal assault on Kenneth with physical aggression. In contrast to Shane, Ron McHale, described in the early pages of this chapter, committed murder. It is alleged that he murdered in an effort to gain respect on the streets. Despite this physically aggressive and homicidal act, Ron's peers *still* considered him a hardcore wannabe. Like Shane, Ron was reproached as a punk who wanted a gangster reputation for which he had no practical use other than impressing his peers. More specifically, students labeled Ron as a working-class, Irish-American, hardcore wannabe who got drunk, played a senseless game called "knockout," and preyed upon a helpless victim (a Scandinavian student) instead of a real gangster or someone else considered tough by street cultural standards.

L.J.D.: [Why did Ron murder the university student]?
KEENAN: [He was playing a game]. Knockout was a game where you go up and punch somebody in the face real hard, see if you can knock 'em out. If you knock 'em out, that's a point.

L.J.D.: Then what happens if you knock 'em out? That means you're down with the gang or something?

KEENAN: No. It's just a game.

L.J.D.: So, I mean, the point of the game . . .

KEENAN: Just to knock someone out . . . . [Y]ou go up to somebody, no reason [hits his palm with his fist], right in their face and knock 'em out. If you knock 'em out, then you got a point. If you don't knock 'em out nothing happens. You just don't knock 'em out. But I don't like that game. . . .

I don't like Ron. I knew him before. He was a dick. Sorry, he is a dick. He, um, was running around with those White kids that thought he was hard and he'd do anything. He was one of those people like, "Oh, I'll do it if you dare me," you know. He's stupid. He is really stupid. I seen him once before [the murder] happened, and he just thought he was on top of the world. And then stabbing somebody to death? For what? Just cause he [the Scandinavian student] talked funny, or just because no reason at all. No reason.

L.J.D.: It that why he stabbed the kid?

KEENAN: 'Cause he talked funny.

L.J.D.: Cause the kid was from [Scandinavia], so of course he got an accent.

KEENAN: That [reason is] ridiculous. . . . (Interview with Keenan)

Oh, yeah, I knew [Ron] before [the murder] had happened. Couple of weeks ago, we had gotten into a fight, not me and him, but him and some other kids, and we were with our friends, like what we were talking about, and I guess they didn't get along, so they just had a fight. But going back to that, umm, that incident. I think it was stupid because, umm, that was a dumb thing to be doing, trying to knock someone out, you know. . . . And I bet you if it was some other guy, like a big black strong guy, they wouldn't have done nothing. Since [the university student] looked kinda sissy, then they just [played knockout]. So, yeah, I think it was stupid. (Interview with Kirkland)

L.J.D.: What do you think about what happened with Ron McHale?

ALI: It's his fault, yo. Killed somebody. . . . Shouldn't have killed him, maybe stabbed him in the leg or something, kill him, nah.

L.J.D.: Why did he kill that guy?

KENNETH: No reason.

ALI: Based-out, drunk. He got caught up in the wrong crowd. He got caught up with people that like to smoke, really smoke bomb [and] everything, man. They probably base heads. (Interview with Ali and Kenneth)

Thus far I have drawn upon interviews and observations to construct ideal-types of the labels "hardcore" and "hardcore wannabe." These were the labels actually used by students, not categories I created for the sake of classifying research findings. The key distinction between the labels is the mutually exclusive concepts "*have* to be hard" and "*want* to be hard." Illustrative quotes and events, excerpted from the more complex realities of Jason, Malik, Shane, Ron, and other street-savvy youths, imply two ideal extremes: urban youths necessarily have to be hard and are, or unnecessarily want to be hard but are not. These extremes differentiate between "hardcore" and "hardcore wannabe." However, these dichotomous categories do not suffice: they allow no middle ground for classifying urban students who have to be hard but *prefer* not to be—that is, students who are considered hardcore but are not becoming gangsters.

For instance, Kwon, the student quoted several paragraphs above, describes himself (and is described by his peers) as hardcore. Due to our shared extracurricular interests, I knew Kwon well.[13] Neither "hardcore" nor "hardcore wannabe" capture Kwon's gangsterlike comportment. Students like Kwon compelled me to construct a third ideal-type, a variation of the gangster theme: the hard-enough urban youth. Like Jason and Malik, Kwon lives in a neighborhood where illicit street cultural activities take place, and he has neighborhood friends who are involved in the drug trade and criminal gang-related activities. Unlike Jason and Malik, Kwon does not take part in such activities himself. Kwon is Korean American. However, because he had a reputation for being able to defend himself (demonstrated in actual fights) and because he associates with Black peers with hard reputations, he is referred to by those peers as a Korean African American. Unlike Shane and Ron, Kwon's gangsterlike demeanor is substantiated by the realities of his neighborhood and his ability to defend himself physically against neighborhood toughs. Even more, unlike the typical hardcore wannabe, the ideal hard-enough student is unlikely to perform for his peers. Unlike the typical hard urban teen, students who are hard-enough are the most likely to reconcile the mainstream demands of school with the demands of surviving the streets.

BEING "HARD-ENOUGH" TO SURVIVE THE STREETS

Recall Kenneth from the jacket incident? Like Kwon, Kenneth is not involved in illicit street cultural activities but lives in a neighborhood where such activities are commonplace. When I pulled Kenneth aside during the jacket-incident altercation with Shane, the following conversation ensued.

> Kenneth said to me, in a calm but serious tone, "Let me go, Tomni.[14] Let me go!" I responded, "No, Kenneth, because if I let you go, you're going to hurt somebody." Kenneth explained, "I know, but Shane talks too much and I want him to know he can't punk me like that." I explained, "I know, Kenneth, but then you'll get into trouble and Shane's not worth your getting into trouble." Kenneth exclaimed, "I don't care, I don't care, let me go, Tomni!" I affirmed, "Well, I care, and I don't want you to get into trouble." Kenneth explained, "You don't understand. [Shane's] been talking about putting his boyz on me, and *you don't live in my neighborhood!* I can't let him punk me like that." I responded, "Kenneth, you're right. I don't live in your neighborhood, so I'm not going to ask you not to protect yourself. But I got your back right now and I'd like to help you settle this right now, right here, without fighting." Kenneth complained, "I always get blamed for stuff I didn't do." I responded, "I know you didn't take Shane's jacket. I would have dropped it on the ground too if Shane had falsely accused me; don't worry, I got your back." Kenneth had calmed down a bit and finally agreed to try to settle things without fighting.
>
> I agreed to mediate a truce between Kenneth and Shane. Kenneth, Shane, and I went to another classroom, away from all the other students. I immediately told Shane that he owed Kenneth an apology and asked him if he knew why. Shane responded, "Because he didn't

take my jacket, Jason did." I confirmed, "Yes, and because you tried to bum rush him and blame him, when he was only trying to give you your jacket back." Shane explained, "I thought he had taken my jacket. That's why I said all that stuff." I said, "You were wrong." Kenneth added, "Man, I really don't want to fight you but you been talkin' smack and making threats about your boyz; I got boyz too, but I really don't want to fight you." Shane apologized, "I'm sorry man, I should have been yelling at Jason, not at you. . . . I'm sorry man." Kenneth accepted and replied, "That's all right man, but you gotta learn not to run your mouth so much." They shook hands and for the moment, things were okay.[15]

Kenneth initially had no desire to fight Shane. He had even tried to walk away and board the bus when Shane initiated the altercation. But Shane persisted, and Kenneth could not afford to be "punked" or "dissed" by a hardcore wannabe. Kenneth had to defend his reputation for being hard. Kenneth knew that the classroom walls had ears; he knew that word would reach his neighborhood that Shane had "stepped to" him. If Kenneth did not face and fight Shane now, he would have to face his "boyz" later and risk losing his tough reputation. If Kenneth allowed Shane to "punk" him now, he would increase his own likelihood of being treated with blatant disrespect on the streets in the future.

The ideal-typical hard-enough urban youth possesses instrumental qualities for avoiding, or at least mitigating, the violent confrontations and illicit entrapments of urban streets. Like Kenneth and Kwon, the hard-enough student carries himself in a way that affirms that he is equal to every physically aggressive challenge. To borrow the words of one student, this means, "If someone's gonna punch you, you *could* beat them up. You stand up for yourself when it comes to fights and you get respect, respect in the streets."[16] Thus, the typical hard-enough student is "down" with or respected by youth on the streets, without being involved in the illicit aspects of street culture.

Some kids on the streets, if you're talking about [being] down, they gotta have respect for you. And you could be positive and you can say, "Naw, I don't wanna do drugs, I don't wanna deal drugs, I don't wanna be around gangs, and if you're friends with people on the street, they'll all respect you and they will continue to be down with you. But if, if you just wanna become like that gangsta image, that'll only last you a couple while, and you don't know who your foes are, so I mean eventually you won't be down anymore. But if you're down with the streets, all you have to do is accept friendship and treat people with respect. (Interview with Casper)

[To be down with kids on the streets], you really don't have to be associated with the things that they do. You don't have to do what they do. But you have to have the same mentality, you have to understand them. You have to understand how they're thinking, and you have to understand that they're doing what they feel is necessary for them. . . . You don't have to do it yourself. You just have to understand what they're doing. (Interview with Gari)

A hard-enough student must also be able to talk authoritatively about using guns and other dangerous weapons even if he has no genuine interest in using such weapons.

Some guy talked to me, he was like, "Yo I took this guy out, I took that guy out, too." I played with him [and said], "Yeah, I had a twelve-gauge shotgun and you know, I was shooting with it and I hit a squirrel." (Interview with Kwon)

This type of student can also prevent a confrontation from escalating by standing his ground and projecting an I-got-nothing-to-prove attitude instead of fighting. For example, Malcolm, the fifteen-year-old Boston student featured in chapters 4, 5, and 6, provided me with the details of one such encounter. When Malcolm was thirteen years old or so, some kids attempted to rob his friend Denton. Malcolm and Denton had stopped for a game of basketball on their way home from working at the Roxbury Multi-Service Center. Malcolm recalled, "[T]hese kids had pushed Denton," and demanded, "We want your jewels!" Malcolm walked across the court, joined Denton, and inquired, "Yo, what's going on." The aggressor responded with a threat, "Shut up, boy, before I smack you." Malcolm guesstimated that the aggressor was approximately ten years old, but he had backup—he was accompanied by four or so youths who seemed approximately eighteen years old. This altercation had taken place about two weeks before the interview, but Malcolm recalled the details:

[This kid said to Denton], "Give me your stuff or I'm gonna smack you." So, [I asked him], "Why you gonna hit him? Why you gonna mess with him? He didn't do nothing to you." And he was like, "'Cause I want to, BOY!" So I had some Doritos—I was hungry too—and a Mountain Dew, so I gave him my Mountain Dew. And he was like, "I want your chips too!" So I gave him my chips. And he asked me to take everything out of my pocket, and I took my cassette tape out and gave it to him. And then he just left. (Interview with Malcolm)

The aggressors were generally older and Malcolm and Denton were outnumbered more than two to one, yet Malcolm could have fought to demonstrate his street prowess. But he preferred to defuse the situation. As a result, Malcolm had to stand his ground with an attitude that conveyed, "You can have my chips because I've got nothing to prove, but I *will* fight if I have to." Without this hard-enough posture, the aggressors probably would have also physically assaulted Malcolm (and Denton), instead of being appeased by Malcolm's chips, soda, and tape.

Like Kwon, Kenneth, and Malcolm, students who are hard-enough usually have a reputation of being good fighters because they have defended themselves in past disputes. As a result, hard-enough students are unlikely to retreat when confronted and will usually fight only as a last resort. Unlike their peers who are wannabes and are constantly seeking opportunities to establish a tough reputation, these students already have a hard reputation. Unlike their peers who are (becoming) hard and are constantly convincing themselves that they have very little choice but to become gangsters, hard-enough students still view joining the American mainstream through schooling as a viable option. They hold this view despite the incongruity between the ideals and norms of schooling and the illicit realities of the streets.

As mentioned above, the typical hard-enough student associates with individuals involved in criminal activities without being seduced by the dark side of street culture. This accomplishment is neither easy nor inconsequential, and it places students who are hard-enough at risk of being misunderstood, mislabeled, and considered guilty by association. One interaction that I had with Robbie, a ninth grade alumnus of the Cambridge program, illustrates the challenges and consequences of being hard-enough to survive the streets. Robbie's ethnic origins are in the Dominican Republic; he considers himself both Black and Latino. I quote him and retell his story from a memorandum that I was compelled to write moments after our interaction.

Robbie's Wisdom[17]

ROBBIE: Last Friday at the high school dance I wasn't even being rude or anything and a cop wanted to do me like Rodney King. But the teachers were there, so he couldn't do anything. What happened was that after the dance, I had gotten my coat from the coat room and I started to leave when I realized that my sunglasses must have fallen out of my pocket. So, I went back to the coat room to get my sunglasses and the policeman monitoring the party said, 'No! Get off the premises!' A gym teacher told me I could stay and look for my sunglasses, and when I told the cop the teacher said I could stay and look, the cop said, 'But what did I say?' Then a school guard peeped around the door from the coat room and said that I could come in and look for my sunglasses. Then the cop said angrily, 'Go ahead! Go ahead!' Before I went to get my glasses, I went to the cop and tried to apologize. I said, 'I didn't mean to disrespect you or get on your bad side. . . .' But the cop interrupted me and said, 'Don't give me that garbage, get out of here, get out of my face and go look for your glasses!' Then I said, 'I can't give you any respect unless you give me respect.' Then the cop said, 'Don't give me any of that garbage! I don't need to respect you. Get your glasses and get out of here!'. . . . I don't like cops. . . . I'm afraid of cops. . . . They'll give you false charges like those phony trespassing charges they gave me in the mall when I spoke up for myself.

Robbie is a very articulate and perceptive young man. He is aware that something is wrong with what he refers to as "the system." During an earlier alumni reunion meeting of the Cambridge program, Robbie had explained, "After I got arrested [for the trespassing charges mentioned in the above quote], I stayed in the house for a month. . . . The police pick on people of color more than White people." At first this statement about not leaving the house seemed like an overreaction. But the more occasions I have to listen to, observe, and converse with Robbie, the more I am convinced that he is not overreacting. He knows he must actively avoid being trapped by the system. He is future-oriented and does not want the injustice of the system to lock him into the present.

Other students, all Black males and Latinos, from the reunion group might second Robbie's sentiments but they do not seem to have thought things through as carefully as Robbie. Robbie seems not merely interested in expressing that something is wrong but also strives to change the system. For example, Robbie writes positive raps and has organized a student group to help his fellow students cope with the pressures they face. I sometimes worry about Robbie: he is so young and yet he endeavors to cope with so much. As the reunion meeting came to an end, Robbie asked me if he could get a ride. We left the meeting a little early, so he could arrive promptly for an SAT preparation course. As we walked to the car, Robbie volunteered, "I'm a sixteen-year-old with the racial tension and oppression of a thirty-two-year-old." He explained that after seeing the movie *Malcolm X*, he felt that his eyes had been opened and that he knew how "the system worked." He expressed that he loved the movie, and that "things haven't gotten better, they've gotten worse." I conversed with him but will not reveal the contents of the conversation that ensued because he shared his views with me in confidence.

At sixteen, Robbie carries the weight of his street cultural associations on his shoulders. In many ways, Robbie is a typical teenager with idealistic views about falling in love and going to college. But in his neighborhood and school on a daily basis, he has to confront, negotiate with, and avoid social forces like peer pressure to act hard, physical and armed confrontations, undeserved encounters with the legal system, negative images and low expectations for young Black and Brown ("Latino") males. Robbie realized that in order to avoid these entrapments, he had to summon the wisdom that he envisions himself possessing at thirty-two years of age. Even leisure activities like "hangin' with his boyz" have been ordeals since, at the very least, Robbie feels a social responsibility to challenge their involvement in or flirtations with illicit activities. And, at the very worst, "hangin' with his boyz" has resulted in an arrest. No wonder he feels sixteen going on thirty-two.

I could share several more anecdotes that exemplify the hard-enough ideal-type, but suffice it to say that the urban youths to whom I affix the label "hard-enough" have no desire to be gangsters, drug dealers, or petty thugs; they do desire to be students. The typical hard-enough student considers shortsighted and pessimistic the hard view that becoming a gangster is the only viable alternative. Unlike their hard peers, hard-enough students do not see their fate as sealed, work relatively hard in school, and do their best to avoid dangerous and criminal street cultural activities. Despite the realities of social marginality, hard-enough students are usually consummate optimists who believe that through schooling, they will become upwardly mobile. But because these students live in their neighborhoods and not in their schools, they must make surviving the streets a priority. As illustrated by Kenneth in the jacket incident as well as other altercations over articles of clothing, surviving or navigating tough streets sometimes means assuming gangsterlike postures in school-based settings. In other words, if during a school-based dispute a hard-enough student has no viable option but to demonstrate his potential to be as ruthless as a gangster, he must do so to maintain dignity and respect beyond the walls of the school.

REAL EXCEPTIONS TO IDEAL CATEGORIES

The three ideal categories constructed in this chapter are derived from a broader set of findings about gaining respect on the streets. These findings are derived from an even broader body of qualitative data on the cultural inconsistencies between mainstream schools and urban streets. I documented numerous inconsistencies while conducting my research but pursued themes that emerged, recurred, and revealed students' preoccupations: "hardcore" and "hardcore wannabe" were two such themes. For instance, I noticed that when street-savvy students in Boston and Cambridge used, defined, accepted, or challenged these labels, they did so with passion and conviction. Hence, specific topics, themes, and events earned their way into this chapter not merely because they occurred frequently, but because they embodied student concerns and preoccupations with street culture.

Ron McHale's murder of a university student, Shane and Kenneth's altercation over a jacket, and other depicted events illustrate the allure of gangsterlike posturing. Yet, as exemplary as these events may be, they are but brief moments excerpted from young and unfolding lives.

In addition to the three ideal variations of a gangsterlike theme, I also uncovered a fourth type of urban student: students who live in neighborhoods where illicit street cultural activities are commonplace but who are sheltered from the streets. These students cannot be categorized as hardcore, hardcore wannabes, or hardcore enough. According to one student, these are the urban "kids ... that don't hang on the streets because their parents always got something planned for them after school 'cuz they don't want them hanging on the streets."[18] My research findings suggest that the students in this fourth category are usually pre-adolescent and female. This book, however, will not examine the experiences of sheltered urban students.[19]

If I had examined the experiences of sheltered urban students, many of whom are female, I would be able to compare and contrast students who frequent the streets with students who do not. And, if in addition to schools and streets, I had observed other milieus where students strike hard poses, this study may have included more girls. For example, Alberta, a student from the Cambridge program, once explained that some girls who consider themselves "gangsta bitches" frequent shopping malls. Within these malls, they walk around with their crew of girls in search of other females to bully. To prove her toughness, the lead bully of the crew will bump aggressively into her target, daring a fight or verbal altercation. I took note of Alberta's story, but given limitations of time and resources, I never conducted follow-up research on hard posturing within shopping malls. A few weeks after my interview with Alberta, while shopping in the Cambridgeside Galleria, I was targeted by a group of girls. As I descended and exited an escalator, the lead member of a group of four or so girls bumped aggressively into me as we passed; then the lead member and group ascended the escalator. I stopped, turned, frowned, and scrutinized their ascent; for a moment I groaned to myself, "What's wrong with her? She actually crossed my path to bump into me!" The girls, especially the lead member, scowled at me while ascending as if to say, "Yeah I bumped into you! What you gonna do about it?" Then, remembering Alberta's story, my frown turned to a smile; my head began to nod as I thought to myself, "So that's what Alberta was talking about!" My reaction seemed to confuse the girls; their scowls turned to stares of perplexity. I turned and walked away. Like the sheltered urban students, tough or hard girls extend beyond the purview of this book. Hence, the categories of hardcore, hardcore wannabe, and hard-enough, while sociologically useful, do not include the numerous gradations of difference among real urban youths.

Of course, urban youths from low-income neighborhoods are not a monolithic group; they wander in, out, and around these ideal categories. For example, individual students sometimes walk a tightrope between being hard-enough and becoming hard, between maintaining street-based friendships and avoiding immersion in the negative aspects of street culture. And, as illustrated in chapters 5 and 6, so-called hard students at risk of becoming thoroughly disenchanted with school or immersed in illicit street cultural activities can become hard-enough with adequate social support and mentoring.

Ron McHale's case particularly exemplifies how real individuals may evade labels that have been affixed to them. Ron was a peer of the students in the Cambridge program, but not enrolled in the program himself. After he allegedly murdered a university student, most students in the program eagerly volunteered their opinions of him. I never conducted formal interviews with Ron but I did arrange several non-contact visits and informal interviews with him at the county correctional facility. My visits with Ron and discussions with his best friend and favorite teacher combine to sketch an urban teen who is hardly gangsterlike by any standard, except for the tragic moment when he allegedly committed murder. Ron seems neither the remorseless monster the newspaper article painted him to be nor the fashionable hardcore wannabe that his peers believe him to be.

THE QUEST FOR CHARISMATIC AUTHORITY

Individual and categorical deviations notwithstanding, there are benefits to analyzing ideal-types of gangsterlike posturing. Because ideal-types are conceptually neat and abstract, they allow sociologists and other researchers to cut to the chase, come to some sort of consensus, and give careful consideration to answers for big and elusive questions like "So what? What does it mean sociologically, that students engage in gangsterlike posturing? Or, what makes gangsterlike posturing a *social* action?"[20]

Whether students assume gangsterlike postures to survive the streets or merely to impress their friends, and whether or not these postures are convincing, street-savvy students often pose in a quest for charismatic authority—that is, these students reside at the relatively powerless urban margins of society yet desire to be viewed as exceptional within their own social circles. Within street cultural contexts, the urban gangster has a certain appeal that is charismatically authoritative.[21] Some students successfully cloak themselves in gangsterlike mannerisms and are seen as hard. These students command respect on the streets. Other students are not so successful and are not considered legitimate sources of authority within street cultural circles. Yet the vast majority of students from my study who don gangsterlike mannerisms do not ultimately desire to be gangsters. Instead, they recognize the necessity and utility of charismatic authority within the socially marginal realm of the streets. Street-savvy students aspire to be active and powerful social agents instead of puppets on the strings of social structure.

Furthermore, most street-savvy youths in this study who don gangsterlike mannerisms want to be students, but they must live beyond the walls and jurisdiction of schools. School walls have "ears" that extend into the toughest of neighborhoods. Therefore, street-savvy students sometimes find it necessary to engage in gangsterlike posturing in both the streets and in school. This last point, substantiated in chapter 2, seems to elude the majority of teachers and other school officials with whom street-savvy students interact.

In chapter 2, I presented the student lament that "teachers just don't understand the streets." Students complain that most teachers have no clue that so-called "disruptive" behavior is sometimes a necessary front for surviving the streets. Distinctions between hardcore and hard-enough notwithstanding, teachers do not even appear to distinguish students who are sincerely hard—or becoming hard—from their trendy hardcore wannabe counterparts. Instead, they lump the vast majority of students who don gangsterlike mannerisms but are not gangsters—that is, the hard-enough students and the hardcore wannabes—in with the few hard students who are becoming gangsters.

As concluded in chapter 2, there is strong evidence from field observations and student interviews that many, maybe even most, teachers in the Cambridge and Boston public school systems are not "down." When teachers are not "down" or street-savvy themselves, they lack the frame of reference for understanding gangsterlike postures. They lack the discerning gaze that allows them to distinguish genuine gangsterlike postures from superficial fashion statements. Unfortunately, as elaborated in the following chapter, "down" teachers appear to be in short supply in both the Boston and Cambridge public school systems and, I suspect, in most schools across the United States that serve street-savvy students.

FOUR

Social Capital, Cultural Capital, and Caring Teachers

The Perspectives of Street-Savvy Students and a Magic Teacher[1]

THE "MAGIC" OF MS. BRONZIC

As Malcolm, a street-savvy ninth grader of African-American descent from a low-income neighborhood in Boston, revisits his experiences with his fifth grade teacher, a look of frustration washes across his face.[2] "Man, I hated her. I always wanted to beat her up. But I knew if I beat her up, I'd probably get expelled or somethin'."

Malcolm explains that his frustration with Ms. Hines stemmed from a disagreement they had had about the black history curriculum:

> February rolled around, and it was black history month. And so [Ms. Hines] is telling me about Martin Luther King, and I've learned about Martin Luther King all my life; what else could I learn about Martin Luther King? So, I [say], "Come on, I want to learn about somebody else besides Martin Luther King for once!" And she [responded], "Well the school curriculum provides me with this, and this is what you've got to learn." So, fine. Then, I think, I called her a racist one day, 'cuz she didn't want to teach us any other black history.
>
> [Ms. Hines responded that the lack of black history] wasn't her fault, it was the school curriculum's fault for not providing it. If you're a teacher, you know what I'm sayin', you're suppose to be able to teach me what I have to know. That's how I see it. So [Ms. Hines] was cornball [crazy].

In contrast to Ms. Hines, Malcolm's memory of his sixth grade teacher, Ms. Bronzic, brings a smile to his face.

> [In the] sixth grade, my teacher was Ms. Bronzic; she was a Jewish lady—man, she was so cool. She was the coolest teacher I ever knew: the coolest white lady teacher I ever knew. . . . It's like, I don't know, but Jewish people, they're cooler than regular white people anyway. . . . She use to tell me how she use to live in Dorchester [Massachusetts] and stuff. And, she's old too, but she never would tell us how old she was. . . .
>
> [Ms. Bronzic] use to always tell me I could do better. And I [would explain] that I did like everybody else did. But her teaching methods, they worked! I don't know, she was magic or somethin'. I remember I did a [book] report on *The Legend of Sleepy Hollow*, and I got an A: it was a hundred percent, the best in the class. But [Ms. Bronzic] made me do it over; she said it wasn't good enough even though it was the best in the class. And I remember her teaching me that way: to always be better than the best. . . . [S]he's the type of teacher that ain't teachin' for money. She'd probably do it for free. She's real cool.

Ms. Bronzic's teaching was effective, in part, because she was able to establish a relationship with her students that compelled Malcolm to work hard and do "better than the best." How is it that educationally productive relationships between mainstream teachers and non-mainstream, street-savvy youths like Malcolm come about and are maintained? Or, from the student perspective, why did Malcolm comply with Ms. Bronzic's demands? The answer, in short, is that Malcolm discerned that building a relationship with Ms. Bronzic was a worthwhile investment in his future as a student. In contrast to Ms. Hines, Malcolm was convinced that due to Ms. Bronzic's commitment to the relationship she would, in Malcolm's own words, "be able to teach [him] what he [had] to know."

PRELIMINARY WORDS ON SOCIAL AND CULTURAL CAPITAL
AND STREET-SAVVY STUDENTS

What is this magic that Ms. Bronzic possesses and Mrs. Hines lacks? Human capital? Social capital? Cultural capital? Or does her magic simply boil down to tender loving care for all her students? The concepts of human capital, social capital, and cultural capital appear with regularity in the social scientific literature. While human capital has been clearly and consistently defined as the knowledge, skills, educational training, and other capabilities acquired by individuals that enhance economic productivity,[3] the other two types of capital elude clear and consistent definition. The concepts of social capital and cultural capital are, nonetheless, central to this chapter.

Theories refined by James Coleman and Pierre Bourdieu, respectively, argue that adequate access to social capital and cultural capital is instrumental to positive educational outcomes. Social capital, briefly defined, refers to resources that result from social relationships among individuals, families, communal groups, social networks, and the like; cultural capital refers to the linguistic and cultural competencies of the dominant group in society. The case study documented in this chapter is important because these theories also suggest that, unlike their mainstream counterparts, at-risk youths have limited access to these types of capital. Therefore, a worthwhile scholarly question about Ms. Bronzic would be, "What roles do *social* and *cultural* capital play in Ms. Bronzic's bag of magic tricks?" More generally, how do social and cultural capital factor into relations between teachers and students of color who are financially impoverished, at-risk, and street-savvy?[4] These questions are addressed in this chapter. However, there is one major difference between this chapter and other works that examine social and cultural capital: the opinions of students like Malcolm will figure prominently in the analyses. In other words, this chapter examines social and cultural capital from the perspectives of urban youths who are mostly Black males and Latinos from economically impoverished neighborhoods.

Sara Lawrence-Lightfoot once observed, "Good schools are ultimately dependent on good teachers—smart, inspired people who have something to teach."[5] Lightfoot's ethnographic research in schools also led her to conclude that empathy, "the ability to place oneself in another's position," is crucial to a successful teacher-student relationship.[6] Consistent with Lawrence-Lightfoot's findings, my interview data suggest that teachers, like Ms. Bronzic, who convince students that they genuinely care, cause these students to feel "'seen' in a way they have never felt seen before, fully attended to, wrapped up in an empathetic gaze."[7] Furthermore, more recent studies have explicitly identified teacher caring as an essential ingredient in productive interactions between teachers and students.[8] Hence, in addition to social and cultural capital, this chapter also elucidates urban students' perspectives on teacher caring.

This chapter integrates literature on social and cultural capital with qualitative interviews and field observations. First, I review the concepts of social and cultural capital. Second, from interview data, I present the perspectives of street-savvy urban youths, especially Black American males like Malcolm, on public school teachers. Third, I take a closer look at the magic of Ms. Bronzic to examine further the roles of social and cultural capital in the teacher-student relationship. Finally, I offer concluding observations that extend beyond an examination of social and cultural capital in the teacher-student relationship. Scholars have simultaneously examined human and social capital[9] as well as human and cultural capital,[10] yet the connections between social and cultural capital remain largely unexamined.

SOCIAL AND CULTURAL CAPITAL: ACCESSIBLE DEFINITIONS

In popular usage the word "capital" refers to accumulated monetary income, assets, or other forms of economic wealth. One defining characteristic of capital is that it can be invested (or managed or manipulated) to produce more wealth. In the social scientific literature, social and cultural *capital* are also considered valuable resources, the exception being that the currency of these types of capital is not monetary (at least not directly). Instead, these types of capital are embodied either in social structures (in other words, reoccurring interpersonal, institutional, or other patterned relationships in the case of social capital) or in cultural structures (linguistic codes or dialects, tastes, customs, beliefs, competencies, and so on, which are shared by a group in the case of cultural capital).

Social Capital

Social capital resides in interpersonal or institutional relationships (that is, social networks or group life) between and among individuals. Therefore, social capital is not the internalized possession of an individual. These relationships function to facilitate individual accomplishments or actions that would be unattainable without such connections.[11] Under ideal situations, social capital is a communal resource residing within a broad ecology of networks between interacting social institutions like community organizations, schools, and households. Coleman refers to this type of broad ecology of networks as a functional community.

> [In a functional community] there [is] "closure" between the adult communities and the communities of youth in ... school: Parents [know] who their children's friends [are] and [know] their parents. The norms that pervade the school are in part those dictated by the needs of youth themselves ... but in part those established by the adult community and enforced by the intergenerational contact that this closure brings

about.... [A] functional community [is] a community in which social norms and sanctions, including those that cross generations, arise out of the social structure itself, and both reinforce and perpetuate that structure.[12]

However, under less than ideal situations and without the mutually reinforcing norms and networks found in functional communities, social capital, in its most essential form, may reside in relations between two individuals as long as the relationship provides socially structured resources (for example, information, trust, norms), which facilitate the achievement of goals that would be unachievable in the absence of the relationship. Hence, a teacher-student relationship rich in social capital should enable positive educational outcomes, at least within the confines of that teacher's classroom. Like social capital, cultural capital figures prominently in successful relations between teachers and students.

Cultural Capital

Cultural capital refers to the inherited or acquired linguistic codes, disposition, tastes, modes of thinking, and other types of knowledge or competencies deemed legitimate by the dominant group or groups in society.[13] With respect to the United States, "cultural capital" signifies the English language, and the dispositions, mannerisms, and other cultural practices of middle- and upper-class Americans—that is, of the American mainstream. The possession of cultural capital allows an individual to maneuver successfully within mainstream or dominant group social settings.

In theory, schools are supposed to be great equalizers of inequality. In reality, many scholars argue that schools are *mainstream* social settings that fortify and reproduce the linguistic and cultural practices (cultural capital) imposed as legitimate by the dominant group in society. Schools discourage and devalue students who, owing to family heritage, possess little to none of the cultural capital of the dominant group.[14] Therefore, students like Malcolm are at a disadvantage in comparison to their mainstream counterparts: these mainstream students' families provide and reinforce the cultural capital valued by schools.

If all things were equal in schools, through the dyadic relationship between teacher and student, social capital and cultural capital typical of the American mainstream would be available in the same degree to all students. However, as I elaborate below, street-savvy urban students rarely benefit from these capital resources. Student interviews suggest that most teachers fail to allocate the social and cultural capital funds to the at-risk urban students who may need these funds the most. From the perspectives of street-savvy students, most teachers just do not care enough to build teacher-student relationships that facilitate positive educational outcomes. Limited school-based access to social and cultural capital resources is particularly problematic for at-risk youths of color because these students are likely to lack the social class and family heritages that ensure alternative means for acquiring these types of capital.[15]

It is rare for bonds like the educationally productive relationships between mainstream teachers like Ms. Bronzic and street-savvy youths like Malcolm to come about and be maintained. This makes it all the more important to investigate the nature of these relationships when they occur. I looked for answers by asking at-risk students for views of their favorite teachers.

CARING AS AN ELIXIR OF EDUCATIONAL SUCCESS

According to the students in my study, the qualities that gave a teacher favorite-teacher status included having a good sense of humor, which makes learning fun yet educational, understanding and encouraging students, being someone whom students can talk and look up to, being concerned about students and having time for them, and believing in students' ability to meet academic requirements. The one characteristic that all favorite teachers have in common is the ability to convince students that they genuinely care. Below are typical responses to the interview question, "Do you have any favorite teachers?"

> [I don't have any favorite teachers in high school] but I like my eighth grade teacher . . . because she'd be like one of us. She'd try to like make jokes and . . . like try to talk slang and stuff. (Interview with Ann)

> I have one favorite teacher. He's my social studies teacher. . . . I like him because of the reason why, he's like fun and I'm learning at the same time. And he's educational to me. He's just someone I look up to. (Interview with Abe)

> One of my favorite teachers is Miss M. . . . I had her when I was a freshman. Yeah, it's probably just Miss M. . . . [She's my favorite teacher] 'cuz like when you're in high school, it's different from elementary school. And like some teachers don't care about you, if you don't do your work, and like, I don't know, she [Miss M.] just be pushing you, you know, to do your work and stuff. . . . [S]he's real good. And if you have troubles and stuff, you can talk to her after school and stuff. She's there for you and stuff. (Interview with Reni)

The students from my study have favorite teachers, but these teachers are in short supply. All too often, these students describe teachers who do not engage them in the learning process—teachers, like Ms. Hines, who make little effort to tailor pedagogical approaches to the unique needs of at-risk urban students. These students describe the majority of their relationships with teachers as devoid of trust, devoid of caring, devoid of viable information and therefore deficient in social capital resources that enable positive educational outcomes. The students in my study perceive that, at best, they have a fifty-fifty chance of encountering a teacher who cares.

> There are some teachers who do [care] and there are some teachers that don't. Some teachers try to reach out to you and then there are others who just don't care, except for the fact that they're just teaching. (Interview with Cher)

> There's some teachers that care. Most of them don't. Most of them go there just for the paycheck. But there's some that care. (Interview with Gari)

> Some of them [teachers] . . . can relate [to students]. Some of them talk to us, but others, they just, just, we're just in there so they can teach us what they have to teach us and that's that. (Interview with Shelly)

Nah, some of them [teachers] don't [care]. Like I said, there's like, one out of every house[16] will probably care for their students, for like one particular student. (Interview with Reni)

Even the students who give teachers the benefit of the doubt feel that those teachers who may care in theory fail to adequately structure caring into the teacher-student relationship.

[Teachers] care about kids. They might not show it all the time, but they do care. (Interview with Abe)

A couple [of teachers] do [care]. I think a lot of them care, but the way they care is, I mean, they don't really show it in the proper ways. (Interview with Casper)

Yeah, it depends [but] most [teachers] do [care], and I guess the other ones they're just trying to learn how to . . . I guess, like it's just mixed up kinda. I guess you know half of them . . . do, and maybe the other half, they just really don't know how to talk to you, you know what I mean? They don't know how to approach it and deal with it [talking to teens]. So, therefore, they might take a situation in the wrong manner, you know, and snap at the kid and, you know, do the wrong thing. (Interview with Timmy)

In addition to describing teacher-student relationships deficient in effectual caring, students describe teachers who lack viable knowledge or information longed for by street-savvy youths. This desired information was not knowledge about academic subjects; instead, it was knowledge about avoiding the illicit demands of street culture (for example, gang involvement, violent encounters, drug trafficking). Although a few students believe that teachers do understand what kids have to deal with on the streets, the most common response is that teachers do not understand at all or do not understand enough. This point was made in chapter 2. While caring, favorite teachers are in short supply, caring, street-savvy teachers are an even scarcer resource.

I think Miss O. does [understand the streets], but I don't know about any other teachers. I never talk to them. (Interview with Taneetha)

Some . . . like my language arts teacher, she'll talk to us about . . . teen violence and stuff, and she'll be like, "You guys shouldn't be on the streets and selling drugs." But some teachers, they just don't care [about the streets]. (Interview with Keesha)

No [teachers don't understand the streets], 'cuz if they [teachers] did [understand the streets], they would talk about it, and none of my teachers talk about it. . . . I want them to talk about it. We could see what they think is going on, and maybe they can help. . . . If all teachers get together [they could help]. [T]he more people, one person can make a difference. You never know. (Interview with Sam)

Overall, the students in my study paint grim pictures about their chances of encountering caring teachers. Grimmer still are their chances of encountering teachers who are "down" with kids on the streets—that is to say, teachers who understand the demands of street culture and social pressure to be hard like a gangster. Regardless of how well a teacher knows his or her subject matter, unless she (or he) can relate, or cares to relate, to the demands of urban street culture, she may not be able to acquire and maintain the interest of the students who must navigate the streets on a daily basis. When teachers are unable to structure caring and viable information about street culture into their relationships with street-savvy students, they may undermine urban students' access to important forms of social capital that facilitate positive educational outcomes.

Caring and Social Capital

Let us recall Coleman's definition of social capital in regard to raising children: "the norms, the social networks, and the relationships between adults and children that are of value for the child's growing up."[17] The student interviews above, like Malcolm's, suggest that caring is instrumental to stable relations between adults and children, or, more specifically, teachers and students. In other words, caring is one important aspect of the social relation between students and teachers that "can constitute useful capital resources for [individual students]."[18]

In his examination of how social relations constitute social capital, Coleman observes, "[I]f A does something for B and trusts B to reciprocate in the future, this establishes an expectation in A and an obligation on the part of B to keep the trust." However, from the perspective of the students in this study, if teacher A shows student B that she genuinely cares, then student B will oblige by engaging in the learning process with teacher A. Persistent exhibitions of caring on the behalf of teachers provide a reliable foundation for street-savvy students to trust that learning *will* take place. Students, even those who assume hard postures, view themselves as owing caring teachers their best efforts.[19]

Unlike adult-to-adult social relations, teacher-to-student relations are asymmetrical: teachers are in a better position than students to possess mainstream social (and cultural) capital resources that students need. Students have little to offer except future promise of educational success. In contrast to non-caring teachers, caring teachers allow students to make such an offer in good faith. From the perspective of students, when teachers care enough to make learning fun, or care enough to encourage student excellence, or care enough to have time for students, students feel obliged to work and assured that their efforts will pay off. Remember, what makes a caring teacher significant or instrumental or a social capital resource is that a relationship with her or him makes "possible the achievement of certain ends that would not be attainable in [absence of a caring relationship]."[20] And in the case of street-savvy students, the achievement would be positive educational outcomes despite the cultural capital deficits or gangsterlike dispositions that these students may bring to the learning process.

Likewise, teacher knowledge about navigating inner-city streets is another social capital resource that obliges at-risk urban students to invest in a teacher-student relationship. As with persistent displays of caring, frequent demonstrations by teachers of street smarts—or a willingness to learn from students about street smarts—provides a basis for student trust. However, student interviews imply that the dissemination of this knowledge also falls under the purview of teacher caring. In other words, teachers who care are those who will acquire and share whatever knowledge is necessary for building productive teacher-student relationships.

So far, student interviews reveal that caring and viable advice about surviving the streets are valuable social capital resources that reside in urban students' relationships with favorite teachers. As will be demonstrated below, these two resources are definitely a part of Ms. Bronzic's bag of tricks.

CASE STUDY: THE "MAGIC" OF MS. BRONZIC

During my interviews with Malcolm, Ms. Bronzic figured prominently: in his nine years of secondary schooling, Ms. Bronzic remained unsurpassed. Whenever I asked him what made her so special Malcolm responded with an air of perplexity and urgency, "I don't know. . . . Her teaching techniques worked!" Initially, I arranged to interview Ms. Bronzic and spend a day with her at school. Eventually, I would spend an additional week observing Ms. Bronzic work her magic.[21]

Below I re-create my school visit with Ms. Bronzic and provide highlights from my interview with her.[22] By bringing social scientific scrutiny to this case study of one teacher, I seek to demystify her bag of tricks; I also intend to assess the role of social and cultural capital in her pedagogical approach.

First to Third Periods

Ms. Bronzic has been a teacher for over thirty years, eighteen of which have been at the sixth grade level. She has taught in the same sixth grade classroom for the last ten years. As you stand in front of the room facing the students, the left wall of her classroom is purposefully and thoughtfully decorated with posters and charts to enlighten the mathematically curious, which are titled Fractions, Measurements, Decimals, and Homework Rules. The back wall displays a series of posters of animated students who offer firm but friendly commands: Retrieve, Plan Ahead, Get Organized, Study in a Quiet Place, Concentrate, Be Prepared, Take Notes in Your Own Words, and Pay Attention in Class. Beneath this series of posters is a banner that summarizes what I observed as an ethos or guiding principle of her class: Kids Have Great Expectations and So Should We.

Ms. Bronzic's desks—a combination of two desks separated by a waist-high storage case—span the front of the classroom. Behind her desks is a wall-length bookcase and cabinet combination. The book cases are filled with supplies, manuals, files, resource binders, flash cards, and thesauruses. As I take in all the scenery of the classroom, the message appears clear: "Ms. Bronzic teaches here and teaching is serious business!"

Ms. Bronzic wears slim-framed reading glasses at the tip of her nose, alternately peering over them while speaking to students and through them while reading poetry. Her businesslike demeanor motivates her charges to sit up straight and pay attention. "All right, this is the last poem in the series," Ms. Bronzic announces before reading "The Ad-dressing of Cats," from the Broadway play *Cats*. She enthusiastically reads the poem line by line, stopping frequently to invite student analyses. All students are paying attention and *none* seem afraid to offer observation, compliment, or critique. Ms. Bronzic reads the last line of the poem and inquires, "What's he doing here? Is [the cat] making fun of us?" A Black male student asserts, "I think he's saying we should respect cats more than humans."

Ms. Bronzic queries students who are not volunteering answers, "What do you think, Ronald? What's going on here [in the poem]?" Once asked, these silent students answer without hesitation. The students who speak most frequently are the White female students in the room. These frequent responses seem more a consequence of these students composing almost fifty percent of the class than of a lack of interest from the students of color. There are nineteen students in class today: eight European-American girls, two European-American boys, two African-American girls, five African-American boys, one Latina-American, one Asian-American boy. Like Malcolm, the African-American students reside in low-income, urban neighborhoods.

After stimulating discussion about the poem, Ms. Bronzic plays the song version of the poem from the Broadway play. There's a baritone soloist, a backup chorus, and abundant fanfare. "That's what I call a finale!" remarks one of the White female students. "What about [the singer's] enunciation?" Ms. Bronzic probes. "He's trying to emphasize his message," exclaims one student. Ms. Bronzic continues, "What's the message you leave with about cats?" "That they're important," affirms one student; "That they're intelligent," affirms another. Ms. Bronzic's interrogations about the poem are interactive and flow in and out of student analyses. Her method is decisively Socratic or dialectical, and her students offer thoughtful evaluations with an ease that suggests to me that this is business as usual in her class.

An exercise that began as a discussion of the content of poetry progresses into a discussion of high culture, and culminates into an assignment on writing poems. For example, Ms. Bronzic shares some other high culture experiences with her students, including having high tea at the Ritz. Returning to the topic of poetry in general and "The Ad-dressing of Cats," in particular, Ms. Bronzic reminds her students of her expectations about the structure of the poems they are to write. "You can structure your poems after [the one I read] but don't plagiarize! What does plagiarize mean?" The students respond in enthusiastic unison, "Copy!"

At this point in my observations and fieldnote taking, I began to discern a pattern in Ms. Bronzic's pedagogical approach. The content of her instruction has changed from poetry to English grammar, but the Socratic method (interactively pushing, probing, prodding, reiterating, and guiding students to answers) of her instruction remains consistent. As I observe and take notes, I sense that Ms. Bronzic is aware of my presence. I silently acknowledge that my presence has influenced class dynamics, yet the influence appears minimal. Based upon the comfort level of the students and ease with which they pay attention and interact, I feel assured that what I have witnessed so far is more class as usual than performance for a guest. Furthermore, I remind myself that I had only called Ms. Bronzic yesterday to ask if I could come this morning; such short notice did not allow ample time for her to orchestrate this class just for me. I definitely seem to be observing a bit of the magic that Malcolm described in his interview.

Fourth and Fifth Periods

After her first three periods, Ms. Bronzic has planning and development time. During this respite from her serious and passionate work as a teacher, she informs me that the students I just observed are "really on point." She has these students for first through third and seventh periods. However, her sixth period class "thinks learning is a joke." The students in sixth period forget to bring their books, pencils, and homework assignments and they laugh and joke too frequently. I ask, "What's the difference between your sixth period and the class I just observed?" "Parental involvement," Ms. Bronzic responds without hesitation, an indication that she has previously given thought to this question. "I can call most of the parents in the class you [just] observed about a problem I'm having with their child and they'll be here immediately. But many of the parents in my sixth period don't even return my phone calls!" Ms. Bronzic's tone is one of frustration and disappointment.

Sixth Period

A student walks into class chewing gum. "Throw away your gum, Rhonda!" Ms. Bronzic's directive is uncompromising. The student's response is mildly apologetic, "Oh yeah, I forgot." Ms. Bronzic continues her admonishment in a calm yet serious tone, "Why do you forget? I've told you no gum in this class all semester. How do you forget something that I tell you every day? We're talkin' gum chewing here, not trigonometry tables." Ms. Bronzic admonishes one Black male student for forgetting his home lesson folder, and, from another Black male student, she confiscates a hand fan that she had previously asked him to put away.

There are supposed to be ten students in her sixth period class, but only five are in attendance today (four Black boys and one Black girl). The students in this class are noticeably less prepared than those in the first class I observed. These students are also more disruptive and have shorter attention spans. However, Ms. Bronzic still *successfully* employs the Socratic method as she teaches this class about adjectives. Just as she had done with her first class, she pushes, probes, prods, interacts, and guides students to answers. The only major difference in her pedagogical approach to this class is that the Socratic method is woven between disciplining and reprimanding students. The pace of this class is slower, but the teacher caring and expectations remain high.

Seventh Period

It is now 12:55 in the afternoon (the last class period of the day), and the class I first observed returns to Ms. Bronzic's classroom. Her pedagogical approach is productive, yet mentally, physically, and spiritually demanding. By "spiritually" I mean that regardless of the preparedness of her students, Ms. Bronzic strives to maintain a spirit or mood that is consistently positive, demanding, and encouraging. Before her sixth period less-prepared class, she had lamented, "I know they're going to come in unprepared. I need to sit down and prepare myself for this class. It's so frustrating to teach when students aren't prepared and parents don't care!"

At the end of the school day, I accompany Ms. Bronzic as she escorts her class outside. As the students depart, a Latino student, who appears to be a sixth or seventh grader, walks quickly pass Ms. Bronzic. She stops him and inquires in a serious tone, "Why did you get an F?" The student fidgets and looks around Ms. Bronzic as if searching for someone. Ms. Bronzic gently grasps his face, cupping his chin and cheeks with the thumb, palm, and fingers of her right hand: "Look at me, look at me! Why did you get an F?" At this point, the student is still looking everywhere except at Ms. Bronzic, but makes no attempt to uncup her hand from his face or otherwise escape her grasp. His response is a confession, "Because I didn't study!" Ms. Bronzic interrupts his explanation and demands in a maternal tone, "Look at me!" The student's response is evasive, "I'm looking for somebody. That's why I can't look at you." Ms. Bronzic persists, "They aren't going anywhere. They'll be there. Look at me! Why did you get an F?" The student elaborates his confession, "Because I didn't work hard or study. I didn't do my best." Partially satisfied with the student's response, Ms. Bronzic releases her gentle grasp, "So what are you going to do the next time?" "The same thing I did before," the student announces in a mischievous but subdued tone as he resumes his quick-paced walk to evade further public scrutiny about his study habits. "What are we supposed to do with that kind of attitude?" Ms. Bronzic turns to me and inquires in a calm yet frustrated tone.

As I witness this encounter between teacher and student, I am impressed that he has allowed Ms. Bronzic to stop him in his tracks and interrogate him. I know nothing about his personal relationship with Ms. Bronzic. However, my interviews with urban, minority male students suggest that unless Ms. Bronzic had a reputation as a caring teacher, this student would not remain generally compliant and apologetic in the face of her *public* admonishment in broad daylight. Instead of compliance, the average, non-caring teacher would have more likely elicited a hard attitude and posture from this student. My day with Ms. Bronzic's sixth grade classes has come to an end. My second, week-long visit to Ms. Bronzic's reveals more of the same pedagogical approach. And, until I can provide an adequate social scientific explanation, I agree with Malcolm: Ms. Bronzic's teaching methods are "magic."

THE DEMYSTIFICATION OF MS. BRONZIC: "MAGIC," "CAPITAL," OR BOTH?

To what degree are social and cultural capital applicable to the dynamics between Ms. Bronzic and her students? What forms of social capital "inhere in the structure of relations" between Ms. Bronzic and her students? What aspects of her interactions with students are left unexplained after an application of the concepts of social and cultural capital? In other words, to what degree do these concepts fail to provide a thorough understanding of Ms. Bronzic's magic?

Accessibility to Mainstream Forms of Cultural Capital

Several past and recent studies suggest that if the students in my study exhibited more mainstream cultural capital, they probably would have encountered more caring teachers.[23] If, instead of African-American linguistic codes and mannerisms that are sometimes gangsterlike and street-savvy, these students possessed mainstream mannerisms, linguistic codes, dispositions, tastes, and appreciations, more of their relationships with previous and present teachers would likely have been replete with social capital resources.

Regardless of the degree of gangsterlike posturing or amount of mainstream cultural capital her students bring to the classroom, Ms. Bronzic sees in *each* child the ability to acquire mainstream cultural codes. She views it as her responsibility to make the dominant "culture of power" accessible to *all* students.[24] For example, similar to the poetry assignment described above, creative writing assignments on fictional books allow for a variety of personally meaningful responses—including street-based experiences—from students while simultaneously reinforcing standard English writing skills. Ms. Bronzic elaborates:

> I never know where the [book] discussion is going to go because I have a certain framework but if they [students] go off into certain tangents because they bring in issues that they're dealing with that have . . . meaning for them [that's allowed]. . . . [W]e might go four, five, six weeks on a book, I mean we go into it so deeply . . . and get into such heavy-duty discussions that it's incredible.[25]

As argued by Lisa Delpit, "If [a student is] not already a participant in the culture of power, being told explicitly the rules of that culture makes acquiring power easier."[26] Explicit in Ms. Bronzic's interactions with students are dominant cultural linguistic codes, "high" cultural rules, appreciations, and social graces. Moreover, valuable opportunities to practice the rules and social graces of the culture of power (cultural capital) is merely one among several forms of social capital resources that inhere in a teacher-student relationship with Ms. Bronzic.

Several Forms of Social Capital

In addition to facilitating student acquisition of cultural capital, and, of course, persistent acts of caring, there are several other forms of social capital that inhere in relations between Ms. Bronzic and her at-risk urban students. Most prominent among these are effective classroom norms, valuable information about street culture, and trust. Ideally, family and communal arrangements would fortify these forms of social capital beyond the walls of the classroom. Ms. Bronzic welcomes but does not depend upon these outside reinforcements. These forms of social capital do not exist by happenstance or coincidence but have been thoughtfully integrated; they are reinforced by both the social organization of her classroom and the ideals of high expectations and dialectical interactions that shape her pedagogy.

Norms

An overarching normative principle or ethos that pervades Ms. Bronzic's classroom is "Learning is serious business!" As exemplified by her request that Malcolm rewrite his *Legend of Sleepy Hollow* paper, Ms. Bronzic is uncompromising in her expectation that students take seriously the work of schooling. Students who do not share her convictions or ideals are not ignored. Instead, they receive both reprimand for mediocre self-expectations and encouragement to work harder.

Other effective norms promote serious work and constrain mediocre work. As exemplified by her segment on poetry described above, Ms. Bronzic compels students to engage in *active learning*. She believes that effective teaching is less about giving information and more about having students analyze information and explain their analyses.[27] As corroborated by Malcolm's rewrite of his *Legend of Sleepy Hollow* paper, another norm in Ms. Bronzic's class is "Substandard work is *not* accepted!"

Ms. Bronzic recalls that the *Legend of Sleepy Hollow* paper was one of several that she had Malcolm rewrite.

> [Malcolm] got a lot of things thrown back in his face to rewrite. My favorite line [regarding mediocre student work] is "Do I look like a garbage collector? You can put that in my circular file because I don't want it!" [Those] are some of my famous lines. Or, "Would you do business with a company that sent you a letter in the mail that looked like that?" He did a lot of rewriting. He did not do it happily but he really improved over the year.[28]

When it comes to enforcing norms, Ms. Bronzic perceives herself as "an equal opportunity disciplinarian" who admonishes all students who fail to take seriously the business of schooling.

Information and Trust

Two other forms of social capital that inhere in the teacher-student relationship with Ms. Bronzic are valued information and trust. Coleman argues that "an important form of social capital is the potential for information that inheres in social relations.... The relations ... are valuable for the information they provide."[29] As evidenced by student interviews above, as well as those in chapter 2, the vast majority of teachers lack viable information about navigating inner-city streets. Students had little to no success with establishing relations of trust with these unempathetic, uninformed teachers. One of the secrets of Ms. Bronzic's success with urban students seems to be her possession of viable knowledge about navigating the streets.

> Oh, I understand the streets. I choose to.... I always tell [my students] you don't have to become a part of it; you can play the game, but you don't have to become part of the streets.... One of my boys used the word "friend" [to describe a street acquaintance]. I said, "I don't think you want to use the word friend.... They are acquaintances of yours, and you play the game. But please, don't let me hear you use the word 'friend' because the word 'friend' to me means something very important...."[30]

Urban students are more likely to trust teachers who talk openly about street culture and give viable advice about avoiding the illicit activities that take place on urban streets. Teachers like Ms. Bronzic facilitate educational success in school without insulting or compromising street-savvy students' needs to survive the streets.

The Power of Humane Investment

Social and cultural capital are significant social scientific explanations for Ms. Bronzic's "magic" but they are not sufficient. Beyond the influences of social and cultural capital, a precept prevails that seems more spiritual, religious, or humanistic than social structural. For instance, Coleman observed that in Catholic schools the precept that "every individual is important in the eyes of God" is derived from religious doctrine.[31] Ms. Bronzic seems to adhere to a similar precept that states, *"Every student is important in the eyes of a caring teacher."* Ms. Bronzic looks into the eyes of her students, past gangsterlike comportment, tough fronts, and other non-mainstream demeanor, and sees the potential for brilliance.

According to Sara Lawrence-Lightfoot, teachers like Ms. Bronzic seem to possess an ability to see themselves and the destiny of humanity in the students they teach. They see all of their students as worthy beneficiaries of their wisdom, information, trust, and caring. According to Lawrence-Lightfoot, such vision is indispensable to good teaching and is all too often absent in the relations between at-risk students and mainstream teachers:

> In schools where teachers do not see their own destinies in the eyes of their [students] there's unlikely to be good teaching going on. In some sense, you have to see yourself reflected in the eyes of those you teach or at least your destiny reflected [in those you teach]. [By destiny I mean] your future after you're long gone. Part of what you're doing [as a teacher] in this [schooling] process is handing it over, is sharing what it is you know and how you perceive the world and your angle on it. What we might call the most pernicious discriminatory behavior on the part of teachers, which is often expressed quite passively, is, it seems to me, when teachers can't imagine themselves in their students at all. When there is no reflection back and forth.[32]

When all her capital resources have been taken into account, a humanistic, altruistic magic remains. This characteristic of humane caring allows Ms. Bronzic, a mainstream Jewish-American female teacher, to look into the eyes of Malcolm, an at-risk, street-savvy African-American male student, and see their destinies as inextricably linked.

BEYOND SOCIAL AND CULTURAL CAPITAL IN THE TEACHER-STUDENT RELATIONSHIP

Ms. Bronzic's humane investment in the lives of her students reveals underdeveloped aspects of both Coleman's social capital model and Bourdieu's cultural capital model. With respect to educational settings, an underdeveloped aspect of both these models is the *dyadic* relationship between teachers and students. In assessing how social capital is structured and maintained, Coleman's analyses of communal and organizational arrangements are more thoroughly developed than those of the dyadic interactions between individuals like teachers and students. Likewise, in delineating the characteristics of cultural capital, Bourdieu's units of analysis are social groups or classes instead of one-to-one interactions between individual social actors—that is, a teacher and a student.

In the absence of adequate family, communal, and institutional arrangements, and in defiance of mainstream views that street-savvy students are culturally deficient, Ms. Bronzic inspires academic excellence. Ms. Bronzic's commitment to students, as well as street-savvy students' deference to caring teachers, is an aspect of individual agency that transcends broader social structural arrangements. At-risk students attended to by caring teachers are not merely passive beneficiaries of social and cultural capital resources. Instead, teachers like Ms. Bronzic *inspire and compel* at-risk youths to participate actively in their own academic success. Caring teachers compel at-risk, street-savvy students who are viewed by the mainstream as "culturally deficient" to view themselves as academically competent. *Every* student is important in the eyes of a truly caring teacher; and, in the eyes of a street-savvy student, *every* relationship with a caring teacher is a scarce but treasured resource.

FIVE

Malcolm

24/7/365

A BLUE AND PURPLE SKY

While accessing one of his earliest memories about hanging out on the streets of Boston, fifteen-year-old Malcolm Winfield describes an incident that occurred when he was nine or ten years old and his older brother, Steve, was fourteen or fifteen. Malcolm recalls a cloudy Easter time evening around 9:00 P.M. Malcolm, Steve, and a couple of their friends are on their way home from the movies.[1] On the way to their neighborhood in the Dorchester section of Boston, the four youths decide to walk through the Boston Commons and hang out at the playground.

Malcolm's voice becomes solemn and cryptic as he relates this story. He specifically remembers this uncanny feeling that something bad is going to happen as they sit on a playground bench and six "dudes" approach the four of them. Malcolm recalls that they are outnumbered twenty to five, but an interview with his brother, Steve, places the ratio at six or seven "dudes" to four—one of the four being Steve's girlfriend. "Yo, Steve, let's be out. . . . Somethin's gonna happen tonight!" Malcolm warns his brother. "Come on man, those dudes aren't thinking about us," Steve reassures his little brother. But Malcolm is right, something bad is going to happen. The six or so youths surrounded Malcolm, Steve, and their two friends. One of the six verbally confronts and accuses Steve, "Yo, ain't you the dude that shot my cousin?" As Malcolm recalls this story, he pauses to laugh at this absurd accusation and clarifies, "We all knew that ain't nobody shoot nobody's cousin. . . . They was just frontin'." Malcolm continues the story, punching the air and mouthing sound effects to mimic the blows, "And the next thing you know, we was all fighting like: SLAP! PAT! PAT! And then we got my brother's coat and ran."

I listen attentively as Malcolm recalls the details about the weather and color of the sky during this rumble—details still fresh in his memory five years after the altercation. "[After the attack] it started to rain and we got on the [city] bus and went home. And the sky was this blue and purple type color. Every time I see that color in the sky, I know something [bad] would happen. . . . [We caught the city bus] and then we was runnin' home after we had dropped off my brother's girlfriend. . . . And then, that same [blue and purple] night, the other friend [that was with us] . . . his brother got shot in the neck, but [luckily] he didn't die. . . . [M]e and Steve was like, "This is a evil night; this is a bad night!"

Thus far, the experiences of street-savvy students have been presented in quotes, vignettes, and narratives. The quotes are comparable to peepholes. The vignettes and narratives resemble windows. Both figurative openings yield limited opportunities to view the lives of street-savvy students inscribed in text. Through these openings I have focused upon gangsterlike posturing. Malik, Jason, Shane, Kenneth, Robbie, and Malcolm have either been labeled by their peers as "hardcore" or "hardcore wannabes," or labeled by me as "hardcore enough." These labels, though sociologically useful as ideal-types, obscure the degree to which these students do not engage in gangsterlike posturing. Street-savvy students do not don gangsterlike mannerisms 24/7/365, in other words, all the time (24 hours a day, 7 days a week, 365 days a year).

The peepholes and windows have not only framed a particular posture, they have been valuable opportunities for understanding the complicated lives of urban and inner-city youths. Maybe for three hours out of a twenty-four-hour day, Shane tries to act hard, or for ten to twenty hours out of a 168-hour week, Jason and Malik are involved in the drug trade. I say "maybe" because I am making educated guesses about total hard or hardcore-wannabe hours—guesstimates derived from interview and observational data that contain implicit rather than explicit clues about the duration of time for which students assume hard postures. However, these hours or moments of posturing, while qualitatively profound, do not quantitatively dominate every waking minute of these students' lives. Although this book has chronicled the hard postures and street-related experiences or exploits of Malik, Jason, Shane, Kenneth, Malcolm, and other students, a fuller, more dimensional story remains untold. For example, as substantiated by the somber subtitle and vignette at the beginning of this chapter as well as by previous quotes and observations, I have characterized Malcolm as hard-enough to navigate inner-city streets. But beneath and beyond this hard-enough characterization, who is Malcolm?

In this chapter, I extend Malcolm's story beyond peepholes and windows by providing his fifteen-year-old biography. At the very least, this allows a larger picture-window view of Malcolm, at most, this story provides an extended biographical dialogue with Malcolm, with me as interpreter. The portrayal of Malcolm that ensues looms more vivid, complex, and multidimensional than those of other students presented in this book. Of course, like Malcolm, all the street-savvy students in this book have life stories worth telling. Yet the purpose of this chapter is not to tell Malcolm's story as "the story" of all inner-city youths. Instead, this chapter uncovers layers, textures, and dimensions that transcend Malcolm's hard-enough posture as a testimony that similar layers exist beneath and beyond the exteriors of *all* street-savvy students. Finally, I tell Malcolm's story in the present tense of his freshmen year in high school (ninth grade). It was at this point that I returned to Boston to conduct follow-up interviews.[2] Instead of translating Malcolm's statements into academic prose, I leave *his* linguistic code intact. Although I have interviewed several individuals who have intimate knowledge of Malcolm's life, his voice figures most prominently.

FIFTEEN GOING ON TWENTY-ONE

It is mid-March in New England. It is also midday. The remnants of a cold winter linger on as spring makes a tentative bid for influence over Cambridge, Massachusetts. Originally from the South, I have now survived eight New England winters, yet every March I find myself wishing that the northern spring would assert itself as promptly and deliberately as its southern counterpart. The temperature barely reaches 40° Fahrenheit, and the sky hangs low and full of thick, heavy clouds that eclipse my best efforts to be bright-eyed and bushy-tailed. I leave my Harvard residence hall at approximately 2:00 P.M. en route to the Roxbury Multi-Service Center (RMSC) in the Roxbury section of Boston, Massachusetts.

I drive from a section of Cambridge dominated by the idyllic campuses of Harvard University and the Massachusetts Institute of Technology (MIT) to the starkly urban neighborhoods of Boston. Once in Boston, I notice fewer trees and green lawns. I see more concrete that expands vertically into buildings and horizontally into sidewalks. I try to fully behold the change of scenery, but am too preoccupied with the traffic—a necessity for coping with the infamously crazy Boston drivers— to note every scenic detail. However, during this commute from Cambridge to Roxbury, I do notice a major change in architecture and landscape: Harvard's red bricks, green lawns, and lavishly maintained facilities contrast sharply with Roxbury's worn Victorian-style residences and rundown storefront properties. Unlike the facilities of Harvard, several buildings in Roxbury appear dilapidated—sturdy and liveable yet in dire need of aesthetic and structural restoration.

During this commute, I am also aware of a socioeconomic transition from affluence and privilege to relative deprivation and disenfranchisement. In both Cambridge and Roxbury, however, the countenances of residents convey an air of belonging. In both locations, people appear to tend to the errands and business of the day. In Cambridge, I observe individuals going in and out of shops, rushing to university classes or other destinations, waiting for buses. In Roxbury, I observe individuals going in and out of shops, rushing to work or other destinations, attending to children, waiting for buses and other forms of transportation. Both sets of residents seem at home as they go busily about their days.

I arrive at the RMSC at 2:30 P.M. full of anticipation and trepidation: I expect that fifteen-year-old Malcolm will be eager to begin telling his life story, yet I worry that, like last week, this energetic ninth grader will simply forget our appointment. Malcolm chose this location as the site of his interview; it is at this center that his mentor, Louis Johnsson, is employed. The RMSC, which sits on the corner of Blue Hill Avenue and Holborn Street, is housed in a four-story building colored by yellowish-beige paint that is worn and peeling.[3] Blue Hill Avenue sustains a constant flow of traffic, which includes police cars and ambulances, publicly accessible transportation (taxi cabs and buses), and commuters in private cars en route between Roxbury and downtown Boston. An audible hum from this stream of traffic seeps through the walls of the RMSC—a constant reminder throughout the interview of the fast-paced urban context. The outside of the RMSC building is mostly basic wood siding except for the bricked lower portion of the first floor. The windows of this building disclose its past and convey its present function: the RMSC building, once an old apartment complex, has been converted into office space, and several old residential-looking windows remain alongside newly renovated office-style windows. On one side of the building, across Holborn Street, is a parking lot and open field. On the front of the building, across Blue Hill Avenue, stands an old meat market that has been closed for at least the last ten years. Next to the meat market is a building that houses Gang Peace and is painted with a mural containing vivid portraits of neighborhood children. Behind the RMSC are post–World War II Victorian-style houses. The RMSC provides an array of services including counseling, housing, emergency services, protecting women who have been battered or sexually assaulted and children who have been abused, and sheltering the homeless.[4]

Malcolm arrives thirty minutes late.[5] Yawning contagiously, he explains that he has been "snoozing" all day and almost overslept our appointment. "It's one of those days when you just want to stay in bed all day," I commiserate while catching his yawn. Malcolm is an attractive, cinnamon-brown, athletic fifteen-year-old who stands about 5'9" tall, weighs 165 pounds, and is still growing. He arrives at the RMSC stylishly, yet comfortably, dressed in hip-hop fashions: beige "Tims" (Timberland boots), baggy blue jeans that are worn but not tattered, and a green army camouflage vest that is orange on the other side. Malcolm explains that the "Tims" and army vest complement one another. Beneath the vest, Malcolm wears a gray, oversized short-sleeved T-shirt that he characterizes as a "Pebble Beach, regular ol' black people's shirt," an indication that many people in his community wear this kind of shirt.

Malcolm has a full head of three-inch-long dreads that he has been growing for about six months. He decided to dread his hair as a deliberate expression of self-presentation and ethnic pride, an expression of what Malcolm refers to as a "new mentality that most people can't get with." When I encourage him to explain his "new mentality," he reflects and admits, "I don't even know yet, I'm still learning, you know." Malcolm momentarily ponders my request for an explanation. Then, with youthful enthusiasm and idealism, Malcolm begins to articulate his emerging mentality. "See, I use to walk around with my hair just nappy. But I had to go one step further, you know what I'm sayin'.... It's representing myself. Knowledge is self. That's how I see it.... I'm not trying to say that it's bad to wear your hair cut low, but do you think that the Egyptians had their hair cut and faded? They had 'fros and stuff. You know they had a little somethin'-somethin' going on. They ain't have no cut. Or, they rocked baldies, you know!" As an overall assessment of his hip-hop fashions, Malcolm asserts, "I try to be on top with my style!"

I first met Malcolm about four years ago while conducting ethnographic research at the Paul Robeson Institute for Positive Self-Development. This institute (detailed in chapter 6) is a supplemental school program that meets on Saturday mornings in which African-American men teach and mentor black boys.[6] At that time, Malcolm was a thin eighty- to ninety-pound eleven-year-old with a closely shaven "cute little peanut head." The phrase "cute little peanut head" is a term of endearment I inherited while coming of age in a black southern community—a phrase used to describe the closely shaven heads of pre-adolescent males. During Malcolm's "peanut-head" days, style did not seem to figure prominently into his presentation of self. In other words, Malcolm appeared to care little if his hair was closely shaven or slightly grown out, "nappy," and uncombed. But now, about four years later, he not only tries to be "on top with [his] style," he also tries to set noteworthy trends for other urban teens to emulate. With a smile and prophetic gaze toward summer trends in hip-hop fashions, Malcolm points to his army vest and declares, "I'm gonna have mad heads rocking this. In the summer mad people is gonna be rocking this." Then (Malcolm gracefully unzips his vest to reveal the orange side) "I'm gonna switch." I feel more like his big sister than an ethnographer as I assert to myself, "Cute little peanut-head Malcolm has really come into a fashionable sense of himself!"

The interview gets off to a slow start. The school holiday, Malcolm's sleeping late prior to the interview, and the overcast, cool and cloudy day conspire and cause Malcolm to yawn frequently throughout the first of our several interviews. Yet, between yawns, I probe and jostle Malcolm's memories of his life. Despite the yawns, Malcolm offers his responses eagerly and earnestly. I continue the interview for over two hours. Eventually, to dimensionalize Malcolm's life story, I will have several informal conversations with him. I will formally interview Malcolm again at home as well as conduct formal interviews with his brother Steve; his grandmother, "Nanna" Helen Winfield; and his mentor and surrogate father, Louis Johnsson.

In appearance, Malcolm looks like the almost-sixteen-year-old that he is; he will celebrate his sixteenth birthday in about two months. However, in conversation, he sometimes seems more like a twenty-one-year-old than a teenager. His opinions on several subjects reveal acquired tastes of someone at least five years his senior. For example, Malcolm prefers not to date "girls his age," because "they don't know how to act." Instead, he prefers to date older seventeen-year-old women. Furthermore, Malcolm can wax eloquent and critical about the difference between east coast and west coast rap. His level of maturity and critique reminds me of conversations that I have had with college students on similar topics and, momentarily, I forget that Malcolm is only in the ninth grade. As we discuss various rap artists, Malcolm expresses his heartfelt concern that in a scenario similar to the assassination of Malcolm X, KRS-1, an outspoken and politically active rap artist, might be targeted for assassination by the U.S. government: "[I]f the white people start listening to what [KRS-1] is really telling [black] people, they ain't gonna like it.... In this country when you start telling [white people] to do what's right, the government don't like it.... Right now, [KRS-1] is still underground, but if he starts blowin' up [gaining mainstream acceptance], it's all over: they're [the government] going to shut him down quick." His favorite rap artist is Nasty Nas from Queens, New York, because Nas tells politically powerful stories in his raps, empowering stories to which inner-city youths relate: "The flow in Nas' raps is just so incredible.... The way the words connect with the beat.... It's just ... it just flows beautifully. Nobody's gonna touch [that is, compare to] Nas. [He's been my favorite rapper] ever since his tape dropped around '91 or '90."

The moments during the interview when Malcolm seems fifteen going on twenty-one are frequent; however, there are several other points during our conversation—for example, when Malcolm shares his love for playing video games—when I am reassured that he finds ample time to be a fifteen-year-old. Likewise, Malcolm's twenty-one-year-old brother Steve has also noticed that Malcolm's level of maturity often seems closer to young adulthood than to adolescence: "All my friends [observe that] Malcolm is only fifteen and that he's real mature. I [respond], 'Yeah, but you know he's fifteen: it comes out once in a while.' I think he's looking for himself and ... he don't care about what anyone thinks of him, he's just gonna do his thing."[7]

"NANNA" AND THE BROTHERS WINFIELD

Malcolm has three brothers whose ages range from eighteen to twenty-one. "I got a sister on my father's side, but I hardly ever see her," Malcolm admits as a matter of fact. He and his two brothers, Steve and Ronald, are being raised by his maternal grandmother, but his brother Kevin "lives with one of [his] mother's best friends." Malcolm clarifies that he and his brothers are close, that they have always "stuck together as brothers." He smiles with affection while characterizing his brother Steve—a tall, lean, "good-looking," athletic twenty-one-year-old—as a "goodie, a good kid." Hints of sibling rivalry are noticeably absent as Malcolm shares his view of Steve. Instead of rivalry or tension, his tone resounds with admiration and fraternal loyalty: "Steve's real important to me. Me and Steve do everything together." I get the sense that Steve and Malcolm are best friends; now I understand why Malcolm, who looks up to his older brother Steve, seems fifteen going on twenty-one.

Malcolm's view of his brother Ronald, who is nineteen years old, appears equally fraternal. Yet along with his fraternity, there is an opinion that Malcolm has formed with reluctance. Malcolm remembers hearing a familial rumor that "[his] older brother Ronald is crazy." Initially, Malcolm did not agree with this verdict on Ronald's state of mind. But Malcolm clearly recalls a conversation that led him to agree reluctantly with his family's verdict: "One time Ronald had came home and he told me that he had shot at these kids. And I was like, 'You shot at some kids? Ronald, *why?*' He was like, ''Cuz, 'cuz they was gonna shoot me.' That's when I knew Ronald was crazy." As Malcolm utters this conclusion, I sense that he still hates to admit that Ronald is "crazy."

Malcolm concludes that his grandmother, Helen Winfield, has caused Ronald's mental decline. Frustration and disappointment begin to dominate the cadence of his speech as he blames "Nanna." Immediately, I want to interrupt Malcolm and lecture to him about all the social structural and institutional sources of Ronald's "craziness" that are well beyond the control of his grandmother, but I attentively listen. "After all," I remind myself, "this is *Malcolm's* life story, not my sociology lecture."

Mrs. Winfield was one of the first parents I met at the Paul Robeson Institute. She is a full-figured—she prefers full-figured to overweight—mahogany-brown African-American woman of average height with a booming alto-pitch voice. Malcolm frequently admits, "Nanna loves to yell!" Even though she lacks the youthful energy that she possessed while raising her own children, Mrs. Winfield has done her best to raise her grandsons. And she has done so without adequate support from members of her extended family. Mrs. Winfield takes a tough love and strict disciplinarian approach to raising her three grandsons.

"Ronald never felt loved by my grandmother. . . . 'Cuz, I remember this one incident in particular where my grandmother had left five dollars on the dresser, and there were so many people in the house. . . . [T]he next thing you know, we couldn't find the five dollars. [I believed that] my grandmother misplaced [the] five dollars, and she got upset. Then she blamed my brother Ronald for taking the five dollars." Malcolm vividly recalls siding with his brother and protesting to his grandmother, "Ronald didn't take the money!" Malcolm quotes Ronald's emphatic objection, "I ain't take the money! I ain't take the money!" Malcolm pauses contemplatively, "How can you distrust your own [grandson]?" Ronald was once a "straight A student," but his grandmother had repeatedly treated Ronald with a disrespect that she never showered upon Malcolm or Steve. "I remember one time my grandmother and Ronald went shopping and Ronald slammed the car door. Then my grandmother hit him with [her] cane in front of *EVERYBODY!* . . . And I know if that was me or Steve, she wouldn't have even thought about hitting us. . . . I know my grandmother always had something against my brother, Ronald. I don't know why. So then one day Ronald just left the house. I guess he couldn't take it any more either. So, Ronald left, but now he's locked up. . . . And I blame my grandmother; I hate to say it [but] I blame my grandmother for Ronald being like that."[8]

As I listen to Malcolm's lecture about his grandmother, I offer quick sound bites of positive observations about his grandmother. I am careful not to force my views upon Malcolm; instead, I interject points here and there as I have always done when conversing with Malcolm. He admits that Mrs. Winfield has been there for them when other friends and family members abandoned them: "We ain't have nobody else [but Nanna]." Malcolm's mother died when he was four years old. At that time, after having raised her own eight children, Mrs. Winfield took full responsibility for ten-year-old Steve, eight-year-old Kevin, seven-year-old Ronald, and four-year-old Malcolm.

EARLY CHILDHOOD MEMORIES

Not knowing where to begin listening to and documenting Malcolm's life story, and eager to hear every detail, I abruptly ask him to tell me about his earliest childhood memories.[9] Fortunately, my abrupt yet well-intentioned attempt to access Malcolm's earliest memories does not leave him at a loss for words. His earliest memories began when he was approximately four years old. "I remember one childhood memory when it was Easter and me, my brothers, and my cousins and my grandmother went to [Boston City Hospital[10]] to see my mother. I remember 'cuz I was looking at the picture yesterday and I was real little." In this picture, four-year-old Malcolm, his three older brothers, two female cousins, and his grandmother are in the hospital and Malcolm, his brothers, and cousins are striking Michael Jackson poses. Malcolm shifts his recollection away from the picture and back to the actual hospital visit. "I was eatin' some type of pudding. And, I was just looking at my mother, and she was sleeping. And that may be one of the last times I saw my mother." To this day, Malcolm does not fully understand why his mother, Barbara Winfield, was in the hospital; he says, "It was a disease called Skerma Derma or something."[11]

When Barbara developed terminal scleroderma, her family knew very little about the disease. "We didn't understand about things. I had never heard about [scleroderma] in my life," Mrs. Winfield recalls.[12] Malcolm's maternal uncle, Mitchell, would eventually get a book on scleroderma and act as both reporter and translator between hospital officials and the family. Mitchell would frequently talk with the doctors and relay their prognoses back to the family. Mrs. Winfield admits that Mitchell dealt with aspects of the illness when the rest of the family "just couldn't deal with it." Mrs. Winfield describes her son Mitchell, one of her twins, as "very intelligent." Her understanding of her daughter's illness derived from a combination of Mitchell's book knowledge and her belief that scleroderma and cancer are "all the same thing." "[Barbara] had [scleroderma] in her hands. . . . Her skin tightened, and [the disease] also destroyed her kidneys."

Before leaving the past, I want to know more about the day of Malcolm's birth, a day of which, of course, he has no memory. Neither Malcolm's brother Steve nor his grandmother can remember the details of the spring day in May when Malcolm was born. Mrs. Winfield does remember a contemporaneous event. She recalls being hospitalized in order to have surgery on her back and asking her pregnant daughter not to come to the hospital: "I told her [not to] visit me because it was too depressing and I didn't want her to come because she was carrying [a child] and I didn't want her to worry [about my back surgery] because she really loved her mother." As for the day of Malcolm's birth, Mrs. Winfield remembers, "Malcolm was a healthy baby, that's all I can tell you. . . . He was born on time. [He developed] asthma when he was little but [eventually] outgrew it." Mrs. Winfield uses words like "spoiled" and "intelligent" to characterize Malcolm as a toddler: "[Malcolm] was walking around spoiled [by] my daughter Anna, his aunt. . . . Oh, he was terrible, rotten, spoiled. . . . I had to get him together. My daughter [Barbara] said, 'Mommy, get him together. . . . Do something [with him].' But he was a live baby, very active and . . . very intelligent." Due to his mother's illness, Malcolm's grandmother and aunt Anna shared the responsibility of caring for him.

Like details about Malcolm's birth, pictures of his mother are scarce. "I have one [picture] and that's of me on my mother's shoulders." Malcolm's tone is sentimental, "We hardly have any pictures of my mother." But memories of Malcolm's mother abound. Both Malcolm's grandmother and brother Steve seem soothed as they conjure her up in words. A gentle smile washes across Steve's face as he remembers her as "a quiet lady [who] kept to herself [and] took care of her kids." Likewise, Mrs. Winfield speaks about her firstborn, Barbara, with dignity and respect, painting a picture of a loving daughter and an attentive mother. "She truly loved [me]. . . . She was very quiet, she wasn't a street person, she loved her children, took care of her children . . . loved her family." As Mrs. Winfield lists these characteristics, I hear pride and loss in her voice. She recalls and reiterates that her daughter "wasn't a worrier like me. . . . She never was a worrier." However, her daughter was a strict disciplinarian whose sweetness could turn to tough love: Barbara believed in spanking her children when they misbehaved. Mrs. Winfield explains, "In other words, like the law that's out now if you hit your children, [Barbara] would have been in jail. . . ."

Both Mrs. Winfield and Steve continue to conjure up daughter and mother, respectively, with tender moments from their memories. I hear a longing in their voices, especially in Mrs. Winfield's, that moves me to sorrow. They both regret that Malcolm was too young to become fully acquainted with his mother. Steve explains, "Malcolm was real young and he didn't really know [our mother]; he didn't talk and hug and share moments with our mother."

By contrast, Malcolm is uncertain about the current fate of his biological father. His earliest memories of his father as "cool" have soured to resentment. Malcolm's father has been virtually uninvolved in his life. "I hardly know him, he's a sucker. If I ever see him, I'm gonna kill him . . . if he's still alive. He's probably dead of something." Malcolm pauses to try to recall what he has been told about his biological father: "But my grandmother told me [that my father] was real handsome. When my mother met him, he worked construction and he was making a lot of money, and he knew where he was going. . . . And then he . . . just fell apart. And then my mother died after that."

BULLY YEARS

When he was four Malcolm observed his mother sleeping in her hospital bed. He recalls, "I was just chillin', yo. 'Cuz, to me, I probably didn't know what was going on. . . . I ain't have a care in the world. And, then . . . everything was cool." Shortly after this visit to the hospital, Malcolm's mother passed away. Not old enough to fully grasp the concept of death, Malcolm initially believed his mother was sleeping. Mrs. Winfield recalls how her daughter's death affected her grandsons: "Steve went into his own shell . . . [Losing his mother] made him . . . very independent. Ronald . . . was very bad, but [both Steve and Ronald] were older than Malcolm. . . . As Malcolm started going to the first grade, second grade, third grade . . . [his classmates] would talk about their mothers, [and] he would rebel."

Everyone has a story to tell about Malcolm's rebellious years. Malcolm has intense memories of his rebellion, but has yet, at only fifteen years of age, to fully understand how his defiance relates to his mother's death: "When my mother died, I started buggin' out." During the early years of elementary school, he "just went wild," "started beating everyone up," and his "grades started dropping." Steve remembers that Malcolm "seemed angry all the time" and that every day he picked his little brother up from elementary school, Malcolm would start a fight: "It seemed like the whole class was after him." Malcolm's bully years lasted from first through fourth grade.

Mrs. Winfield tells the story of a "little incident" that occurred when Malcolm was in kindergarten; unlike many of Malcolm's bullylike fights, this incident was in self-defense, not striking out. In kindergarten, Malcolm was very protective of ten-year-old Steve. With a loving grin, Mrs. Winfield refers to the incident she is about to describe as "something funny that can go into [my] book." Steve and Malcolm were going to school and some girls who admired Steve began to playfully touch and pull on Steve. To one of these girl's surprise, Malcolm kicked her in the knees and exclaimed, "Leave my brother alone!" Malcolm was either too young or too protective to embrace the concept of pre-adolescent crush. Mrs. Winfield gives a full body chuckle, "Malcolm wasn't even as tall as her knees [and] he kicked her." As far back as Mrs. Winfield can recall, Malcolm has been, and remains, fiercely protective of his older brothers, especially Steve.

As Malcolm graduates from kindergarten to the first and then second grades, his fighting becomes much less defensive and much more aggressive. Steve describes one fight that especially "sticks out in [his] mind." As usual, Steve goes to pick Malcolm up from school. One student that Malcolm has previously bullied approaches him, pins him down, and demands, "I want you to leave me alone and stop pickin' on me in class!" Malcolm agrees, "Okay, just let me go." Once he is released, Malcolm chases, catches, and beats the boy so severely that Steve has to stop the fight. Malcolm also remembers this fight; he smacks his left hand with his right fist to re-create the impact of the blows he delivered. Malcolm recalls the intensity of the fight and his rage, but his motivation for fighting still eludes him. He does not know why he became so angry and belligerent: "I don't know why [I fought this student]. Somebody was talkin' trash or something. Back then, it really didn't matter to me as long as I was fighting. Woooooh, I was hurtin' that kid; and my brother, he didn't want to break [the fight] up because I was winning, but he had to break it up."

Malcolm's bully years continue into the fifth grade. However, it is a year earlier, during the fourth grade, that he and about "ten little kids" form a crew. He and his "boyz" from this crew run "around trying to beat people up." Instead of backing down from bigger kids in the neighborhood who "wanted [Malcolm's crew] to chill," Malcolm and his boyz threaten to "beat them up after school." While in the fifth grade, Malcolm stops being a bully. In depicting his years as an elementary school ruffian, Malcolm offers matter-of-fact observations instead of apologies and regrets. Now, at fifteen years of age, he feels neither shame nor pride about having been a bully.

Steve and Mrs. Winfield link Malcolm's fighting to the death of his mother. Louis, Malcolm's surrogate father, blames both the death of Malcolm's mother and the absence of his still-living but uninvolved biological father. Malcolm has yet to soul-search for the source of his anger, but he clearly remembers why he stopped being a bully. "When I use to fight, it's not like I use to ever lose, but, it was just, I got nothing out of it. So I stopped fighting." In an earlier interview, Malcolm had attributed the cessation of fights to his participation in the Paul Robeson Institute and the influence of Louis:

[The Institute] turned me around . . . because I use to love to fight and sometimes I would win and sometimes I wouldn't. Most of the time when I have a fight or something, I end up regretting it afterward. Then when I came into [the institute] everybody was having fun and I just realized that there wasn't a need to fight, 'cuz it didn't make any sense to me. . . . Everybody was having fun. And [I learned] if somethin' starts escalating into a conflict, you can just resolve it with words. You don't need violence. [I've learned that] anyone can have a fight every day, but it takes a man not to have a fight every day.[13]

A SHADOW, MENTOR, AND FATHER

Malcolm is about twelve years old and in the sixth grade. It's Saturday morning at the Paul Robeson Institute. Mrs. Winfield approaches Louis, an assistant director and mentor, and requests, "The next time you're over the house, I'd like to talk to you about something."[14] The next day, Louis pays a visit to the Winfield residence. Mrs. Winfield explains why she had approached him at the institute and requested his undivided attention: "I don't want to put any pressure on you or anything, but [the other] night Malcolm told me that he considers you his father!" Louis did not expect this news yet he is not surprised by Mrs. Winfield's announcement; he and Malcolm have grown extremely close over the three or so years since they had first met at the Paul Robeson Institute. But, at the same time, Louis does not know what to think. His concern about everything that could go wrong between (surrogate) father and son sparks heartfelt questions: "God, what do I do with this information? How do I make sure that I don't mess up . . . or hurt [Malcolm's] feelings . . . or disappoint him? The transition from big brother or mentor to fatherhood will be a significant change, a serious responsibility." Louis shares his questions with his girlfriend, who is not supportive: "How could you allow [Malcolm] to say that? He's not your son and that's not fair to his biological father."

This advice does not sit well with Louis.[15] His worries persist: "How can I ignore Malcolm's regard for me? Shouldn't I be less concerned about what's fair to Malcolm's biological father and more concerned about what's fair to Malcolm?" Long before his meeting with Mrs. Winfield, many of these soul-searching questions had raced, briefly and quietly, through his mind. But since Mrs. Winfield's announcement, these questions have become incessant, amplified. So, Louis meditates, prays, and soul-searches in an effort to gain some insight. Finally, his thoughts echo his heart's resolution: "God inspired Malcolm to have those feelings for me. There wasn't anything that I did [other than] be a friend and support Malcolm. . . . [Therefore] it is not my place to tell him that I will not be his [surrogate] father . . . if he looks up to me like that." A few days later, Malcolm asks Louis, "Is it okay that I consider you to be my father?" Louis responds without hesitation, "Yeah, sure, it's okay man. . . . You know you're like a son to me anyway."

A few months pass. During this time, Malcolm gets into a little trouble with the police. Louis provides discipline, guidance, and support; he weaves the roles of father and mentor. That spring, when Louis attends the Spring Unity Breakfast, an annual event sponsored by Concerned Black Men of Massachusetts, he has an important announcement to make. Before giving the benediction, Louis brings Malcolm up on the stage with him. Without going into detail, Louis explains the ordeal that he and Malcolm had gone through as a result of Malcolm's arrest and publicly affirms his paternal love, responsibility, and respect for Malcolm.

> [W]hen we get involved in young peoples lives, they develop strong feelings—love and appreciation for [us]. It's not our place to step on those [sentiments]. . . . It's like a flower trying to grow. . . . It's not fair to the flower to step on it when all it's trying to do is blossom and show its beauty to the world. The flower is not trying to hurt anybody or do anything wrong to anybody. . . . I don't see Malcolm's feelings [about me] and his expression of those feelings as being anything but love and appreciation for me. I love Malcolm like my own son. God has put it in my heart to call Malcolm my son.

The audience responds with enthusiastic applause and a standing ovation. Some members of the audience are moved to tears by Louis's speech. Malcolm, still standing beside Louis, looks as though he is about to cry tears of joy. Louis hugs him, "Everything is going to be okay, man!" Late that evening, once back at his residence, Malcolm redelivers Louis's speech for his grandmother. Shortly thereafter, Mrs. Winfield phones Louis: "Malcolm's soooo proud. He's walking around with his head up high!"

Louis Johnsson is an attractive almond-brown African-American man in his early thirties, who stands about 6'1" tall and weighs approximately two hundred pounds. Athletic, sturdy, and professional are three adjectives that often arise when those who admire Louis's "look" describe his appearance. His hair, mustache, and goatee are closely shaven as if to comply with military standards. Whether dressed in business or casual attire, Louis is one of those people who can coordinate clothes and wear them well; he looks "professional" even when he wears jeans and a T-shirt. Only sixteen years older than Malcolm, Louis looks more like Malcolm's older brother than surrogate father. Until Malcolm carved out the role of surrogate father, Louis had initially thought of himself as more of a big brother-type mentor to the students at the institute.

I meet Louis Johnsson in an office at the RMSC to interview him about his involvement in Malcolm's life. He tells several other stories about Malcolm, and I tell him that I remember when he made that touching speech at the Unity Breakfast. I was in attendance and can still remember the looks of surprise, elation, and pride that flashed across Malcolm's face. I have known Louis for about five years; he was one of the first teacher-mentors at the Paul Robeson Institute with whom I became closely acquainted. In addition to being a mentor, Louis is director of Boys to Men, a mentoring program for the alumni of the Paul Robeson Institute, and vice president of Concerned Black Men of Massachusetts.

Louis and Malcolm first met when Louis was twenty-five and Malcolm was nine. Louis remarks without conceit but with conviction, "If I had not been involved in Malcolm's life . . . there's no telling where he would have ended up." I have known of Louis's beneficial influence upon Malcolm's life for the last five years and, previously, had come to a similar conclusion myself. Actually, all those I know who know of Louis's involvement in Malcolm's life agree that, over the past five years, Louis is the best thing that ever happened to Malcolm. I ask Louis to say more. Louis's response reveals a conviction born of 20/20 hindsight, commitment, and pride: "[Once Malcolm] got settled with me and realized that I wasn't going anywhere, that [knowledge] developed a sense of peace and calm within him and I think it was at that point that . . . he went from being a very angry young man to [being] not angry, but a more loving and a more understanding and a more peaceful young man. . . . I couldn't ask for him to have a better attitude about life in general."

Louis's convictions derive from several key interventions made by him on Malcolm's behalf. He has several stories to tell about how he successfully got Malcolm to see that fighting was only one alternative, and often a poor one at that, among many ways to resolve conflict. For example, once when he was ten or eleven years old, Malcolm rode his bicycle to a neighborhood high school basketball court to play basketball and, shortly thereafter, returned to his residence "without his bicycle, with a busted lip . . . [and] scratches on his face." His grandmother called Louis to explain what had happened, and Louis asked to speak to Malcolm. From Mrs. Winfield's tone, Louis was really worried that Malcolm had been brutally beaten, but once on the phone, Malcolm had assured Louis that he had not sustained any serious physical injuries. Malcolm had gone on to recount that while he was playing basketball, someone said something insulting about his mother, and he had responded by punching him. Malcolm had not realized that his offender had come with two friends. All three had jumped Malcolm and "busted up" his bike. Louis's response to Malcolm was, "Well, let's think about what happened."

Louis and Malcolm talked through the chain of events that led up to Malcolm being "triple-banked" (physically assaulted by three people at once) and helped Malcolm to realize that he had reacted with his fists before using his head, before "realizing the whole situation." That was not the last time that Malcolm got into a fight, but it was "from that point that . . . he started to really look at what was happening to him." Louis had told Malcolm, "You know . . . you were fortunate this time, man. . . . [None of your attackers was] somebody who could hurt you seriously

... or kill you.... But next time you may not be so lucky." Before he became involved with Malcolm and had these heart-to-heart conversations, Malcolm seemed to have a belligerent disposition. Malcolm's motto was "[You] don't take no stuff from anybody ... no matter what size they are!" Louis adds that at that time, "[Malcolm] was small [but] sometimes the small guys are the ones who are the quickest to fight." But after a few heart-to-heart, man-to-man conversations, Malcolm started to realize, "Hey, wait a minute, something's wrong here"—that is, fighting usually doesn't solve anything.

Louis goes on to tell several stories about Malcolm, including the one about the first time Malcolm was arrested, the arrest to which Louis had referred in his speech at the Unity Breakfast.

> Malcolm is twelve years old. He leaves a local apartment complex with some friends, and they all begin to run to a subway stop on the Red Line near the University of Massachusetts. There is a police station close by, and the state police are over at this apartment complex investigating a crime. When they see Malcolm and his friends running, they pursue. One of the police officers catches up with one of the runners, wrestles him down to the ground, and pins him against a fence. Malcolm is the only one from his group of "boyz" who runs back to assist his friend. In defense of his friend, Malcolm begins mouthing off to the police officer. The officer responds, "Get out of here. Go about your business. This is not your concern!" Malcolm disagrees with the officer's command and continues to verbally defend his friend. The police officer warns, "If you don't get out of here, I'm going to arrest you!" Malcolm is steadfast in his verbal defense. Then, as he had warned, the police officer arrests Malcolm. Ironically, the officer releases Malcolm's friend upon confirming that he was not the suspect they were looking for.
>
> They take Malcolm to the police station and hold him in order to teach him a lesson about the consequences of defying police authority. The police call Mrs. Winfield, and Mrs. Winfield pages Louis. Louis and Steve go to the station and find Malcolm sitting behind a desk watching television. A few police officers comment to Louis, "He's a great kid, but he just talks a lot.... Take him home and get him out of here." As they are leaving the station, Malcolm defends himself and pleads with Louis for leniency, "I didn't do anything, Louis. I didn't do anything!" Louis and Malcolm revisit the events that had transpired and, after talking things through, Malcolm understands that he could have responded to the altercation in a manner that would not have resulted in an arrest. Louis empathizes with Malcolm: "There's nothing wrong with you saying what you think about the situation, but [you argued with the police officer] to the point where [your argument] developed into another situation."

The second time Malcolm was arrested, the circumstances were a bit more serious.

> Malcolm is thirteen years old, and it is evening time. Malcolm and his friend Stanley have just left a community center in Dorchester and are walking home. A van pulls up: "Hey, you guys want a lift?" Malcolm is acquainted with the driver and the five passengers, six guys all together, so he accepts the ride. Instead of going straight home, they decide to ride around for a little while. But before driving around, the driver makes a quick stop at his residence to do something; then, just as they are about to leave the driver's residence, six to seven police cars pull up behind the van. With red and blue lights flashing, the officers

approach the van with guns drawn, force the driver and seven passengers out of the van, and command them to lie face down on the pavement. The officers arrest and handcuff their suspects.

At midnight, Mrs. Winfield calls Louis and informs him that Malcolm has been arrested and is in jail. She is so upset that she cannot recall the few details that the police had provided; she only remembers the location of the police station and the name of the police officer. Louis calls the police station and speaks with one of the arresting officers, who gives his version of the story. The young men were riding around Dorchester and Roxbury, passed by a shopping mall, and recognized a white girl that they all knew. The young lady was selling sweatshirts on the corner. They confronted her, a verbal altercation ensued, and they took her sweatshirts and T-shirts. She had reported that one of the robbers was wearing a ski mask.

According to Malcolm's version of the story, the altercation involving this girl occurred before he boarded the van. But—according to the police version of the story—Malcolm, his friends, and the stolen items were in the van when the police made their arrests. Malcolm did not have any of the stolen items in his possession, but he did own a ski mask, the kind that covers the nose and mouth, but not the whole head. While listening to the police officer's account, Louis remembers his warning to Malcolm, "You need to get rid of that ski mask because people use that kind of stuff to do crime. . . . And . . . if you're walking around with it on and police see you with it on . . . they're going to think that [you're a criminal]." At the time of the arrest, Malcolm was not wearing his ski mask, but the police officer explains that they found the mask in his bag. Nobody else in the van had a ski mask, so Malcolm is now a key suspect in the investigation of this incident.

The officer states that after having interrogated Malcolm, he is convinced that Malcolm is telling the truth that Malcolm was not present when the others confronted the girl and stole her merchandise. But the incriminating evidence against Malcolm remains: the ski mask and the victim's claim that Malcolm was at the scene of the crime. Malcolm and Stanley are the only juveniles; all of the others are over seventeen years old. The police officer also informs Louis that it would be a waste of time for him to come to the police station tonight: "We are not going to release [Malcolm] if you come down here because he has to go before the judge tomorrow morning."

The next morning, Louis goes to the police station, but due to an intervening incident involving seven female arrests, Malcolm's hearing is postponed until early evening. Female cases are always given priority over male cases in order to expedite the process and prevent them from having lengthy internments in overcrowded jails. It looks as though Malcolm's hearing will be further postponed until the next morning and he will have to spend another evening in jail. Louis returns to his office and asks to be contacted as soon as possible. Later that same day, Officer Jones, an African-American female, calls Louis at work: "Come and get Malcolm. . . . What time can you be here? I get off [in a few hours] . . . please come [to the station] before I get off from work." When Louis and Mrs. Winfield arrive at the station, Officer Jones explains that the courts are backed up and that they cannot officially release Malcolm. But from talking to Malcolm, she does not want him to spend another night in jail. "Don't ask any more questions, just [take Malcolm home and] be here tomorrow morning at 9:00 to meet with the judge."

The next morning, Louis returns to bring Malcolm before the judge. By coincidence, the judge and the court-appointed lawyer know Louis. They are also familiar with the work of

Concerned Black Men. In presenting Malcolm's case, Louis talks about all the activities Malcolm participates in at the institute as well as other beneficial activities that have grown out of Malcolm's involvement with the institute. After verifying with the lawyer from the district attorney's office that the police never found the weapon, the judge sets a trial date, places Malcolm on probation, and releases him to the custody of Louis and his grandmother.

Recalling Malcolm's overall reaction to this second arrest Louis points out, "It really scared him. He didn't know what was going to happen. I think the reality [and gravity] of the situation really hit him when they put him in a jail cell, took away his shoes and shoelaces, and took away his belt. He was treated ... [as though] he was a criminal." Today the police station has more space, but two years ago when Malcolm was arrested, the station was severely overcrowded. "They had adult criminals all in the same cells [with juveniles]." When Malcolm was initially released by Officer Jones, he seemed dazed by the whole experience. "He wasn't scared, he wasn't nervous, but he was very puzzled. He didn't know what to think. He wasn't sure what to do. He had all his [possessions] in his hands—[that is], his jacket, his belt, and shoelaces. His personal valuables were in a plastic bag.... So when Malcolm came out, he really looked disoriented." Malcolm was hungry and exhausted from not sleeping the night before. "[His grandmother and I] took him home, sat him down, and talked with him for a little while, but it was very clear that he really didn't want to talk. So I didn't press him [that evening]," Louis recalls. Eventually, Malcolm's disorientation developed into concern for his future.

The next morning, while waiting to go before the judge, Louis, Malcolm, and Mrs. Winfield talked for three to four hours about Malcolm's future, about the direction in which Malcolm's life was heading. Louis and Mrs. Winfield wanted to believe Malcolm's version of the story but they were well aware of all the street-based "accidents" waiting to happen, and the foolish, shortsighted decisions sometimes made by adolescents. So Louis made it clear to Malcolm that from the day of his hearing to the three or so weeks leading up to the day of his trial, he had to be extremely careful. Any little infraction could result in Malcolm's arrest and incarceration until the trial date. The thought of being incarcerated again was not in the least bit appealing to Malcolm. As Louis remembers the gravity of the situation, the tone of his voice grows solemn, "[F]rom the day that the judge [placed Malcolm on probation] to the day when his [trial was held], I pretty much became Malcolm's shadow. When he got out of school ... I would be there every day after school waiting for him. Sometimes I'd go to his classroom.... And from the time that I would get finished here at work, if I had someplace to go, I took him with me; if not, I took him straight home. To make sure that there was no area where he could get in trouble ... his grandmother told him he couldn't go outside [after school]. He was on punishment.... Interestingly enough, during that [three- to four-week] period ... we became even closer."

Malcolm did not believe that Louis would actually become like a shadow. He did not believe that, given his demanding schedule, Louis would be there for him *every day*. Louis indicates that shadowing Malcolm was no easy feat but his love and commitment to Malcolm left him with no other viable alternative: "Whenever I scheduled appointments, I made sure that I didn't schedule them during the time [when Malcolm] was getting out of school ... to make sure that I could be there every day. And, he became ... a better person because I didn't allow him to just go and do what he wanted." After Malcolm's trial and being found not guilty, Malcolm asked Louis if he would continue being his shadow. "As much as I would love to," said Louis, "and as much as you would love me to, [I can't]. But I will tell you this, I'll keep coming up to your school when you least expect it."

Two years later, Louis's discipline and support continue to cast guiding shadows over Malcolm's life. It is apparent to me through my interviews with Malcolm that he feels indebted to Louis: "If it wasn't for Louis, I know for a fact [that] I'd be outside selling drugs, stealing cars ... I'd be doing everything [illegal]." I ask Malcolm to tell me more about Louis's positive impact, and Malcolm is at a momentary loss of words. He pauses and gathers his thoughts, "[Louis] taught me how to use my brain to better myself.... I still know how to sneak somebody if I have to but I ain't gonna do that.... Louis always told me that I was different. He always told me I had wisdom beyond my years.... And [over] the last two years, me and Louis grew [closer]."

A TYPICAL SCHOOL DAY

The alarm clock sounds at 5:30 A.M. Malcolm has set the alarm extra early to allow for "snooze" time. The alarm sounds every ten minutes, and he hits the snooze bar until 6:10 A.M. He gets out of bed and turns on some hip-hop music, any other genre would be too mellow to rhythmically sway him to full consciousness. He jumps in the shower, soaps up, washes to the beat, bass, and flow of the music, gets out of the shower and selects his clothes for the day. Malcolm carefully matches pieces from a limited wardrobe of baggy and oversized hip-hop fashions. He thinks to himself, "I need some new gear!" When it comes to shoes, Malcolm only wears Reeboks. "These size ten Reeboks are making my feet hurt. I've got to get some new ones," he reminds himself. After he finishes dressing, Malcolm begins the morning ritual of searching for his keys. He scolds himself, "Every day it takes me ten minutes to find my house-keys." Like clockwork, and to complete his ritual, Malcolm yells the magic question to his grandmother, "Nanna!!! Where's my keys?!!" His grandmother returns his yell, "I don't know! You're the one that came in the house with them!" As usual, this magic combination of searching and yelling causes his keys to materialize. Malcolm grabs his keys, checks to make sure his schoolwork is in his backpack, and leaves for school at 7:00 A.M.[16]

Malcolm describes the typical morning ritual that precedes his school day in the ninth grade. Once he gathers his thoughts to describe his classes and activities, he seems bored by the thought of answering my question. Surprised by my interest in such a mundane topic, Malcolm makes sure he has understood my question. "A regular day ... from start to finish?" Earlier during the interview, as Malcolm had provided highlights from his elementary school years, he had described a student who was highly critical of his teachers, frustrated with their pedagogy and curricula, and yearning for more information. Once he had reminisced past the sixth grade, however, there was a noticeable change in the tone of his voice, a decline in passion about schooling memories. Now, as he describes his ninth grade experience, I detect no ambivalence in his voice. The dissatisfaction with, frustration with, and critiques of schooling turned into apathy.

Malcolm's apathy is new. From first to third grade, he recalls his teachers and principal as generally caring and supportive. From fourth to eighth grade, I had observed and conversed with him over the three- to four-year-period that I conducted ethnographic research and follow-up observations at the Paul Robeson Institute. When we conversed last spring, Malcolm, a rising high school freshman, seemed curious about high school. So, as Malcolm—now a rising sophomore—provides highlights of his elementary and middle school years in the Boston public school system, I have a clear memory of the animated, enthusiastic, albeit frustrated "little student" that he used to be. Malcolm conjures up this "little kid." "Fourth grade was the year that all my teachers was telling me [that] I'm like the smartest kid in the classroom. . . . [It was] from third grade to fourth grade [that] all my grades went back up really high." Malcolm's fourth grade teacher had asked her students to read a book, the title of which now eludes him: "It was [called] *Sunbeams* or something." The rest of his classmates took a "whole year to read this book," but Malcolm finished it during the first term. He imitates his fourth grade teacher's voice: "You can read pretty well, Malcolm! I'm going to give you another book." Malcolm also read this second book at an accelerated pace. To emphasize the quick pace of his reading, Malcolm snaps his fingers: "[Those books] wasn't nothing to me, and I wanted something challenging."

Malcolm's request for more challenging work was a recurrent plea during his later elementary school years. With the exception of sixth grade, Malcolm's requests for more challenging and engaging work constantly clashed with curricular limitations and teacher excuses. For example, in response to his request for more engaging books, Malcolm's fourth grade teacher had informed him, "Well, we don't really have the materials." Malcolm had sighed a frustrated and disillusioned "Fine!" Implied in the tone of this one-word declaration "Fine" I hear several synonymous responses: "You teachers just don't give a damn!" or "You teachers just don't care," or "That we-don't-have-the-materials response is just a convenient excuse. If you really cared, you'd find the materials," or, a slightly different sentiment, "You're insulting my intelligence so just forget that I asked to be challenged." Malcolm cannot recall the name of this fourth grade teacher: "[She was] this white lady. . . . She was skinny. She was tall [and] she dyed her hair blond all the time." Malcolm's next words are almost drowned out by the sound of a police siren shrieking down Blue Hill Avenue: "She was pretty nice to me. . . . So I didn't give her any problems." Powerless in a teacher-student relationship that was "nice" but otherwise academically unproductive, Malcolm no longer pressured this teacher to provide more challenging work.

In the fifth grade, Malcolm continued to read above grade level: "When I got to the fifth grade, my teachers were telling me that my reading levels and everything were above [grade level]." It was also during this time that Malcolm's career as a bully came to an end: "[In the third and fourth grades] I was chillin' out slightly [from being a bully], but I was totally chilled by the time I got to the fifth grade." Malcolm sounds both proud and frustrated as he tells me how his knowledge of black history began to expand, a byproduct of the curriculum at the Paul Robeson Institute. Malcolm's frustration stemmed from his fifth grade teacher's inability to keep pace with the Institute's curriculum. His fifth grade black history paled in comparison to that taught at the institute.

Malcolm's memories are more detailed and his voice more passionate as he looks back at an episode in the fifth grade: "This time I really got into black history and Louis gave me *Malcolm X* to read. I read [this book] and [thought], 'Wow, this dude went through a lot.' So then, I'm sitting in class and there's this white kid ... [named] Maxwell Smith." At this point, a smile of self-confidence washes across Malcolm's face. "I [quizzed him], 'Yo Maxwell, you ever hear about Marcus Garvey?.... You ever hear about....' I was just giving him random names in Black History, and he said 'No' to all of them. I [encouraged], 'You should read about these people. These were some great people. Then February rolled around and it was black history Month....'" As Malcolm shifts gears in this recollection from quizzing Maxwell to Black History Month, his air of confidence decreases and frustration appears. "The teacher's telling me about Martin Luther King, and I've learned about Martin Luther King all of my life.... [That's the one black man] that everybody knows about. [I tell the teacher], 'All Black History Month [and] all we learned about is Martin Luther King.... C'mon, I want to learn about somebody else besides Martin Luther King for once!'" Malcolm impersonates the voice and mannerisms of his fifth grade teacher— a "white lady" who "had to be about a hundred and four"—as he imitates her response in a grandmotherly tone, "Well the school curriculum provides me with this [information on Martin Luther King], and this is what you've got to learn." Just as he had reacted when his fourth grade teacher had invoked this curriculum excuse, Malcolm responded in exasperation, "Fine!" In this "Fine!" I hear, "You're insulting my intelligence so just forget that I asked you to teach me more." Malcolm then concludes, "Ms. Hines is cornball."

While on the subject of frustrating moments from the fifth grade, Malcolm recalls how his teacher had taught them that when the Europeans came to America there were not "enough people to help build the colonies." So, to alleviate this man-power shortage, "[The Europeans] went to Africa and got these people to help build the colonies." When Malcolm protested that "these people" were enslaved Africans, his teacher agreed, but her historical account of slavery continued to anger Malcolm and insult his intelligence. "[She made slavery] sound like everybody had fun." This teacher had also taught them that Columbus discovered America. "I was fed up with her at that point.... I told her that I read that the Vikings had been to America before Columbus; and before the Vikings, [Africans] were there. [But] she told me, 'No, no, no.' And I [responded], 'Forget it, I don't even want to talk to you about it.'"

Ms. Bronzic—Malcolm's sixth grade teacher—met and surpassed his standards. But since the sixth grade, his stories about schooling reveal neither frustration nor excitement. His seventh and eighth grade school years proceeded without memo-rable schooling incidents—at least without classroom incidents that excited or frustrated him. He recalls "just sliding by" and "hanging out in [the classroom of] the Young Graffiti Masters Art Program."[17] The one incident he does recall with pas-sion during this time was that he fell in, and was pushed out of, love, Now, as Malcolm lists the ninth grade classes he currently attends—"music, trumpet, and drumming and ... just basic classes like math, science, reading, writing, [and] social studies"—I hear detachment or apathy. I am not certain which one of these sentiments best characterizes Malcolm's attitude; I am certain that this nonchalance was absent during his elementary school years. Even when Malcolm identifies his current social studies teacher, as his "coolest [ninth grade] teacher," the enthusiasm in his voice does not compare to his earlier fervor for Ms. Bronzic.[18]

BEYOND THE WALLS OF THE SCHOOL

It is early in the summer before Malcolm's seventh grade school year. Malcolm pays a visit to the residence of one of his boyz, Ivan. He arrives to find Ivan talking to a girl that Malcolm has never seen before, a girl with whom Malcolm immediately falls in love. He learns that her name is Camille. One day, Malcolm, Ivan, Camille, and a few other friends all go to Franklin Park. Malcolm has been waiting for the right moment to ask Camille for a date. This group of friends runs around the park, mischievously disrupting golf games by throwing golf balls at golfers and skipping over rocks through a pond. Finally, Malcolm finds himself alone with Camille when this group dissolves into conversational teams of two or three people. Malcolm gathers the nerve to ask Camille to go out with him and is surprised and delighted when Camille says yes. Malcolm informs Ivan that he has asked Camille for a date. Ivan inquires, "What did you say? What did she say?" Malcolm answers, "She said, 'Yes!'" Malcolm senses jealousy in Ivan's question; Ivan also likes Camille, but has not gotten around to asking her for a date. Malcolm has beaten Ivan in the race for a date with Camille and he gives himself a pat on the back: "Ivan moved too slow; so he got rolled on." While Malcolm dates Camille, Ivan calls her frequently, "Camille, you should be with me, [not Malcolm]."

Camille is the first girl with whom Malcolm wants to spend quality time, the first girl with whom he could just "chill." They go to the movies, play video games, go bike riding. Sometimes they ride their bikes and purposefully try to get lost so that they can find their way back home. On one such trip, they leave from Malcolm's home in Dorchester at 10:00 A.M., ride through Cambridge, and end up way out in the suburbs. They ride all day and finally, after a day full of fun and adventure, they return to Malcolm's place at midnight. Malcolm thinks to himself, "Me and Camille are real tight!"

One day, Ivan has a party. Before going to this party, Malcolm and Steve, his older brother, catch a movie. Malcolm arrives late to the party and laughs when he sees his friend J-Tee, a natural comedian, dancing by himself in the corner and making a funny noise with his mouth to amuse his friends, "Duh-duh-duh duh dee , duh-duh-duh, duh-duh, duh-duh." As usual, everyone else laughs at J-Tee too. Malcolm yells across the room, "Yo J-Tee, where's everybody at?" J-Tee yells back, "I don't know?" As the night progresses, Malcolm notices that Camille and Ivan are not at "Ivan's" party. So, Malcolm goes home, spends time with his brother Steve, and goes to bed.

The next morning, Malcolm sits on the steps to his apartment building and listens to some hip-hop tunes by rap artist Dr. Dre. He looks up to see Camille approaching. Immediately, before she says a word, Malcolm can sense the purpose of her visit. Malcolm, reading her mind as well as her body language, acknowledges, "You came to break up with me?!!!" Camille retorts, "No, I wouldn't put it like that. But you know ... " Malcolm interrupts, "It's Ivan!" Camille agrees, "Yeah!" "Alright, peace!.," says Malcolm in a sharp and dismissive tone.

Camille was Malcolm's first love. They had dated for three months without any negative incidents. In fact, they had done "everything" together. The news that Camille prefers to date Ivan leaves Malcolm devastated and heartbroken.

As Malcolm relates this story about Camille, two things are apparent to me: first, Camille was his first love and, second, her decision to date Ivan did not merely hurt Malcolm's feelings but also robbed him of his innocence about being in love. When I ask him what he felt when Camille told him she was dating Ivan, he responds, "I was real upset!" Malcolm sighs, "You could talk to Louis about it.... Louis knows, Louis knows.... I was broke, I was, woooooo, I was in the house for another three months." I look for other negative consequences of this breakup with Camille. There is a pensive pause. "Yeah. My schoolwork dropped and there is [no friendship with Ivan]. Nobody likes him anymore.... Nobody is friends with him, he has no friends 'cuz he's a real, devious, conniving dude...."

It has been almost three years since Ivan and Camille betrayed Malcolm; yet from the fury in Malcolm's voice, it seems as though this incident occurred yesterday. However, Malcolm directs his fury solely toward Ivan. Since that day when Camille broke his heart, she and Malcolm have never dated again, but they have sustained a friendship. "Me and Camille are like this," he explains, raises his right hand and twisting his middle finger tightly around his index finger. "We're real close.... [But] she's just a friend. She's just a [close] friend!"

I do ask Louis to tell me about Malcolm's first love, and he clearly recalls the moment of breakup. Malcolm had paged Louis, and Louis was on the road when he returned the phone call. "Me and Camille just broke up.... [S]he doesn't want to see me any more." When Louis asked him how he was feeling, Malcolm became extremely quiet and said he did not really know how he was feeling. Louis was so concerned that he went to Malcolm's apartment, took him out to the front steps so they could have some privacy, and sat with him for a while. Louis admits, "We really didn't talk about Camille a lot ... we didn't really talk much at all, because, I could tell he was feeling bad, so I didn't want to pressure him. But I think he just wanted to have me there and have some company. [He just wanted] to be able to lean on me.... I think the most important thing was just helping him get through that period because he seemed very disappointed and very hurt. He got over it to some extent ... and to the other extent, I think it still haunts him today."

When Malcolm first shared this first love, I was amazed to learn that he and Camille were still friends. But now, as Louis provides his version of the same story, I fully understand how and why Camille and Malcolm's friendship had been salvaged. Louis had encouraged Malcolm to "pick up the pieces and keep on moving." But he had also advised, "[C]ontinue to be friends with [Camille] if it is possible ... [unless] it becomes a situation where there's a conflict and your girlfriend or her boyfriend has an issue with [this friendship]. [If this situation occurs], then you should back off.... But if [Camille's] willing to just be friends with you, then that's a good thing." Malcolm has definitely taken Louis's words to heart.

The Malcolm in this first-love story contrasts sharply with the hard-enough kid depicted in the vignette that introduces this chapter. But the real Malcolm is not *either* hard-enough to survive the streets or sentimental enough to fall in love and pine over a broken heart. The real Malcolm is *both* hard enough *and* sentimental, *both* tough *and* vulnerable, *both* a naive adolescent *and* a savvy young man. In other words, the real Malcolm is *both* an exemplar of the hard-enough ideal-type *and* a dynamic individual who transcends static categorization. And although my ethnographic presentation of Malcolm's life story has illuminated layers, textures, and dimensions of Malcolm's life, the real, multidimensional Malcolm defies even the most thoughtful, scholarly attempts to categorize him neatly. The real Malcolm possesses a fifteen-year old outlook on some matters and a twenty-something perspective on others. He is haunted by memories of a loving mother, vexed by the absence of his biological father, and inspired by the shadow of his surrogate father. Within the mind of the real Malcolm, boredom with school is juxtaposed against not-so-distant memories of his passion for academic knowledge. The real Malcolm is *neither* a mere pawn determined by street culture *nor* a invulnerable social agent in total control of his destiny. Instead the real Malcolm is *both* a victim limited by social structures like the streets *and* a social agent who makes choices and has dreams.

If dreams sufficed, then the real Malcolm would overcome the barriers of classism, racism, and anti-inner-cityism—by "anti-inner-cityism" I refer to bigoted views about inner-city youths—and other "isms" with the mere power of his will and labor of his hard work. Dreams do not suffice. Study after study reveals that social structural constraints, economic barriers, classism, racism, inadequate school facilities, and a host of other constraints are real and influential.[19] Hence, by expecting dreams and hard work to suffice, we confuse our mere windows of understanding on Malcolm's life with the complex, panoramic, lived reality that is Malcolm's life—the complicated reality within which he must sometimes be hard-enough to survive the streets.

I close this chapter with a narrative and a poem. The narrative describes the events that transpired one afternoon when I hung out with Malcolm to talk about his life outside of school, including sojourns from home, through the streets, to work, and to one of his frequent hangouts, the YMCA. The poem, written by Malcolm, expresses his perspective on violence: Malcolm accepts blatant forms of violence as universal phenomena but concludes that outsider proclamations against urban graffiti are but one example of the subtle yet powerful forms of symbolic violence directed toward his youth-based urban culture on a daily basis. I start and end this chapter with events that take place beyond school walls, because school is merely one of several settings in Malcolm's life. In reality, he spends more time outside the walls of the school. I start with a narrative about the streets and end with a poem about the streets to illustrate that the streets are *both* a site for illicit, dangerous activities *and* a place for positive social support and interaction. I close with Malcolm's voice in order to advocate that voices like his belong among the experts, politicians, and scholars who debate and prescribe what is best for inner-city students. I hope the young man that you see now is much more complicated and multidimensional than the hard-enough kid you saw at the beginning of this chapter and in the earlier chapters of this book. As you read the narrative and the poem that follow, please bear in mind a point asserted earlier in this chapter: of course, like Malcolm, all the street-savvy students in this book have life stories worth telling.

FINAL SOJOURNS

Malcolm is completing his ninth grade year and has recently celebrated his sixteenth birthday. It is the midafternoon of a day early in the month of June. I meet Malcolm at home in Dorchester. I park my car in front of his apartment complex, and we walk through his neighborhood to get to the nearest subway station. As we walk, Malcolm points out a couple of places where he and his boyz hang out on the streets. We pass by Victorian-style houses in an assortment of conditions: well-kept, weather-beaten, falling apart, abandoned. We pass a couple of poster boards advertising the feature films *Mission Impossible* and *Dragon-heart*. Malcolm likes the first movie, but regards the second as unconvincing: "They were on to something with the talking dragon but without more sorcery and knights and stuff, the dragon is far-fetched." As we walk through the streets of Malcolm's neighborhood, I recall an opinion about the streets that Malcolm had shared a couple of months ago. Alongside stories about fights, muggings, arrests, and shootings on the streets, Malcolm shared good memories about the streets. He had fond memories of games of hide 'n' seek, cookouts, and water fights. He smiled as he recalled the times when "you open the fire hydrants and just play in the [water from] the fire hydrant all night. And then the cops [would] come and turn [the fire hydrant off]. Then you wait about an hour and turn it back on." Malcolm had complained, "[T]he news [media] only tells the bad things [about inner-city kids]. The news will never tell if a black kid got a scholarship or something [positive]."

When we arrive at the subway station and board the train, the vast majority of passengers waiting for and riding on the train appear to be Black or Hispanic (non-white). When the train arrives at South Station, a few White passengers sprinkle into the subway car but the car never fills to capacity; we seem to have hit the midafternoon calm before the rush-hour storm. We arrive at our destination in downtown Boston and walk to an old building that looks as though it was once an industrial sweatshop. I imagine that years ago, garment workers labored here for long hours and in close quarters.

We walk five flights of stairs to the studio of Artists for Humanity. "This is where I work, Tuesdays through Thursdays, from 3:00 P.M. to 6:00 P.M. Somedays it be boring, other days it's fun," Malcolm comments as we walk over to his work area. This is a spacious art studio shared by many artists. Sometimes the artists are given assignments, like T-shirt designs, on which to work; otherwise, they can work on their own projects. Malcolm explains, "All the artists who work here are teenagers. . . . Our bosses are a white lady and her partner."

We walk around, and I try to take in the view. The room is filled with paintings of various styles and sizes. Figures of art are propped against walls, placed on easels, and pinned on bulletin board-sized canvases. Malcolm introduces me to coworkers whom we pass by as we make our rounds. Once back at Malcolm's work area, he shows me two of his paintings. He has titled one *The End of the Beginning of Nothing*. This is an abstract painting with dark, somber colors—a cloudlike layer of black over a thin layer of green over shades of blue. The colors appear to melt one into one another. Malcolm has titled the second painting *The Perfect Black*. He explains, *"The Perfect Black* comes from the Egyptian symbol." There are two dark brown, almost black, pyramids against a yellowish backdrop. I mention that I am impressed by Malcolm's art.

We leave Artists for Humanity to take the train back to Dorchester. In contrast to our earlier subway ride, this time the subway car brims full of people returning from work; some people are nodding, some are reading papers, some seem to stare aimlessly into space or look pensive. Malcolm reads *Graphotism International* (Issue #7). This magazine showcases graffiti art from all over the world. Looking over Malcolm's shoulder, I notice colorful, vibrant graffiti work, painted on walls, buildings, and other urban sites in London, Amsterdam, and Paris. I look away from this magazine and around the subway car; most of the passengers appear to be Black, a few White faces appear here and there.

We walk back through Malcolm's neighborhood to his house. The rain foils my plans to literally hang out in the streets with Malcolm. Since this morning, the weather has been unconducive to hanging out on the streets; light rain has changed to heavy downpours and back to light rain followed by more heavy downpours. We stop briefly back at Malcolm's apartment and then drive to the nearest YMCA.

As we enter the Teen Center room at the Y, Malcolm informs me, "This is a typical day for me, Tomni!" The furnishings of the Teen Center include a sofa, coffee table, armchair, and footstool that are worn but sturdy. Extra chairs adorn the periphery of this room. The recreational choices include a WF Superstars Wrestling video game, Ping-Pong tables, a pool table, and a boom box sound system. One wall of the room holds a large chalkboard, written on in multicolored chalk. Another bears a bulletin board full of job announcements and other newsworthy scraps of paper. I look around at the teens in the room. Two faces familiar to me are present: one of Malcolm's coworkers and one of Malcolm's classmates from the Paul Robeson Institute. All the teens are "rocking" oversized shirts or jackets, baggy jeans or pants or shorts, and rugged Timberland boots or brand-name sneakers. At any given moment, the number of teenagers in the room seems never more or less than ten; all appear to be youths of color. Malcolm greets some of his friends, and they begin reading, critiquing, and complimenting the contents of the latest graffiti magazines.

I challenge Malcolm to a game of pool, beat him, and sit down on the sofa. I want to play him again but do not think I will be so lucky the second time around. I strike up a conversation with Alana, the Teen Center director, an African-American woman in her mid-twenties. We talk about teenagers and agree upon several points: "Too many so-called 'experts' who talk about young people have very little hands-on, face-to-face interactions with young people," and, "Too many nonprofit, youth-based organizations don't give kids a say in their own youth centers." Alana explains, "I remember how difficult my teenage years were and I bring this understanding to my work as a youth specialist at the YMCA." She speaks highly of Malcolm and of how she is often amazed by him. She complains about adult leaders and so-called "role models," "Children don't believe in adults anymore because they know too many adults who lie and too many adults who don't practice what they preach."

I sense Malcolm's presence. I look behind me to see Malcolm kneeling behind the sofa with his chin propped on the back of this sofa between my head and Alana's. He gently breaks the news that he has plans to go out on a date and wants to know what my plans are. "Tomni, what are you doing now?" Malcolm inquires. I read the tone of his question and jokingly respond, "Malcolm, so you're kicking me to the curb?" He retorts, "Yeah, kinda, but you know I love ya." I suspect that Malcolm has made plans to go "mackin" with his boyz and the last thing he needs is a thirty-something female ethnographer tagging along. I say good-bye to Alana, give one of the kids from the Teen Center a ride home, and drop Malcolm at the Huntington subway station. Malcolm bids me farewell, "All right Tomni, peace!"

Three and 21/95 [3/21/95]

by Malcolm Winfield

Violence is everywhere . . . and everything.
Violence cannot be stopped because violence always finds a way to survive.
Violence is probably the oldest negative in the universe. . . .
I don't know why violence exists, but it probably exists for a reason.
As a graffiti artist, of course, when I see it, I don't get mad.
But when I see people trying to stop graffiti, I do get mad.
Because those people, whoever they are, want to stop my culture.
A few days ago, when I was driving downtown—well not really downtown . . . more like
lower Roxbury—I saw a sign that said, "Do you want to stop graffiti in your neighborhood?"
with a question mark and an outline of a dead man's body in the background.

Now that's real violence to me, my community, and my mind!

part III

Solutions, Broader Implications, and Policy Suggestions

SIX

Shadows, Mentors, and Surrogate Fathers

PATERNAL EMBRACE

Malcolm recalls his first day at the Paul Robeson Institute in vivid detail. "This lady, Sharon Greene, knocked on my door." Malcolm raps three times on the table to help re-create the moment when Sharon Greene woke him from a deep slumber to drive him to the institute. At that time, he was nine years old and in the third grade. "Gotta go! Let's go!" Malcolm mocks Sharon's commands. Malcolm recalls being confused and responding, "What? Huh?" Sharon inquired, "Didn't you get the letter in the mail? You gotta go to the Paul Robeson Institute today!"

Malcolm is a member of the first class to enroll in the institute during the 1989/1990 school year. He smiles as he pictures how other students from his public school were present and how a man named Phil Simmons introduced him (Malcolm) to Louis Johnsson. Malcolm's smile turns into an expression of awe, "Louis just blew my mind. . . . He was doing what he wanted to do. [Louis] had just got out of college, was working for Digital, [and he was] making the type of money he wanted to make. And I thought to myself, 'I wanna do that. . . . I wanna strive for perfection just like Louis. . . .'"

As time passed, and Malcolm's relationship with Louis grew stronger, Malcolm boasted to others that Louis was his father. Other students would retort, "That's your father? That ain't your father!" Malcolm still remembers the moment during the Unity Breakfast (banquet) when Louis silenced these responses of disbelief. Malcolm reenacts Louis's speech before the crowd at the banquet.

> Some time ago this young man right here [asked] me if he could call me Dad. . . . I didn't put that in his heart for. . .him [to want me] to be his father. God put that [desire] in his heart. . .

Malcolm has never forgotten Louis's speech. In front of a room full of witnesses, Louis adopted Malcolm and a surrogate father-son relationship was born. Malcolm remembers being elated: "I didn't know what to do, I just hugged him for an hour."

The Paul Robeson Institute for Positive Self-Development is a supplemental school program, held on Saturday mornings at Northeastern University, in which African-American men teach and mentor Black boys.[1] The boys who attend the institute reside, predominantly, in single-parent, low-income households in the Boston area. According to an assistant director, approximately seventy-five percent of the students are from single-parent, low-income households, and roughly twenty-five percent are from double-parent households.[2] The pages that follow provide answers to one overarching question: From the perspective of students, how do teachers at the Paul Robeson Institute interact more effectively with boys from inner-city neighborhoods than the teachers in the Boston public schools?

The institute was founded by the Concerned Black Men of Massachusetts, Incorporated (CBMM), a nonprofit, tax-exempt organization with the clear-cut mission to embrace Black boys within a community of Black male teachers, mentors, and role models. According to a document from the Paul Robeson Institute information packet:

> In the fall of 1989, CBMM, under the leadership and auspices of its Standing Committee on Education initiated The Paul Robeson Institute for Positive Self-Development. The Paul Robeson Institute was founded to provide a vehicle of educational, emotional, and personal support to young Black males and their families. Predicated on the ground that Black children and their families are at acute risk in today's society, the institute was formed to provide a range of early intervention and self-awareness options for elementary age youth and their families.[3]

CBMM selectively recruits, screens, and orients the men who become mentors and teachers. More specifically, all men who pass the selection process are expected to act as mentors. Some of these mentors, based upon their credentials, are recruited to teach. I refer to this latter group as teacher-mentors. All mentors volunteer their services.

CBMM works with school officials in the greater Boston area to identify Black male students in the third, fourth, fifth, and sixth grades who are at risk of failing in the public school system. The curriculum of the institute is designed "to impact academic skills in the areas of reading, writing, math, science, test-taking, and computer literacy through class sessions" and tutoring.[4] Hence, teacher-mentors at the institute teach a formal curriculum of reading, math, science, and black history. But all mentors assist with the informal curriculum by modeling culturally sensitive coping mechanisms that facilitate smooth transitions among Black culture, school culture, and street culture. When Malcolm and other members of the first group of students graduated from the institute, CBMM founded an adjunct program called Boys to Men to extend mentoring support to alumni of the institute. Louis Johnsson became the director of Boys to Men.

A guiding belief or school ethos pervades the halls, corridors, and classrooms of the institute: young, urban, Black males from low-income backgrounds are entitled to the same American dream as their affluent, mainstream, White male counterparts. Or, more specifically, young, Black males, regardless of their socioeconomic origins, can be lawyers, doctors, scholars, and good fathers, as well as athletes and working-class laborers. Paul Robeson, after whom the institute is named, embodies this ethos. According to Dean Lewis, the director of the institute, "We decided to name this institute after Paul Robeson because he was an athlete, scholar, singer, actor, lawyer ... a renaissance man. He was many things that these boys want to be."[5]

The institute is not a public school. However, an analysis of the way in which this institute *supplements* the Boston public school system provides valuable examples of the interactions, support networks, opportunities, and the like that are in short supply in the Boston (and Cambridge) public school systems. These are the types of interactions that street-savvy students need to thrive in any school setting. The dominant practices of the institute, which reflect, project, and sustain the ethos preached by mentors, include an elaborate mentoring process, responsible manhood rituals, opportunities for learning, and calling the bluff on hard postures. After elaborating these practices in the pages that follow, I define the success of the institute on the terms of students and parents; then I present the challenges that persist in spite of this success.

Mentoring

The prevailing practice of the Paul Robeson Institute is that of mentoring. Mentors at the institute are coaches, big brothers, surrogate fathers, disciplinarians, motivational speakers to whom the boys can relate and emulate. These men cast a variety of positive shadows over impressionable young boys. In other words, as illustrated by Malcolm's relationship with Louis, these boys walk in the shade of positive, accessible role models. The variety of roles that mentors incarnate will be evident throughout this chapter, but the director's role as mentor is particularly important. Dean Lewis is the embodiment of the charismatic leader described in social scientific literature on effective schools. He is the mentor to whom other mentors, students, and parents look for guidance and inspiration. The following excerpt from my fieldnotes illustrates how the director, Dean Lewis, guides and inspires.

Today is physical activity day, but I [L.J.D.] can't play with the boys because I have to meet with the parents. One of the parents who arrived for the meeting gave Dean [the director] a box of pencils and pens. Dean thanks her and exclaims, "The parents are hooking us up!" In the midst of the boys' playfulness and running around Dean asserts, "Hotep!"[6] The boys respond, "Hotep!" and silence fills the room as the playfulness quickly subsides. Dean explains, "When someone comes to the center of the room/circle, I want you to stand. And about cleaning up, I don't care who made the mess but I want everyone to clean it up. For example, see this mess right here, I'm going to clean it up because this is my institution." Dean looks over at one of the boys who hasn't quite started to help clean up and says in an encouraging yet authoritative, tone, "You're my 'boy' so you know I'm going to be watching you." Dean then directs his attention at all the boys in the room, "Today is games day. Anyone who didn't eat [breakfast] but wants to should go to the kitchen. [The rest of us] should break down the tables and get ready for Harambee.[7]

After everyone assembles in the Harambee circle, Dean goes to the middle and explains, "When a brother [mentor] comes to the center of the circle and says 'Hotep!', I want you all to say 'Hotep!' and stand up." Dutch comes to the center of the circle and says "Hotep!", and the boys stand up and respond in an united chorus, "Hotep!" Another brother [Larren], who wears a beautiful African kente print jacket, comes to the center and says "Hotep!" The boys stand up and respond, this time out of unison, "Hotep!" Dean comments on the boys' lack of unity and energy in responding, "They late, they dissed you [referring to Larren] just like they dissed me and Dutch. Let's try again!" Another [mentor] comes to the center of the circle and says, "Hotep!" The boys respond, almost in complete unison, "Hotep!" Dean notices, "Those two [boys] were late. Let's try again." Louis walk to the center of the circle and say, "Hotep!" The boys, now over-anxious to respond in unison, respond in a slightly staggered chorus, "Hotep!" Dean challenges [and encourages], "They late, they late. . . . Let's try it with a teacher."

Harambee fizzled out at the end as the boys began to turn their attention to what would happen after Harambee, for example, games. Dean recaptures the boys' attention and leads the energy. Dean directs the boys attention to the Nguzo Saba sign with the seven principles [of Kwanzaa: unity, self-determination, collective work and responsibility, cooperative economics, purpose, creativity, and faith[8]]. He asks about eleven boys to carry the sign around. He explains, "This is called the moving buildboard. It takes unity for these boys to carry this buildboard around because it's too heavy for one to carry. . . . What does Umoja mean?" There's no answer from the boys. Dean probes, "What example did you just see?" Some boys respond, "Unity!" Dean instructs the boys to continue walking the sign around while he describes [the term] "kujichagulia" (self-determination). He points out how one of the little brothers [students] was more determined than the others to take the sign around.[9]

Like the director, the men who staff the institute take their roles as mentors quite seriously. The teacher-mentors persistently defy, challenge, and deconstruct negative Black male stereotypes. This aspect of mentoring reigns most salient. Not only do the men of the institute preach about the varied and sundry accomplishments of Black men like Paul Robeson, Martin Luther King, Marcus Garvey, and Malcolm X; these men, themselves, are living challenges to negative stereotypes like O-dog (mentioned in chapter 3), the epitome of the hardcore urban Black youth. These men are scientists, engineers, teachers, deans, coaches, ministers, professors, fathers, working-class laborers, and unemployed men with good hearts.[10] Furthermore, although it is more common that the men mentor the boys, sometimes the boys mentor the men. In other words, sometimes there are discussions and forums during which the boys update the men on what it is like to be young inner-city males who must cope with social pressure to act hard like a gangsta.

Hence through the process of mentoring, teacher-mentors at the institute provide alternatives to seductive gangsterlike stereotypes of inner-city males; mentors model alternative types of masculine behavior that the boys view as realistic for successfully navigating the negative aspects of street culture. And mentors develop and nurture compassionate perspectives about street culture that dissolve hard (tough) student attitudes and facilitate cooperation between teachers and students. Students appreciate that many mentors at the institute grew up under similar situations and therefore relate very well to street-savvy students. For example, the teacher-mentors often mix urban slang with standard English and, according to the boys, this conveys empathetic understanding. While enrolled in the institute, Malcolm voiced a sentiment popular among students there:

[When the mentors at the institute] use slang, it makes me feel like they're in tune with us. . . it makes us feel closer to them, like they're [the mentors] your age but you know they're not so you gotta respect that. But, on the other hand, you can talk to them the same way you would talk to your friends but not disrespectfully.[11]

Complaints like those made by Malcolm about his public school teachers in chapters 4 and 5 are rarely the complaints made by students at the institute about mentors. When students complain at the institute, the complaints are typically about the amount of parental attention that the men heap on the boys, the paternal and fraternal embraces that hold the boys to high standards. The following student complaint was the result of the director's admonition that students should not behave like "Silly, Silly, and Silly, Incorporated," but like leaders, instead.

KAREEM: Why y'all always picking on me?

DEAN: Why are you always putting yourself in a situation that gets our attention?

KAREEM: I don't want your attention.

DEAN: What do you want?

KAREEM: [Silent. Sucks his tongue in frustration.]

DEAN: Rahjid, you taught Kareem. Tell me how you met him.

RAHJID [a mentor and Boston public school teacher]: I met Kareem two years ago by fate. He was running down the hall in school.

DEAN: There it is [an example of Kareem's propensity to get into trouble].

KAREEM: Y'all always picking on me!

DEAN: And we're going to keep on "picking on you" [mocks Kareem]. We're not going to let you get away.[12]

In short, through the mentoring process that values the cultural assets and experiences of inner-city life, the students at the institute come to feel themselves as *valued*, *validated*, and *understood* members of a community that recognizes their unique experiences.

Rituals

Another prevalent practice of the institute not found in the Cambridge or Boston school systems is a practice I call "responsible manhood rituals." Every Saturday morning session starts with a ritual called Harambee. During Harambee, the boys stand in a circle and rap in unison about the seven principles of Kwanzaa. The rap is recited in an enthusiastic, rhythmical call-and-response chorus:

Umoja means unity! . . . *Umoja means unity!*
Umoja means unity! . . . *Umoja means unity!*

Kujichagulia! . . . *Kujichagulia!:*
Self-Determination! . . . *Self Determination!*

Ujima! . . . *Ujima!* . . . Ujima! . . . *Ujima!*
Collective Work and Responsibility! . . . *Collective Work and Responsibility!*

Ujamaa! . . . *Ujamaa!* . . . Ujamaa! . . . *Ujamaa!*
Cooperative Economics! . . . *Cooperative Economics!*

Nia means Purpose! . . . *Nia means Purpose!*
Kuumba means Creativity! . . . *Kuumba means Creativity!*

Imani! . . . *Imani.* . . . Imani! . . . *Imani:*
Means Faith! . . . *Means Faith!*

They also often recite a poem titled "I'm a Proud Young Black Man."[13]

> I am a PROUD young BLACK MAN
> I ASPIRE to become a PROUD BLACK MAN
> I will ACHIEVE my goal by:
> Loving my GOD, AND MY PEOPLE,
> STRIVING for EXCELLENCE
> KNOWING my ENEMY—IGNORANCE
> SUPPRESSING my ENEMY WITH KNOWLEDGE
> FOR I AM A PROUD YOUNG BLACK MAN

Rap and Afrocentric poetry are cultural expressions to which inner-city youth relate and appreciate. Even more, the teacher-mentors stress that these raps and poems are words that they, themselves, strive to live by and that the boys should also live by. These and other oratorical rituals are meant to be meaningful recitations, words that figure prominently in the minds of the boys when they are away from the institute and are specifically designed to counteract the self-destructive images, beliefs, and statements that sometimes emanate from street culture (and mainstream culture) about the worthlessness of Black male lives.

Opportunities for Learning

Another salient characteristic of the institute is one I call opportunities for learning. I borrow a definition of this concept from an article by Aage Sørensen titled "Schools and the Distribution of Educational Opportunities."[14] According to Sørensen:

> There are elaborate theories of learning, emphasizing cognitive structures, memory processes, and motivational states. There is also an elementary fact about learning: one cannot learn what one has not had an opportunity to learn. An opportunity for learning is the presentation of a certain amount of instructional material.... Students are exposed to opportunities for learning outside the instructional settings of schools. They might be taught by parents, experiences and experimentation, and by each other. All these sources of opportunities for learning are relevant, but for the learning outcomes most relevant for educational attainment, schools have quite an extensive monopoly.

For many street-savvy students at the Paul Robeson Institute, the opportunities to learn from in-class incidents that challenge negative black male stereotypes and promote positive black male images are just as important as the opportunities to learn math, science, and black history, or other basic skills relevant for educational attainment. Although the boys at the institute range from eight to twelve years old, several have already formed an opinion about what it means to be a Black man. As discussed above, a typical Saturday morning at the institute overflows with opportunities for the boys to learn, by example, from the teacher-mentors that Black men are not a monolithic group. *Black* men are working-class laborers as well as lawyers, doctors, professors, and good fathers in the real world, and not just make-believe television professionals like Dr. Huxtable from *The Cosby Show* or Mr. Banks, an upper-class

Black attorney from the popular show *Fresh Prince of Bel Air*. And from interacting with positive role models the boys have several occasions to learn that a *Black* man can admit, "I don't know," or "I'm sorry," and still be hard-enough to hang in the streets without such an admission making him less of a man (or a boy). During a parent meeting, the director of the institute explained:

> [T]he men sometimes learn things along with the boys (for example, parts of the brain demonstration) and are very open about letting the boys know that they (i.e., the men) are also learning.[15]

At another parent meeting the director explained:

> If [the mentors] are wrong, we'll apologize right in front of the kids. We teach [the boys] that men can work in the kitchen, can hug, cry, and do other things.[16]

And, as captured in the following fieldnotes, the students have ample opportunity to say "I'm sorry." These notes document the events that occurred after a class session during which many of the sixth graders had been disrespectful to Doc, the science teacher-mentor. I missed the disrespectful event but observed the apology.

> I missed it, but apparently the sixth graders had dissed Doc in a big way and they upset Doc. This is a difficult feat because Doc is a very even-tempered individual. . . . [The director] wanted to make sure the boys knew that dissing Doc was something that would anger all the mentors and something that had severe consequences for the boys. [The director] and other mentors told the boys that the men were going to have a meeting to discuss this incident and that the boys should also have a meeting to decide what they were going to do. . . . The boys decided that they would publicly apologize to Doc. Before lunch, the sixth graders lined up and one by one they walked over to Doc and said, "I'm sorry, Doc." During the Circle of Love, four of the sixth graders made a public apology. [The individual and public apologies were the boys' ideas, not the mentors'.] Doc hugged the boys, and they hugged him back with big smiles. Doc accepted the apology and apologized to the boys because he had promised them a guest speaker and that person hadn't shown up.[17]

In addition to learning that being a man means sometimes having to say "I'm sorry," the boys also have opportunities to learn that becoming a man is a maturing process far more complex than growing taller or knowing how to fight.

> After the students circle up for Harambee, Dean [the director] asked one of the little brothers (students) to come to the center of the circle. [The director] says to this student and all the students in the circle, "Look at this little brother. He grew a few inches and now he's walking around this morning acting like, 'I'm the man, I don't have to do that [help set up for breakfast].'" Dean explains, "You might be 'the man' but you aren't a man. Dean asks another student to come to the center of the circle because this student had gotten into a fight. Dean told the student that he would have one of the [mentors] talk to him [the student] about fighting. Dean explained to all the boys in the room, "We don't play that" [we don't tolerate fighting].[18]

Such interactions have literally transformed the attitudes and behavior of some students who were initially prone to disruptive behavior. Recall Malcolm's assertion from chapter 5:

> [The institute] turned me around . . . because I use to love to fight and sometimes I would win and sometimes I wouldn't. Most of the time when I have a fight or something, I end up regretting it afterward. Then when I came into [the institute], everybody was having fun, and I just realized that it wasn't no need to fight, 'cuz it didn't make any sense to me. . . . Everybody was having fun. And if somethin' starts escalating into a conflict, you can just resolve it with words. You don't need no violence. [I've learned that] everybody can have a fight every day, but it takes a man not to have a fight every day.

As illustrated by the above excerpts from field observations, some of the lessons these boys learn outside of the instructional setting of the Paul Robeson Institute (for example, that real Black men are hard), must be addressed so that some students will more readily accept the instructional material most relevant for educational attainment. More importantly, just as a student cannot learn what he (or she) has not had the opportunity to learn, a student may not learn if he (or she) has an attitude that prevents him from seizing the opportunity when presented. Hence, the institute not only provides its students with several opportunities to learn, teacher-mentors are also extremely attentive to whether the students are receptive to learning. For example, when students are unable to concentrate due to some tragic event (like a shooting homicide in a student's neighborhood), the mentors will preempt a science or math class and allow the boys to discuss how they are coping with this incident or similar incidents. As explained by the institute director during a parent meeting, "We don't want to do the same thing that teachers do in school. We may spend fifteen minutes teaching and more time getting to know your son."[19]

Calling the Bluff on "Hard" Postures

Through mentoring, rituals, and opportunities for learning, the institute reinforces its guiding belief in the viability of young Black males and sustains a positive school ethos for inner-city youth. Moreover, these practices reflect the mentors' deep cultural insight into what life is like for students beyond the walls of the institute. Teacher-mentors have the requisite cultural resources (experiences, language, mannerisms, dispositions, and so on) to relate to inner-city youth. Furthermore, several students who attend the institute already possess positive attitudes toward school; the mentors reinforce these attitudes. But a major difference between the institute and the public school system is the mentors' ability to deal successfully with the students who are becoming hard or are hardcore wannabes as described in chapter 3. Teacher-mentors are quick to challenge and call the bluff on hardcore behavior. In doing so, they de-escalate incidents that would otherwise end in student suspensions or expulsions. One morning, during the Harambee ritual, the following interaction occurred between Dean and a student.

DEAN: Can I get a round of applause for mathematics [student applause] ... for science [student applause] ... for African-American history.... [the director turns to a fifth grader prone to being disruptive] Your dad said you and I could "knuck" any time. You know what "knuck" means? First you hit me, then I hit you. I'll let you go first. You want to start?

STUDENT: Really? Yeah! [Student looks at Dean, who towers 6'6", and on second thought] No!

Later that morning, during a science class on nutrition:

A student raises his hand and tells Ike [the teacher-mentor], "Please ask Andy [a student] to take his foot off my seat. I asked him to stop." Andy was the student Ike [and the director] had words with earlier. Ike immediately asks Andy to leave [the room], and Andy says, "I only had my foot on his seat a little." Ike responds, "I'm not arguing.... Leave!" Andy says to Ike, "I'm going to punch you in your face." [The director] happens to be on the second floor and says to Andy, "You come with me, and when your father arrives, I'm going to bring you with your father to Ike so you can 'punch him in the face!'" [Later that morning, Andy apologized to Ike.] [20]

Teachers at the institute are not quick to suspend or expel disruptive students; instead they are quick to remind students of the high expectations held by mentors.

Dean explains to students, "Larry [a student] is having some problems. Most of them aren't even his fault. [turns to Larry] We know you're going through changes. I'm not going to reprimand you but ... just remember respect. When you diss other people, you diss yourself. I want you to remember to respect yourself." Dean continues talking to and about students in the center of the circle, "[Michael's] brilliant, but sometimes he uses his brilliance to do the wrong things. And that's what happened this week [when the student started a fight]. But we know you can do better. Right!?"[21]

Although mentors condone temporary hard posturing and tough fronts for the sake of safe passage through urban streets, mentors are quick to help students to realize the long-term consequences of disruptive and hard behavior. And on the rare occasion that a student is suspended due to tough posturing, he is made fully aware of the reason and is expected to use the suspension to reflect upon his behavior. For example, when Malcolm first arrived at the institute his bully-prone tendencies resulted in a suspension. Yet this suspension differs substantially from its public school counterpart.

L.J.D.: How would [a] kid be treated at [a Boston public school] if he ... stepped into the classroom using profanity, tryin' to pick fights with people.

MALCOLM: Aww man, he would either be seriously hurt by one of the students, or probably suspended. 'Cuz teachers at [a Boston public school] suspend you like that [snaps finger]. [Malcolm gives examples.]

L.J.D.: What would happen at the institute if a kid came in using profanity, tryin' to pick a fight?

MALCOLM: Well first ... they try to calm him down. Then after he gets calmed down, they'll tell him why he shouldn't be doing this [being disruptive] 'cuz ...

L.J.D.: They ever do this to you?

MALCOLM: Um huh [yes]. . . . I never got in trouble for disrespecting a teacher [at the institute] [except] just once when I swung at Dean [Motley].

L.J.D.: You swung at Dean, the tallest man in the institute? What were you thinking of, Malcolm?

MALCOLM: I don't know, I was mad.

L.J.D.: And what did they do when you swung at Dean?

MALCOLM: They suspended me . . . for one Saturday.

L.J.D.: Did they talk to you about it?

MALCOLM: They said I needed time to myself to think about what I did. If I would have met Dean on the street and I swung at him, I would have been done [lost the fight]. Especially if I didn't know him.[22]

Student interviews reveal that unlike their public school counterparts, mentors at the institute are willing, able, required, and not afraid to confront hard behavior. Through such attentiveness, teacher-mentors become acquainted with the concerns of individual students. Then the mentors make sure that they send out frequent messages to the students that address emerging concerns, messages to which street-savvy students can relate. In this way, the ethos of the institute is constantly updated to keep pace with emergent phenomena unique to inner-city students. And, instead of feeling misunderstood or dismissed or academically unchallenged, students feel that their needs and concerns are being addressed. Through their cultural insight and appreciation of what life is like for street-savvy youths, mentors are able to provide viable advice and alternatives about avoiding illicit street cultural activities.

STUDENT AND PARENT TESTIMONIES

It seems worthwhile to provide a few more detailed testimonies from students and parents that convey the general sentiment about the success of the institute. From data like those below, I inferred that submersion in an *empathetic* community of values or ethos was the major determinant of success for street-savvy, inner-city youth. A positive school ethos lays a foundation upon which other effective school criteria are either reinforced or undermined. Field observations and interviews suggest that there may be a positive correlation between feeling understood and being motivated to impress and cooperate with one's teacher. Hence, this section allows a peek at some of the most insightful, compelling, and representative sentiments expressed during field research, interviews, and surveys. This provides a little more exposure to the data and the opportunity to agree with, supplement, or challenge my conclusions about the ethos of the institute.

Ronell, fourteen years old, ninth grade (alumnus of the institute)

L.J.D.: Is the institute different from [public] school? . . . In what way?

R: It's more fun, you get more freedom. . . .

L.J.D.: Would you say that your teachers at your [public school] understand what kids have to deal with today?

R: No. The teachers . . . you see I like my teachers, but I only got one Black teacher, and um . . . you know, the White people . . . um [student hesitates to finish response]. . .

L.J.D.: This is your opinion. And when I write up my paper, I'm not going to say, "Ronell said, 'The White people . . .'." I'll say, "A student said . . ." So this [interview] won't follow you.

R: See mainly, the Black teachers, you know, know what I'm going through. [They] live in the ghetto and stuff. But White people, they don't live in the ghetto.

L.J.D.: Can you tell me, like, some of the things . . . you're going through growing up?

R: The violence, you know, I'm always watching my back, and I'm growing up fast and stuff like that.

L.J.D.: Would you say the men at the institute understand what you're going through?

R: Yeah, yeah . . . 'cuz . . . it's like they always tell me, "You remind me of me when I was little." And the stuff I'm going through, they must have been going through.

L.J.D.: So you can relate to them, and they can relate to you?

R: Yeah.

L.J.D.: Do you think the institute has made an impact on your life? . . . How do you think your life would be different if you never attended the institute? Would your life be different? Would you be a different Ronell?

R: Yeah, I'd probably be a gangsta.

L.J.D.: You think you'd be a gangsta?

R: Yeah.

L.J.D.: What would you be doing?

R: I'd probably be robbin' people, sellin' drugs, you know [hangin'] on the streets. [But] the institute set me on the right track.

L.J.D.: How did they do that?

R: They just . . . how do I explain it? It's like they opened up a doorway, you know, for me to learn better about my culture and stuff. I just like that. . . .

L.J.D.: Tell me more about the doorway . . .

[Student is at a loss for words.]

L.J.D.: Like you were saying, [the mentors at the institute] sit you down and they can relate to you. And your teachers in the Boston schools don't do that?

R: No, [they don't].[23]

Kogee, thirteen years old, eighth grade (alumnus of the institute)

L.J.D.: Did the institute have a positive influence on your life?

K: Yeah, I guess so. It taught me right from wrong. It taught me how to do things . . . like not follow behind people [but] to be a leader and not to follow everything everybody else do because, what they do, sometimes they lead you into a bad place.

L.J.D.: Do you think you'd be a different Kogee if you never attended the institute?

K: Most definitely.

L.J.D.: How would you be [different]? . . .

K: I would always be fighting.

L.J.D.: Kogee use to fight a lot?

K: Always.

L.J.D.: So what got you to stop fighting?

K: Them [the mentors at the institute] giving me positive role models, and [my] looking up to people and being like, . . . I see Louis [an Institute mentor], and how he acts this way. I should strive to learn how to act the way he does and set goals for myself.

L.J.D.: Now, do you think the teachers at your [public school] . . . understand what it's like to be a young Black male growing up? What you have to deal with?

K: No, my teacher [is] White and she grew up in the suburbs too. I don't think they [the teachers] understand . . . where we're coming from because they always give us a "for instance" [an example] and say things like, if you do something wrong, they'll tell you the way they [the teachers] think they will [should] correct it, not the way you think that you will be able to correct it, the easiest way for you. They give you [an example of] the easiest way for them to correct it.

L.J.D.: Can you give me an example?

K: Growing up around where my way is, like if you walk away from somebody [who's threatening you], they'll just think you're more of a punk and just beat you up. Like say the first time you're about to get into a fight, and the teacher will tell you just to, um, just walk away. But you know that the best thing for you to do the first time . . . if you was to ever get into a fight is to thump the person, is to fight the person or just talk it through and . . . make it seem like you ain't gonna go out [allow yourself to be beaten] this time. But not [talk it through] in a way that you want it [the conflict] to escalate.

L.J.D.: Your teachers at [your public school] just tell you to walk away from it.

K: Um nun, [yes] . . .

L.J.D.: What about the men at the institute?

K: Yeah, most of them understand what it's like to grow up, um, around urban areas. So they can relate to most of the things that you want. Like, they can relate . . . and put it [compare it] to a certain part of their life. . . . For instances, they can relate to more of what you're saying [and] . . . relate it to things that happened in their life. . . .[24]

As argued throughout this book, although social pressures may encourage students to don gangsterlike mannerisms, most inner-city youths are not hard and ruthless gangsters. This is true for the majority of the students at the institute. But, as indicated in the above quote, students like Ronell and Kogee, who would likely end up as expulsion statistics in the public school system, learn to thrive in the school setting of the institute. Kogee was once prone to disruptive hard behavior and resistant to learning but is now more likely to avoid a fight. He now has aspirations to be a "scientist and if [he] can't be a scientist [he'll] just fall back on boxing."[25] Ronell had previously been kept back a grade in the public school system for one year. However, during this past school year Ronell applied to a promotion program and was skipped from the seventh to the ninth grade.

In addition to feeling that the institute has a positive impact on their lives, Paul Robeson students also assert that the institute provides them with substantially more black history than their public schools. When I conducted a joint interview with Kogee and Bill, they criticized their public schools' black history curricula. This was a sentiment expressed by several students at the institute.

KOGEE: (At the Paul Robeson Institute they have) more subjects like black history, not just plain history. 'Cuz what they teach you in class [at school] is booty, it's just not true. At the institute, I feel what they're teaching us is real, it's not fake. It's not like somebody took like some information and twisted it around to fit their own needs. . . . At the institute, they teach black history . . . instead of learning about some other race of people, some white people [who] twisted information. . . .

BILL: 'Cuz [the institute teaches] us more black history, it's not fake. . . . 'Cuz at school they tell us to bring black history books, and we never use them. We don't do any work in black history [in school]. . . . They only talk about two or three] black women, Harriet Tubman and Sojourner Truth . . . and Rosa Parks. . . . They [at school] act like they didn't know anything about any black people.

KOGEE: At my school, they only talk about two black men, Malcolm X and Martin Luther King. [At the institute], they talk about lots of black people that's not in the history books.[26]

Boys like Kogee, Ronell, and Bill are inspired and motivated to work hard by mentors at the institute. The mentors are able to look at these boys and not see gangstas, hopelessly disruptive students, or school-failure statistics. Instead, the mentors see themselves, when they were younger. In the mentors, these boys are able to see themselves when they are older. The mentors compete successfully with the streets for Ronell and Kogee by providing them with viable street-savvy alternatives and advice about being hard, fighting, or avoiding a fight, or about being a leader and not a follower. My interviews and field observations indicate that teachers and administrators in the Cambridge and Boston public schools could learn a lot from these mentors about understanding and relating to urban youth in general and Black males from inner-city areas in particular.

Parents surveyed corroborate the above testimonies about the positive impact of the institute.[27] More specifically, parents cited changes in the behavior of their sons, like an increase in confidence toward schoolwork, decrease in anger, more self-control, and improved knowledge of black (African and African-American) history as the most tangible results of the institute.

Parent 1:
Zamaine can freely make positive observations regarding his behavior. When he is wrong, he can say, "I was wrong." Should [the] situation come about when he is angry or frustrated, he can express it clearly. . . . [The institute] has had a positive effect on my son Zamaine. I feel that his self-esteem and attitude has improved greatly. . . . Zamaine is in a L & D [learning disabilities] class. . . . As Zamaine grows into manhood, I want him to work hard to improve his academics and understand he is responsible to be a positive role model. [The institute] has assisted and continues to assist in these areas.

Parent 2:
[Thanks to the institute and] ongoing counseling dealing with hyperactivity . . . [t]here has been a [positive] change in Larey's grades. Also, his attitude has changed very much. Larey was aggressive and angry a lot. Larey is much more obedient at home and at school. I personally feel that the lack of his father's involvement in his rearing process had caused Larey to act in [a negative] manner. Larey is doing okay now.

Parent 3:
[My son] shows more self-confidence. He expresses himself more both written and verbal. . . . He knows a lot more about history and current events, which he didn't know before [attending

the institute]. . . . [Because of the institute] [h]e shows more self-control He has a very positive attitude toward life and learning in general. He was always looking forward to be there
[at the institute] on Saturday morning; he found it very interesting and enjoyable.

Most parents at the institute indicate via surveys and/or interviews that they have
observed, at the most, positive changes in their sons' grades and, at the least, positive
changes in their sons' attitudes and confidence about schoolwork. However, a
handful of parents indicate that although they believe in the work of the institute,
for some reason, they have not observed improvement in grades and have observed
only marginal improvements in attitudes. One parent explained that her son's failing
grades in school had nothing to do with the institute. Instead, there seemed "to be
some personal problem the [public school] teacher [had] with her son."[28] Another
parent explained that for the first three years that her son attended the institute, she
observed positive changes. But during his last year at the institute, she observed a
negative change. Her son's grades constantly improved until he was placed in an
advanced work class in his public school. This parent also believed that the negative
change was influenced by "local peer pressure." These two parents' observations are
not the norm; the most frequent sentiments expressed by parents are stories of success about the impact of the institute upon their sons' attitudes toward school.

Interviews and group discussions with students of the institute reveal that the
boys who frequently attend the program sustain or acquire positive attitudes toward
schooling. But for the boys who attend infrequently, such claims cannot be made.
Why some boys stop attending or fall through the cracks while several succeed is a
research question worthy of further exploration. Although I did not directly explore
this question, indirect observations yield a few hypotheses.

Some boys may fail to attend for reasons ranging from not wanting to miss Saturday morning cartoons—the institute holds classes on Saturday mornings from
8:30 A.M. until 12:00 noon—to being involved in another Saturday morning recre-
ational/sports activity to not having adequate parental support and encouragement.
As mentioned above, parental cooperation and support are key to students' success
at the institute. Furthermore, some students may stop attending because they do not
find the work of the institute of interest. Nonetheless, the institute has far more of
a problem with accommodating all the boys who want to attend than with absen-
teeism or low interest.

In addition to the students with irregular attendance, there are a few students who
attend the institute frequently, yet show limited or marginal signs of improvement in
attitudes toward schooling or grades. Since the institute opened its doors in 1989, the
number of students sometimes rises so quickly that the ratio of mentors to students
is too low. For example, in 1989, the ratio of mentors to students was 1:2; by the
1992 school year (to 1996), the ratio of mentors to students had decreased to 1:5. A
low mentor-to-student ratio affects the ability of mentors to consistently monitor
student progress outside of the institute via frequent correspondence with public
school teachers. Furthermore, the mentors at the institute are volunteers. Many have
full-time careers in addition to their work at the institute. Hence, the increased student enrollment forces mentors to rely more and more upon parents to consistently
monitor student progress with public schoolwork. While several parents keep men-

tors informed of student progress, others are not so diligent. Finally, some students may fall through the cracks because one Saturday morning a week is not supplement enough to overcome the negative impact of street culture and other disadvantages that erode positive student attitudes toward schooling.

Despite the shortcomings listed above, the overall story of the Paul Robeson Institute illustrates the positive impact of an empathetic ethos upon the attitudes of street-savvy students. It is also a compelling tale about shadows of guidance cast by influential mentors.

SCHOOL ETHOS, RITUALS, AND ROLE MODELS

My research on the Paul Robeson Institute indicates that the ethos, ritualized practices, and role models of any school are major determinants of the success or failure of students. As discussed in chapter 4, most schools have an ethos and ritualized practices that value the cultural capital of the mainstream; these schools may doom non-mainstream students to failure.[29] Hence, schools that merely embrace and transmit mainstream American language, mannerisms, cultural expressions, experiences, and appreciations legitimize existing social inequalities and maintain a status quo that accepts the failure of inner-city youth, especially Black males (and Latinos).

Teachers who fail to convey empathetic understanding about the demands of the streets are likely to have a difficult time motivating and eliciting cooperation from street savvy students. Consequently, if schools are going to compete adequately with the streets for street-savvy youths, schools must possess the cultural resources to create an ethos or community of values sensitive to what life is like for such youths. This ethos must confront and challenge limited and negative images of Black males as hard gangsters, drug dealers, irresponsible fathers, and so on. Teachers must adequately (that is, realistically) address attributes and practices that many urban youths bring into the classroom without categorically devaluing the cultural experiences and coping mechanisms of these youths. With the proper school ethos, rituals, and role models, teachers may not be able to take students out of the inner-city, but teachers will become attentive and sensitive to the way inner-city experiences and tough fronts have affected their students.

SEVEN

Fear of the Dark

The Vilification of Urban Students

Race has become metaphorical—a way of referring to and disguising forces, events, classes, and expressions of social decay and economic division far more threatening to the body politic than biological "race" ever was. Expensively kept, economically unsound, a spurious and useless political asset in election campaigns, racism is as healthy today as it was during the Enlightenment. It seems that it has a utility far beyond economy, beyond the sequestering of classes from one another, and has assumed a metaphorical life so completely embedded in daily discourse that it is perhaps more necessary and more on display than ever before.

—Toni Morrison, *Playing in the Dark: Whiteness and the Literary Imagination*

"OH SHIT! GANG BANGERS!!!"

One fall evening around 8:30 P.M., I was driving four of my "little brothas" or "mentees" back to their respective residences. My teenaged passengers were ninth graders at the time. Two self-identified as Black American (even though both had one parent who was White and another that was Black), one self-identified as Cape Verdean, and the other described himself as Dominican (from the Dominican Republic). All four teens were frequently racially categorized as Black by onlookers who knew nothing about their specific racial-ethnic origins. Earlier that day, I had picked them up after school at approximately 2:00 P.M. They had spent from midafternoon to early evening hanging out with me in the college residence house where I served as a resident assistant. They had played basketball at a university gym, then I had treated them to dinner in the residence house dining hall. After dinner, they had played video games and watched television in the common room of the dorm. Eventually, against their protests, I had announced that it was time for me to take them home. All of them had unanimously sighed, "Ah Tomni . . . c'mon. We want to chill a little longer." I had retorted, "Y'all know I love ya, but it's getting late and I'm going out tonight." Shortly thereafter, all five of us were in my car. I, the driver, and one of my little brothas sat comfortably up front after the other three had crammed into the backseat of my sporty Subaru X-T Coupe, a backseat designed to comfortably seat two people. My front seat passenger had found a rap tune on my car radio, and all five of us were nodding our heads to the bass-filled beat of the music. As I stopped for a red light, the driver in the car behind me applied his brakes a second too late and bumped into the back of my car.

I got out of my car to inspect the damage as the driver who bumped my car—a man who appeared to be European American and in his late twenties or early thirties—jumped out and asserted in a tone that conveyed arrogance, "It was just a little bump. Your car is okay!" My little brotha in the front opened the passenger-side door of my car, pulled his body half way out, and inquired, "Is everything alright, Tomni?" I responded, "Yeah . . . everything's fine." At that moment, this arrogant driver looked up and suddenly realized that I was not the only passenger in the car. The only one of my little brothas' faces that he could see was the one who got out of the car. But this arrogant driver glanced briefly through the back window at the other three heads—heads covered with knit skullcaps due to the cold weather and bopping to the beat of the rap tune playing on the car radio—and his arrogance turned to fear. "OH SHIT! GANG BANGERS!!!" he exclaimed, jumped quickly into his car, and drove around my car through the red light. I got back in my car and, once the light turned green, continued en route to take my passengers home. We all laughed at this driver's ignorance and cowardice. Sadly, the misconception that this driver had about my little brothas was so typical that, though a bit startled, I was not surprised when he recoiled in fear. However, after a wonderful evening of hanging out with my little brothas, laughing at their jokes and vicariously enjoying their stories about being in the ninth grade, I drove back to my residence dismayed, angered, disappointed, concerned, and overcome with several other discouraging emotions. That driver's hallucination that my ninth grade passengers were gang bangers was but a drop in a pool of similar delusions held by many others including teachers, social workers, local store owners and employees, and the police.[1]

The previous chapters of this book brim with quotes, vignettes, and narratives from my formal interviews and observations with street-savvy youths. However, there are hours of interactions, like the vignette above, that remain undocumented in field-notes because these interactions occurred when I was hanging out with these teens as their friend, mentor, or "big sister," not as a researcher. There were seven students in particular, four with whom I am still in contact to this very day, to whom I became a mentor. The non-research—based context of the vignette above is the reason why I have not identified my little brothas with pseudonyms used earlier in this book. And it was often when I was hanging out with my mentees on their terms that I witnessed violent assaults upon them like that recounted in the vignette above. The assaults were not those of physical violence; they were assaults of symbolic violence.

Symbolic violence, as defined by Pierre Bourdieu, manifests through "the subtle exercise of symbolic power waged by a ruling class in order to 'impose a definition of the social world that is consistent with its interests.'"[2] The exclamation, "Oh shit! Gang bangers!," would be relatively harmless if it were merely the outcry of a random individual. It would be justifiable if my mentees had actually been gang bangers. But, my mentees were not, are not, gang bangers and the arrogant driver's outcry is anything but the sentiment of a random individual. As I elaborate in this chapter, it is the tendency to look at Black and Brown males, not see them and, then, assault or insult them with stereotypes and negative racial icons that exemplify the subtle and pervasive exercise of symbolic power wielded by the American mainstream.

While in graduate school, I frequently invited my mentees to my dormitory and visited them in their homes.[3] As I helped these students to navigate mainstream institutions like schools, colleges, courts, governmental agencies (for example, the Department of Social Services), and businesses of potential employment, two things became even more apparent to me: (1) the agents of mainstream institutions often regarded these students as "little thugs"; (2) these students were disappointed that the agents of mainstream institutions regarded them as "little thugs." Sometimes these students joked about these vilifying hallucinations and threatened to say "Booooo!" to those who held them in fearful regard. When these students felt that the only way to gain respect was through fear, they would joke about using this fear to their advantage instead of being victimized by it. But most of the time, they complained that it was difficult to prevail against the wild, vilifying imaginations of teachers, social workers, probation officers, judges, police officers, and mainstream citizens. Despite these students' best efforts, they were often caricatured as little Black thugs on their way to becoming big Black menacing thugs or gangsters or gang bangers or drug dealers or criminals.

Several sources have led me to conclude that the vilification of Black males is a common, yet taken-for-granted, American practice. This conclusion is not a news flash. In this chapter, however, I draw attention to the symbolic violence embedded in this American practice. This exercise of symbolic violence is evident in (1) the racialized alibis of individual American citizens who, like Susan Smith and Charles Stuart, have committed heinous crimes; (2) the political strategies and agendas of presidential campaigns; (3) news media accounts of urban crime; and (4) even in the supposedly creative imaginations of science fiction writers. This list does not begin to exhaust the manifestations of this American pastime, but it does reveal its pervasiveness.

Over the years of researching and writing this book, I have endeavored to make sense of this practice. My quest has been encouraged by those who persist, "You're the *expert*. Why do *you* think people are so afraid of these kids?" In this chapter I answer this question as well as another: What's *Star Trek* got to do with symbolic violence? I add my voice to scholarly claims about the racialization of Black males.[4]

"BASEBALL, HOTDOGS, APPLE PIE AND [BLACK VILLAINS]"

In the 1970s, Chevrolet aired a commercial that sang the American traditions of baseball, hotdogs, apple pie and Chevrolet.[5] By linking the name of Chevrolet to these icons, this car company sought to emphasize its line of cars as an American tradition. The insertion of Black villains into this Chevrolet ditty strikes a dissonant chord and makes audible another American tradition, a tradition that Americans would rather ignore than sing about. Those who vilify urban teens would likely deny that Black villains belong in this ditty. Joe Feagin and Hernán Vera (sociologists), Katheryn Russell (a criminologist), and Toni Morrison (a Nobel Prize-winning literary scholar) are merely four scholars among many who argue otherwise. The vilification of Black males *is* as American as apple pie and is an older tradition than baseball and Chevrolet.[6]

"Negative Racial Icons of National Dimensions"

In *White Racism: The Basics,* Joe Feagin and Hernán Vera document several examples of how Blacks in general and Black men in particular have been maligned as "negative racial icons of national dimensions."[7] For instance, in Dubuque, Iowa, where Black residents make up less than one percent of the overall population, White residents opposed a city council diversity plan to attract a modest number of Black families by conjuring the "fictional black threat to jobs" as well as stereotypes of Blacks as "welfare queens" and "criminals."[8] Feagin and Vera elaborate:

> For a city whose population included such a small proportion of black residents, the range of antiblack myths that surfaced seems substantial. One local rumor warned that armed gangs were coming to Dubuque from Chicago, and in the language of racism "gang" can become code for "any group of young black men."[9] Several young white Dubuque men interviewed by a *Toronto Star* reporter about their support for the white supremacists movement spoke in stereotyped terms of blacks threatening the purses of older women, of black male advances to white women, and of black vandalism.[10]

In addition to White supremacists in Dubuque, Iowa, Feagin and Vera reveal how the racialized culture that pervaded the Los Angeles Police Department (LAPD) contributed to the dehumanization and brutal beating of Rodney King in March of 1991. Apparently, in the eyes of the police officers who beat Rodney King, he epitomized the Black villain. Yet Feagin and Vera substantiate that though King's physical stature—Rodney King stands six feet tall and weighs 225 pounds—"could be intimidating to some ... he is not the giant monster that White officers portrayed him as at the Simi Valley trial."[11]

Some may counter Feagin and Vera's claims by arguing that the White supremacists in both Dubuque and the LAPD represent a racist fringe in the United States, a fringe that reveals nothing about core American ideals and traditions. But the most indicting evidence Feagin and Vera provide of this American tradition is not the examples of White supremacists in Dubuque, Iowa, or the racist culture within the Los Angeles Police Department. More compelling evidence is revealed by the actions of mainstream Americans like Charles Stuart, and powerful Americans like Presidents George H. W. Bush and Bill Clinton.

In October of 1989, Charles Stuart plotted to murder his pregnant wife, injure himself, and then blame these heinous crimes on a Black male attacker. Once Stuart's plan was carried out—apparently Stuart shot his wife and injured himself shortly before driving to the Mission Hill area of Boston, Massachusetts—he carphoned the Boston police. Stuart described his fictitious attacker as a Black man "with a wispy beard, about 5'10" tall ... wearing a black jogging suit with red stripes and driving gloves with the knuckles cut out."[12] The Boston police conducted a massive search for a Black criminal who existed only in Stuart's imagination and arrested a real man, William Bennet, identified by Stuart in a police lineup.

A year before Charles Stuart's racial hoax, during the 1988 presidential campaign, George H. W. Bush's television advertisements aired images of Willie Horton, a convicted felon who was Black and male. In addition to these television ads, the Bush campaign used Horton's image in brochures, campaign letters, and campaign speeches to defeat Michael Dukakis for the presidency of the United States. The common hallucination encouraged by the Bush campaign was that if Dukakis were elected president, then the "Willie Hortons"—that is, Black male criminals—would run wild in the streets and communities throughout the United States. Bill Clinton also manipulated mainstream fears of Black violence. During the 1992 presidential campaign, Bill Clinton attacked Sister Souljah, a Black female activist and rap artist, "for comments she reportedly made to *Washington Post* reporter David Mills."[13] In an attempt to explain the anger, frustration, and alienation of urban Black gang members, Souljah implicated the disregard that White Americans have for the loss of Black lives in urban communities. She explained that those Black gang members who believe and resent that the (white) government does not care if Blacks kill Blacks, may care even less if Blacks kill Whites.[14] By condemning Sister Souljah's comment, Bill Clinton proved "he could stand up to the so-called interest groups (code words used increasingly to mean black, latino, feminist, and gay groups) in the Democratic Party."[15] However, Clinton's attack upon Sister Souljah also suggested that he was less sensitive to the actual loss of black life in inner-city communities than to mainstream voters' hallucinations about black-on-white crime. The Clinton campaign viewed attacking Sister Souljah and thereby allaying mainstream delusions as a politically advantageous strategy.

Hence, in a country where White Americans comprise 70 percent of all arrests and where "80 percent of all crime involves a victim and offender of the same race,"[16] Charles Stuart, George Bush, and Bill Clinton tapped into a mainstream belief in Black male criminality, a myth that each one of them manipulated for personal gain. Stuart's hoax as well as Bush and Clinton's campaign strategies "depended on the common white belief in black criminality, and [they] worked."[17]

The cases of Dubuque, Rodney King and the LAPD, Charles Stuart, George Bush, and Bill Clinton are just a few examples elaborated by Feagin and Vera, and they elaborate them with far more detail, complexity, and evidence than the summaries above. Feagin and Vera observe, "It is likely that a majority of whites today view young black males in most everyday situations as potentially dangerous."[18]

The "Criminalblackman"

In *The Color of Crime: Racial Hoaxes, White Fear, Black Protectionism and Other Macroaggressions*, Katheryn K. Russell refers to this common white belief in black criminality as "the myth of the *criminalblackman*."[19] Russell explains how this abstraction or myth is rendered more concrete—or in more scholarly terms, is reified—by a variety of sources including "reality" police television shows like *Cops*, rap music videos, and many local nightly news programs. Like Feagin and Vera, Russell provides ample evidence of a common belief in black criminality by enumerating several white-on-black racial hoaxes like that committed by Charles Stuart.[20]

In addition to Stuart, Russell enumerates sixty-seven racial hoaxes reported in newspapers across the United States that occurred between 1987 and 1996. Russell points out that "these sixty-seven cases represent only a fraction of all racial hoax cases, since most racial hoaxes are not classified or reported as such."[21] One of the most infamous examples was the racial hoax perpetuated by Susan Smith. In 1994, Smith drowned her two sons—Michael, who was three years old, and Alexander, who was fourteen months old)—by restraining them in their car seats, and allowing her car to roll into the John D. Long Lake located outside of Union, South Carolina.[22] As reported by Barbara Vobejda of the *Washington Post*, Smith claimed "a black man forced her at gunpoint from the car" and kidnapped her sons.[23]

Out of the sixty-seven hoaxes listed by Russell, 70 percent "involve Whites who fabricated crimes against Blacks."[24] Russell admits that though a racial hoax may be perpetuated by a member of any racial-ethnic group and against a member of any racial-ethnic group, white-on-black hoaxes, like those committed by Charles Stuart and Susan Smith, are particularly problematic. Russell elaborates:

> Anyone, of any race, who perpetuates a hoax with a Black villain should face criminal punishment.... Racial hoaxes that target Blacks, create a distinct, more acute social problem than hoaxes that target people of other races. Blacks in general and young Black men in particular are saddled with a deviant image.... Racial hoaxes are devised, perpetuated, and successful precisely because they tap into widely held fears. The harm of the racial hoax is not limited to reinforcing centuries-old, deviant images of Blacks. Hoaxes also create these images for each new generation.[25]

As eloquently phrased by Charles Laurence, a reporter for the *Daily Telegraph*, Smith, like Stuart, gave her hoax "initial credibility by picking just the right character for the role of carjacker. A black man, of course: the bogeyman of honest Americans, of all races, who live in fear of crime.... The carjacker in the sinister knitted cap, of course, existed only in Smith's imagination and the national prejudice."[26]

Feagin and Vera, as well as Russell, argue that this myth of Blacks as deviants predates contemporary television images, presidential campaigns, racial hoaxes, and white supremacists in Dubuque, Iowa, and the LAPD. Feagin and Vera argue that the "tendency to view people of African descent as deviant or criminal is centuries old."[27] Feagin and Vera elaborate:

> [A]nti-African images were imported by the colonies, where images born in European ignorance were used to justify the subjugation of Africans bought and sold as slaves. Negative images of African Americans were accepted by the framers of the Declaration of Independence and the U.S. Constitution. Prominent European Americans in the early history of this nation were slave holders, including the southerners George Washington, James Madison, and Thomas Jefferson.... Writing in *Notes on Virginia*, Jefferson argued that what he saw as the ugly color, offensive odor, and ugly hair of African American slaves indicated their physical inferiority and that their alleged inability to create was a sign of mental inferiority.[28]

Russell maintains that the slave codes, black codes, and other statutes institutionalized racist ideas about Black Americans. The slave codes were enacted in various states from the early 1600s to the mid-1800s in order to dehumanize and regulate the lives of American slaves; formal and informal black codes were enacted from the mid-1800s through the mid-1900s to dehumanize and regulate the lives of African Americans. Russell explains that as time marched forward from the 1600s to the

1900s, "[o]ne constant remained as the slave codes became the Black codes and the Black codes became segregation statutes: *Blackness itself was a crime.*"[29]

When the driver in the opening vignette of this chapter bumped my car and fled the scene after vilifying my teenaged passengers as "gang bangers," he invoked symbolic violence and continued an age-old American pastime or tradition. This dehumanizing tradition should be socially condemned, but is as taken for granted as "baseball, hotdogs, apple pie, and Chevrolet." The case of Ryan Harris that follows further substantiates and updates Russell's assertion: blackness, especially urban blackness, itself is still a crime.

The Murder of Ryan Harris

The news media are instrumental in disseminating villainous images of Black males. Presidents Bush and Clinton, as well as individual citizens like Charles Stuart and Susan Smith, have relied upon print and broadcast media to animate sentiments and symbols that vilify Black males. Though examples of the new media's complicity abound, the coverage of the Ryan Harris murder case exemplifies vilification run amok.

Ryan Harris, an eleven-year-old African-American girl from the Englewood section of the South Side of Chicago, was brutally murdered in July of 1998. Two African-American boys, ages seven and eight, were arrested for her murder. Evidence eventually cleared these little boys of her murder. This evidence included semen found on Ryan Harris's body that the boys were too young to produce, as well as the degree to which her head had been bashed using a force that exceeded the strength a seven- or eight-year-old boy could muster. However, had it not been for DNA evidence that linked a twenty-nine-year-old convict to the scene of the crime, these two preadolescent boys would have probably been falsely accused of this heinous crime. This time, instead of a fictitious Black criminal conjured up by Charles Stuart or Susan Smith, the news media (and police) projected the mythical image of the *criminalblackman* upon *preadolescent boys*! Alex Kotlowitz, one of the journalists who initially covered this case, acknowledges the news media's complicity and his jump to unfounded conclusions.

> Like many other journalists, I was drawn to the case: What went wrong in these two boys' lives? What do we do with such young killers? But as my colleagues and I would learn, we should have been asking, "Were they guilty?"[30]

Kotlowitz continues:

> Had these boys been white or middle class, would other journalists and I have looked at our own children and asked the obvious: Were children so small (the tallest was 4'2") capable of such brutality? Were such young children capable of sexual assault? We often don't listen particularly well to voices that don't sound like our own. And in fact, from the moment these boys were arrested, Englewood residents were telling reporters they didn't believe these boys had killed Ryan Harris. Were we really hearing what they were saying?[31]

The answer to Kotlowitz's question, "Were [the journalists] really hearing what [residents] were saying?" is, "No." The journalists (and police) paid little attention to the residents of Englewood. In the midst of the media frenzy surrounding the case, the little boys were transformed into criminalblackmen. Though all signs pointed to their innocence, it took DNA evidence to exonerate them. Richard Roeper, columnist for the *Chicago-Sun Times*, initially stoked the frenzy. He now describes the media response as an "invasion of Englewood" during which journalists ignored Englewood residents, jumped to conclusions, and presumed the boys were guilty.[32] In addition to the myth of the criminalblackman, another force behind the media frenzy was the desires of journalists to make their careers. Roeper admits, after retrospection, that he and other journalists should have taken a different approach than presuming the boys were guilty.

> Reporters can make careers on a case like this. [But] the career to be made was to maybe step back away from the frenzy and do the solid reporting that some people eventually did that would show us that what we thought at the beginning was not true.[33]

Despite the retrospective regrets expressed by journalists like Kotlowitz and Roeper, the news media's response to the Ryan Harris murder case is more the rule than the exception.[34] These media espouse, build upon, and disseminate mythical images that are powerful, stigmatizing, and symbolically violent. As observed by Martín Sánchez Jankowski, "[T]he sociological consequence [of mythical images] is that images have a way of maintaining themselves in the public's mind and in the absence of quality information and analyses, these images have become the primary prisms through which people construct an understanding of social reality."[35] Images of villainy, criminality, and malevolence were the primary prisms through which the preadolescent boys were viewed despite the existence of quality evidence that the boys were harmless and innocent.

IMAGINARY SPACE, THE FINAL FRONTIER?
(OR, WHAT'S *STAR TREK* GOT TO DO WITH IT?)

I have been a fan of *Star Trek*, the futuristic television series produced by Gene Roddenberry, since I was seven or so years old. I was particularly impressed with Lt. Uhura, the Black female communications officer who diversified the crew with dignity and grace that challenged prevailing stereotypes of Black women. Of course, by today's standards, the original *Star Trek* series and crew of Captain Kirk (of European-American descent), Lt. Sulu (of Japanese descent), Lt. Uhura (of African descent), Ensign Chekov (of Russian descent), and others—notably Scotty, Mr. Spock, and Dr. McCoy—are incredibly Eurocentric and patriarchal, despite this multiethnic cast of characters. This science fiction television show was, however, light years beyond other shows and Lt. Uhura was an inspiring role model. By the way, *Star Trek* producers derived "uhura" from "uhuru," which is Swahili for "freedom."[36]

Three decades after Captain Kirk and crew, there have been four new *Star Trek* series: *The Next Generation, Deep Space Nine, Voyager,* and *Enterprise.* Of the four,

Deep Space Nine has a 1990s counterpart to Lt. Uhura: Captain Benjamin Sisko. In this twenty-fourth century science fictional universe, Captain Sisko has been freed from twentieth-century stereotypes of Black males: he is the commanding officer of a station in a valuable quadrant of space and he is the emissary to an entire planet of spiritual people known as Bajorans. Captain Sisko is a loving, nurturing single father to his teenaged son, Jake, and was also a loving husband until the death of his wife. Captain Sisko exudes brilliance, charisma, courage, spirituality, as well as a host of other positive qualities including integrity, consideration, and compassion. He challenges the American tradition of characterizing Black males as deviants and villains and is, figuratively, galaxies away from one-dimensional, hard, remorseless, gang-banging characters like O-dog described in chapter 3. In this final frontier of space—or, more realistically, in this final frontier of the imaginations of science fiction writers—Black males are finally freed from traditional, limiting, dismal, symbolically violent characterizations. Well, not exactly. For example there are a couple of episodes—"Far beyond the Stars," and "Shadows and Symbols"—in which Captain Sisko is emasculated or devitalized. In these two episodes, Captain Sisko's emasculation may be pure coincidence. There are other episodes, one in particular, with blatant racialized symbols and undertones. *Deep Space Nine* episode fifty-two, titled "The Abandoned" is one such episode.[37]

Before describing this episode, a bit of background information may be necessary for those who are unfamiliar with the species, or more literally, races of *Deep Space Nine*. Among the many species who inhabit this futuristic world, there is a race of beings called the Jem'Hadar. The Jem'Hadar are a race of genetically engineered warriors. Like human beings, they walk upright, have two eyes, two ears, one nose, and one mouth. But, unlike humans, the Jem'Hadar, all of whom appear to be male, have grayish-colored, lizardlike skin, small horns that frame the periphery of their faces, and long, straight black hair that grows only across the top portion of their skulls. The look of the Jem'Hadar is so non-human and the special effects makeup is so elaborate that sometimes I cannot clearly discern the apparent racial-ethnicity of the actors beneath the make-up. Note other character traits of this genetically engineered race of savage warriors: they are ruthless, remorseless, murderous villains who, by design, desire to hunt and kill others. Furthermore, the Jem'Hadar have been genetically installed with a control mechanism: their bodies are genetically engineered to be addicted to a liquid substance referred to, in accordance with its color, as "white."

In episode fifty-two, "The Abandoned," an infant is found within the wreckage of a ship docked at Deep Space Nine. Although its metabolic rate is accelerated—eventually causing it to grow from infancy to preadolescence to young adulthood in a few, maybe two, weeks—this baby appears healthy. The exact species of this "young visitor" is unknown, and it otherwise appears human, except for an oblong-shaped star or flowerlike pattern in the center of its forehead. The baby (actor) used to represent this unknown species as an infant appears to be a honey-brown, black male, six months of age. Likewise, the actor used to represent this unknown species at eight years old (in human years) appears to be an ebony-brown preadolescent Black male. Similar to the infant, this preadolescent appears mostly human except for a couple of small, star-like patterns on his forehead and a slight blotchiness to his dark, grayish-brown, almost black skin.[38] Unlike the baby, whose presence and appearance remind Captain Sisko of his son, Jake, as an infant, the preadolescent's expression is serious and tough; but both the baby and preadolescent are, noticeably, Black and male. The airtime during which the infant's face appears on the screen amounts to ten, maybe fifteen, seconds and the preadolescent's, thirty to forty seconds. The preadolescent briefly questions Captain Sisko in a monotone that is slightly inquisitive but remarkably serious for an eight-year-old: "Who are you? . . . I need food. . . . Where am I? . . . "

In a few more hours or so, this young visitor matures from a preadolescent to a teenager who seems sixteen to eighteen years old, a growth rate that appears natural for its species. As a teenager, the species of this "visitor" is finally discernible: he is a Jem'Hadar. As a teenager, he has finally developed, as mentioned above, grayish-colored, lizardlike skin, small horns that frame the periphery of his face, and long, straight black hair that grows only across the top portion of his skull. This teenaged Jem'Hadar also manifests symptoms of his genetically engineered addiction to some sort of "isogeneic enzyme": he shivers, feels sick, and has pains in his head and chest. This teenaged male desires nothing but to fight, to maim, to kill; he is tough, arrogant, and remorseless. And despite the attempts of Odo, one of the crew members, to teach this young, ruthless warrior that there is more to life than fighting and killing, this young visitor desires three things: to reunite with other Jem'Hadar, to fight, and to kill. Bumper Robinson, the actor who plays the teenaged Jem'Hadar, is a young Black male.

As an in-class exercise on focus groups, I showed "The Abandoned" to seventeen students who took my graduate seminar on qualitative methods.[39] The racial majority of these students was White/European, and the gender majority was female; however, seven were students of color (Asians and Blacks), five were "international students," and four were males.[40] As moderator, I asked the students, "Which, if any, of the following four messages/stereotypes were the most apparent in 'The Abandoned': gender, race, class, and/or nationality?" In addition to racial stereotypes, these students clearly identified gender and cultural—both middle-class culture and American culture—stereotypes, and a few students indicated that Captain Sisko challenged prevailing stereotypes about Black males. However, ten students identified racial stereotypes or messages as the most apparent in the episode. Admittedly, this response rate may have been influenced by the fact that the moderator was African American, yet there were students—one of whom was also a Black female—for whom race was not the most apparent stereotype. One student, a European-American male, wrote that this episode conveys American racial traditions, traditions that included the vilification of Black males. In the openended portion of the survey he completed after viewing "The Abandoned," this student expressed:

> The episode started out heavy on the gender stereotypes. It seems that even thousands of years in the future, a little bit of cleavage or a few soft words can make rich men foolishly part with their money. However, as the show progressed it became less focused on gender and much more focused on race. I should explain that I have always considered the *Star Trek* "universe" of alien races to be comprised of stereotypical analogies to racial categories on earth today. For instance, on the old show Spock and his race [of Vulcans] were stereo-

typed as Asians: Cold, logical, calculating, emotionless. Klingons were Blacks: Strong, aggressive and irrational. The new *Star Trek* added, among other [races], the Ferengi: A Jewish stereotype of short creatures with big ears and bulbous noses who make up a merchant class of highly skilled financiers. This show's ["The Abandoned"] racial theme almost worked like an argument from *The Bell Curve*. As hard as the civilized White master [Odo] tried to help his Jem'Hadar—(another African American stereotype)—pupil on a path to self-improvement, [this Jem'Hadar's] genetic make-up prevented him from learning or overcoming his agressive, anti-social nature. I think it's no surprise that no Klingons (the other "Black" alien race) were in the episode and that the actor who played the Jem'Hadar was always African-American.[41]

Another student, an African-American female, wrote:

Race [was the most apparent stereotype]. The idea that there is a proclivity towards violence among a certain people that need to be shown a way they can live nonviolently. The way the founder, Odo, tried to deny the inferiority/superiority issue but later admitted that the difference was too great among some [races] to make them civilized, mirrored a stereotypical and racist belief in the U.S. The addiction to a substance controlled by those of a greater species was also disturbing and brought to mind the drug trafficking issues between black communities and whites. And [the most racist belief was] that this violent species was born a black child [who] grew into a science fiction equivalent of a black man.[42]

I acknowledge that the students from this graduate seminar may not be representative of those who view *Star Trek* episodes on a regular basis, and those who identified the racial stereotypes of "The Abandoned" as among the most apparent may be more sensitized to racial subtexts and traditions than the typical viewer of *Star Trek*. However, similar to Toni Morrison's content analyses of American literary works, these students saw racial stereotypes reified or rendered more concrete in "The Abandoned." Even in a futuristic television show dedicated to promoting diversity, the age-old "tendency to view people of African descent as deviant or criminal" persists.[43] The failure of *Star Trek* writers to break away from the practice of vilifying Black males indicates the symbolic and metaphorical utility of this tradition.

"STICKS AND STONES ... AND METAPHORS"

In contrast to my analysis of the Jem'Hadar episode in which the writers link blackness to ruthlessness, I entertained the idea that Captain Sisko's emasculation in other episodes may have been pure coincidence. However, like Joe Feagin, Hernán Vera and Katheryn Russell, literary scholar Toni Morrison would argue—and I agree—that very little in the American popular imagination about blackness can be chalked up to coincidence. As stated by Morrison, little remains uninfluenced "by the four-hundred-year-old presence of, first Africans and then African-Americans in the United States," a presence that has "shaped the body politic, the Constitution, and the entire history of the culture."[44] Hence, American literary writers are unlikely to link "Whiteness" to impotence. Likewise, *Star Trek* writers are less likely to link White captains like Kirk, Picard, Janeway, or Archer to the Earth's history of classism or sexism than they are to emasculate Sisko and link him to Earth's history of racism.

The writers are much more likely to cast Captain Sisko, a Black character, in some degree of negative light or, more figuratively, imagine him in some sort of negative and traditional dark. Yet a clearer indication of the symbolically violent tendencies of the American popular imagination manifests in "The Abandoned": stereotypes materialize in the use of a Black baby and preadolescent male to signify a race of brutal warriors *before* this "young visitor" develops the horns and lizardlike skin that are characteristics of its species. These writers and producers used a Black baby and preadolescent boy, both of whom wear very little special effects makeup, to allude to and symbolize the full-grown Jem'Hadar prone to tough, savage, ruthless behavior and addicted to an "isogeneic enzyme," a sort of liquid cocaine or crack.

If blackness and whiteness—not to mention maleness—were neutral concepts, then any baby or preadolescent with mere, subtle markings on its forehead could have portrayed the Jem'Hadar. If these were neutral concepts, Charles Stuart would have blamed the murder of his wife on any criminal, not a "Black" one, and Susan Smith would have claimed that she had been carjacked, without particularly emphasizing that the carjacker was a "black man with a gun."[45] If blackness, whiteness, and maleness, or more specifically black-maleness, were neutral, unsymbolic, unloaded concepts, there would be no myth of the criminalblackman upon which the Bush and Clinton campaigns could rely for political gain. Similar to Stuart, Smith, Bush, and Clinton, the writers and producers of *Deep Space Nine* knew that a phenotypically or symbolically "White" baby and adolescent with very little special effects makeup, flashed across the screen for seconds and uttering a few monotone words, would not have epitomized toughness, villainy, or ruthlessness in the minds of an American television audience. Even in the final frontier of science fictional space, writers and producers engage in what prize-winning novelist Toni Morrison refers to as "playing in the dark."

Morrison uses the metaphor "playing in the dark" to capture how White American literary scholars imagine and construct blackness and whiteness to reflect America's racial hierarchy. The intent of these scholars may not have been racist, per se. Yet irrespective of non-racist intentions toward Africans and African Americans, racialized metaphors in American literature have, among other things, facilitated color coding and thereby reified racial stereotypes. Although Morrison uses "playing in the dark" to apply specifically to American literary writers—and I borrow it here to apply to science fiction writers—this metaphor applies to the more general American mainstream tradition of linking "Black" males and villainy. To figuratively capture this widespread tradition, which extends well beyond works of fiction, the metaphor "*playing* in the dark" does not suffice. I would describe Charles Stuart and others like Susan Smith who concoct racial hoaxes to conceal heinous crimes as "hiding in the dark." I would describe Bush's and Clinton's campaigns as "politicizing the dark." Journalists were "preying or capitalizing upon the dark" as they covered the Ryan Harris murder case. Finally, "fearing, afraid, or scared of the dark" characterizes the actions of the arrogant driver (described in the opening vignette of this chapter) and others who fear street-savvy students who are "Black" and male. In this chapter, I have cast light upon "the dark" to reveal its violent and stigmatizing impact upon street-savvy students.

Why are we so afraid of Black (and Latino) urban students from low-income neighborhoods? "The dark" has become a dehumanizing prism through which Black males are viewed. "The dark" as metaphor and stereotype blinds us to the reality and complexity of the lives of Black (and Brown, that is, Latino) street-savvy students. What does *Star Trek* have to do with symbolic violence? In the final frontier of imaginary, *futuristic* space, writers re-create and reify age-old stereotypes. Urban students compete with pervasive, distorting fictional images from literary and science fictional sources to be seen as fully human instead of monsters or Jem'Hadar.

Feagin and Vera would probably describe these acts of playing, hiding, politicizing, preying upon, and fearing "the dark" literally instead of metaphorically as white racism: "White racism can be viewed as the socially organized set of attitudes, ideas, and practices that deny African Americans and other people of color the dignity, opportunities, freedoms, and rewards that this nation offers White Americans."[46] I agree with Feagin and Vera, but emphasize that even if those who play, hide, politicize, prey upon, or fear "the dark" view themselves as humanitarians and non-racists—as is probably the case with *Star Trek* writers and producers—their actions have negative consequences for urban students who are young, Black males.

Black urban students, or more specifically the students from my study, frequently interact with self-described "non-racist," "nonviolent" individuals of various racial-ethnic backgrounds including African Americans, individuals who verbally assault, insult, or imagine them as "gang bangers" or "thugs." My students live and interact within a society that, historically and contemporaneously, labels them as "deviant criminalblackmen." My students compete with pervasive, distorting fictional images from literary and science fictional sources to be seen as fully human instead of monsters. In my expert opinion, Black and Brown urban students' frequent exposure to these multiple mechanisms of symbolic violence is, at the very least, debilitating and frustrating. Even more, as indicated by Malik's story in chapter 2, this violent tradition may contribute to the social forces that push street-savvy students out of school.

As revealed in chapter 1, researchers have clearly identified the social-structural forces (for example, historic discrimination, residential discrimination and segregation, lack of viable job opportunities, concentrated poverty, inadequate school facilities) that limit the life chances of urban students from low-income communities.[47] Fewer researchers have devoted time to exploring, in the words of Dana Y. Takagi, how "race as a constructed ideology—common sense and popular thought [and] stereotypes" is equally as important.[48] This "common sense and popular thought"—these myths embodied in racialized metaphors or symbols impose themselves as real. Metaphorically playing, hiding, politicizing, preying upon, or fearing "the dark" has the illusion of being harmless imaginings, sentiments, strategies, reactions, and so on. Yet, as I have argued from the start of this chapter, these practices are harmful acts of violence. Unlike those who engage in blatantly racist or physical acts of violence, those who engage in symbolic violence may not even be sensitized to or aware of "the many established ways of acting, feeling, and thinking that perpetuate antiblack racism."[49] Many American mainstream practices fall under the rubric of symbolic violence. Feagin and Vera list but a few of them:

Symbolic violence resides in relentless stereotyping, the media's exclusionary standards of beauty, and the educational system's insensitivities to the needs of multicultural communities. Symbolic violence can include white [police] officers' hostile words and body language, which reveal disrespect for black people and culture, as well as white officers' show of force in black communities when they stop and interrogate black men just because they are black. Symbolic violence is expressed in images of blacks as inferior or as "gorillas in the mist." Many whites in all sectors of society acquiesce or participate in acts of symbolic violence even though they disapprove of physical violence.[50]

Symbolic violence also includes fictional constructs of blackness, racial hoaxes, political strategies, news media feeding frenzies, and the exclamations of passers-by who see Black urban youths who are not criminals and recoil, "Oh shit! Gang bangers!" Sticks and social-structural stones may break urban youths' bones, *and* violent words, metaphors, and symbols can also hurt them!

EIGHT

Policy Implications for *Individuals* in Positions of Influence

"TO SEE THINGS AND PEOPLE BIG"

In *Releasing the Imagination: Essays on Education, the Arts, and Social Change*, Maxine Greene borrows novelist Thomas Mann's distinction between seeing the world small and seeing the world big.

> To see things or people small, one chooses to see from a detached point of view, to watch behaviors from the perspective of a system, to be concerned with trends and tendencies rather than the intentionality and concreteness of everyday life. To see things or people big, one must resist viewing other human beings as mere objects or chess pieces and view them in their integrity and particularity instead. One must see from the point of view of the participant in the midst of what is happening if one is to be privy to the plans people make, the initiatives they take, the uncertainties they face.[1]

Tough Fronts, generally speaking, embraces the view of things big and sees schooling and the streets from the students' points of view. The chapters herein have provided access to the plans students make, the initiatives they take, and the uncertainties they face. This is especially true of chapters 2 through 6, where students define the streets, differentiate between hardcore and hardcore wannabe postures, critique unempathetic teachers, praise "down" teachers, and respond favorably to mentors. And though the introduction, chapter 1, and chapter 7 provide more contextual, cultural, and structural findings, these chapters also shed light on the unique situations of urban students. The students of this study have figured prominently throughout this book; they have never been reduced to statistics or percentages or test scores or "accountability measures."

In sculpting a concluding chapter on the policy implications of this study, however, I feel trapped between things small and things big. As a sociologist, and as revealed by chapters 1 and 7, I am trained to see things or students small, from the distanced perspective of a system—for example, a school system or district, a political system, a cultural system, an economic system, an ideological system, and so on. From this things-or-people-small perspective, my policy suggestions should be broad-based and call for school reforms that are fundamental and systematic. I should be "preoccupied with test scores, 'time on task,' management procedures, ethnic and racial percentages, and accountability measures, while [I screen out] the faces and gestures of individuals, of actual living persons."[2] On the other hand, as an ethnographer who hangs out with urban youths, I embrace the things-or-people-big perspective; I document the faces and gestures of actual living persons and report my findings with great attention to the details of everyday life. While both points of view are useful and necessary, the major findings of *Tough Fronts* best support policy suggestions that see things big. Once again, Maxine Greene's words echo my sentiments:

> When applied to schooling, the vision that sees things big brings us in close contact with details and particularities that cannot be reduced to statistics or even the measurable. There are the worn-down, crowded urban classrooms and the contrasting clean-lined spaces in the suburbs. . . . There are shouts, greetings, threats, the thump of rap music, gold chains, flowered leotards, multicolored hair. . . . For the one seeing things large, there are occasionally teachers who view every act as "a new beginning, a raid on the inarticulate / With shabby equipment always deteriorating / In the general mess of imprecision of feeling, undisciplined squads of emotion" (Eliot, [1943] 1958, p. 128). But there are also other kinds of teachers: those without a sense of agency, those who impose inarticulateness on students who seem alien and whose voices teachers prefer not to hear. *Yet the eager teachers do appear and reappear—teachers who provoke learners to pose their own questions, to teach themselves, to go at their own pace, to name their worlds. Young learners have to be noticed, it is now being realized; they have to be consulted, they have to question why.* (emphasis added)[3]

"Yet the eager teachers do appear and reappear . . ." The students in this study, though they lament that most teachers do not understand the streets, praise the eager teachers like Ms. Bronzic (chapter 4) who appear from time to time. They praise the eager youth workers and mentors like Dean Lewis and Louis Johnsson (chapters 5 and 6) who appear from time to time. They even praise the eager students, like Robbie (chapter 3), who appear from time to time. Thus, I write my policy suggestions with eager teachers, youth workers, and mentors in mind. Though I will briefly discuss broad-based social policies, the bulk of my suggestions for school reform are offered for use by individuals. By pitching policy suggestions toward individuals in positions of influence, I commend those who are already making a difference in the lives of urban students like those in this study. I seek to facilitate the appearance and reappearance of more eager teachers, youth workers, and mentors.

By drawing attention to the influence of individuals, I do not suggest that individual enthusiasm trumps social structure; it does no such thing. I do not subscribe to the American myth of rugged individualism that exclaims, "[I]t is the moral fabric of individuals, not the social and economic structure of society that is . . . the root of the problem."[4] On the contrary, at the root of the problem *are* social structures that constrain, oppress, and impose upon individuals. And in fairness to the teachers who are not eager to interact with street-savvy students, their lack of enthusiasm is probably enhanced or facilitated by the support structure of schooling. By that I mean, these teachers may not be supported by superintendents, mayors, state legislators, and so on, to better teach urban students who are at risk. Even worse, these teachers may be underpaid, overstressed, and underresourced. By drawing attention to those teachers and other individuals who remain eager, however, I illuminate the degree to which they resist, contest, protest, and challenge social-structural constraints. By seeing "things or people big," these individuals fine-tune and supplement the process of schooling to meet the unique needs of street-savvy students. They raise hope for schools as great equalizers (or, at least, adequate minimizers) of inequality.

HOPE FOR SCHOOLS AS GREAT EQUALIZERS OF INEQUALITY

Some of the most recent broad-based school reforms that target urban public schools include raised standards of learning to render teachers and students more accountable, the radical decentralization and restructuring of entire school districts, and school choice or vouchers.[5] These reforms embrace a view of "things or people small" and, to reiterate Maxine Greene's words, are more "concerned with trends and tendencies rather than the intentionality and concreteness of everyday life." Some of these reforms call for longer school days and longer school years without adequately addressing why urban students from low-income communities tend to have low attendance rates. For example, the students in this study feel pushed out of the present school system because teachers express little respect for their lives beyond school walls. Longer days and school years do not address the lack of teacher empathy, the myth of black inferiority, or the American tradition of vilifying Black males; all of these factors contribute to rates of low educational achievement. Furthermore, as discussed in chapters 2 and 4, some street-savvy students refuse to cooperate with non-caring teachers, and without student-teacher cooperation, the realization of higher test scores and other accountability measures are destined to fall short. Hence, instead of enhancing the ability of schools to minimize inequality, broad-based social policies may reproduce failure rates for street-savvy students. The remaining pages of this chapter aim to reignite hope for schools as equalizers of inequality.

Late nineteenth and early twentieth century social scientists described public schools as great equalizers of inequality. More specifically, these scholars believed schools were instrumental in providing children from disadvantaged backgrounds with the requisite values, skills, and competencies for entering the American mainstream.[6] According to this belief:

> [Public] schools have been designed to open broad horizons to the child, transcending the limitations of the parents, and have taken children from disparate cultural backgrounds into the mainstream of American culture. They have been a major element in social mobility, freeing children from the poverty of their parents and the low status of their social origins. They have been a means of stripping away identities of ethnicities and social origins and implanting a common American identity.[7]

Despite this ambitious dream about the power of schooling, study after study reveals that social economic origins are linked to rates of educational success. In other words, schools are not great equalizers of inequality; instead, schools tend to reproduce inequality. Students who hail from social backgrounds of affluence surpass their economically disadvantaged counterparts in achieving positive educational outcomes.[8]

Instead of giving up on schools that serve students who are economically disadvantaged, there are various educational innovations designed to make schools better equalizers of inequality. These innovations are too numerous to list. For example, according to Michael Fullan in *The New Meaning of Educational Change*:

> It is impossible to estimate the number of innovative programs. In New York City's board of education, for example, 781 innovative programs were piloted between 1979 and 1981.... And that was a quiet period compared with the innovation boom since 1983 following the release of *A Nation at Risk*. If we broaden the term innovation to include all educational changes occurring through legislation, new and revised curricula, and special projects—in short, any practice new to the person attempting to cope with an educational problem—it is clear that change is common fare for school people.[9]

The findings of this book may be of use to a variety of educational innovators, but they contribute most directly to research efforts to make schools more effective at minimizing inequality. The findings contribute most directly to effective schools research and the reforms inspired by the effective schools movement. Effective schools research "has been controversial, but it offers useful ideas about how to improve education that continue to be provocative even now that the educational agenda shifts from equity to excellence and rebuilding the nation's capacity to compete in the international markets."[10]

Effective schools research resurrects the early-twentieth-century faith in public schools as levelers, or, at least, minimizers of inequality. Instead of identifying the mechanisms associated with schooling that reproduce social inequality, effective schools researchers enumerate the factors that allow schools to reduce the inequality preexisting in society. For example, several studies demonstrate that some urban schools predominantly serving impoverished Black students successfully provide these students with the skills necessary for escaping poverty.[11] These effective schools generally have the following characteristics: (1) principals who are effective leaders, visionaries, and role models for teachers and students; (2) teachers with high expectations of all students regardless of the socioeconomic background of these students; (3) a school environment or climate free from vandalism, violence, and disciplinary problems and otherwise conducive to learning; (4) a school-wide emphasis on the acquisition of basic skills; (5) cooperation between parents, teachers, and administrators that encourages and facilitates student achievement; and (6) a pervasive and positive school ethos or community of values sensitive to the needs of students. In contrast to the influential "Coleman Report" of 1966, which claimed that *quantitative* school factors are less powerful than family background factors in determining educational success, effective schools researchers argue that *qualitative* factors like those above affect student achievement more than the student's family background or socioeconomic origins.

In addition to the six factors above, my research suggests that effective schools for street-savvy students must have the following qualitative characteristics: (7) "down" teachers who understand the code of the streets and provide viable advice about securing safe passage through the danger zones of street culture; (8) ritual practices and curricular content designed to deconstruct debilitating, pervasive stereotypes about ethnic minorities from low-income communities, especially myths of black inferiority and villainous caricatures of Black and Brown males; (9) access to positive male role models who can challenge limited definitions of masculinity and who have the insight and experiences to call the bluff on hardcore behavior; and (10) links to viable economic opportunities in the formal economy that render participation in illicit, underground economic activities unnecessary. My research findings suggest that schools with these characteristics will facilitate positive educational outcomes for street-savvy students. Sadly, my research findings also suggest that the schools serving the students of this study met few, if any, of these ten effective schools' criteria.

Critics of the effective schools research categorize it as unrepresentative and simplistic.[12] They do not return to the Coleman Report's conclusion that public schools are inherently less powerful than family background in determining student achievement. Instead, they argue that many schools "serving predominantly low-income or black students, may be lacking in most or all of the characteristics of an effective school."[13] Nevertheless, proponents uphold that research on effective schools is important because of the "diversity of research and methods that have produced similar conclusions and because of the *common-sense power* of its principal claims" (emphasis mine).[14] I summarize and supplement these common-sense claims with the hope that they are of use to individuals who are eager to improve classrooms and schools for street-savvy students.

"DOWN" TEACHERS FOR STREET-SAVVY STUDENTS

Research findings on the Paul Robeson Institute (chapter 6) shed particular light upon the effective schools criterion of "teachers with high expectations of all students." High expectations devoid of empathy for life on the streets may inadvertently push street-savvy students out of school. In addition to high expectations, teachers should strive to understand what life is like for street-savvy students. In other words, in order to effectively serve the needs of street-savvy students, public schools need more down teachers. As defined by the students in this study, there are two types of "down" teachers: (1) teachers who understand the code of the streets, and (2) teachers who may not personally understand this code but care enough to learn about the challenges of street culture from their students. Teachers who care but do not understand the code of the streets will at least take the time to hear students out. And the one thing that both types of down teachers have in common is that students can talk openly to them about the pressures of street culture. A call for more down teachers is not a call for more Black or Latino/Latina teachers, per se, if skin color is the only thing these teachers share with students. This is a call, instead, for teachers who not only value the cultural capital of the American mainstream, but who do not implicitly or explicitly devalue the cultural assets necessary for surviving urban streets.

Schools need down teachers who not only have high expectations of all students, but who can help urban youths to successfully navigate the illicit aspects or danger zones of street culture by providing such youths with viable alternatives, viable advice, and if necessary, productive disciplinary responses. These disciplinary responses, like those described in chapter 6, should help students to understand the long-term consequences of gangsterlike posturing instead of condemning the short-term, strategic function of hard postures or tough fronts. As I have said in earlier chapters, well-intentioned advice from teachers like "just say no" and "just walk away" reflect a lack of understanding of the code of the streets or the realities of survival on the streets.

Finally, to serve street-savvy students more effectively, teachers must assert and reiterate that inner city students from low-income backgrounds, especially Black males and Latinos, are not suspension, expulsion, and dropout accidents waiting to happen. Teachers must assert this to themselves and to the street-savvy students with whom they interact. However, instead of a solo performance, these teachers should be part of a chorus of school officials; they should be part of a concerted effort of school policies, practices, and rituals that declare, loud and clear, "Urban students from low income communities can excel in school!"

I do not profess to have all the answers about how one becomes down with street-savvy students, but the following are steps in the right direction.

1. Get to know, personally, street-savvy students on their own terms. This knowledge is best acquired by spending quality time in urban communities and at sites where urban students hang out. If such site visits are not feasible, then hold discussions and forums within schools that allow street-savvy students to enlighten teachers about the realities and challenges of street culture.

2. Learn to value the ethnic cultures of street-savvy students. Gloria Ladson-Billings has found that successful teachers of ethnic children may not always share their students' ethnicity, but these teachers do share an appreciation of their students' cultural orientations and abilities.[15] However, appreciation for the ethnic culture(s) of students is not a cure-all. Lisa Delpit cautions, and I agree, that "culture is but one tool that educators may make use of when devising solutions for a school's difficulty in educating diverse children."[16] Nonetheless, teachers who value their students' culture, like Marva Collins and Jaime Escalante, are "quietly going about the job of producing excellence in educating poor and culturally diverse students ... students considered uneducable by public schools."[17]

3. With respect to the *few* students who move beyond posturing to fully internalizing gangsterlike beliefs, become familiar with the complexity of social-structural forces that constrain and negatively affect urban communities and become sensitized to the code of the streets that ensues from such forces. The works of William Julius Wilson and Elijah Anderson, revisited in chapter 1, provide a wealth of information on constraining social structures (*Bad Boys: Public Schools in the Making of Black Masculinity* by Ann Arnett Ferguson is also highly informative).

4. And, if social scientific studies are not your cup of tea, read biographies that portray the complex realities and constraints of inner-city life that may influence some urban youths to become hard. From Claude Brown's *Manchild in the Promised Land* to *The Autobiography of Malcolm X* to *Monster: The Autobiography of an L.A. Gang Member* by Monster Kody Scott, there are several works that,

without condoning gangsterlike behavior, reveal the *human vulnerabilities* of those who become hard. One biographical work that I highly recommend is Fox Butterfield's *All God's Children: The Bosket Family and the American Tradition of Violence*. Butterfield documents the family history and life story of Willie Bosket, who has been called "the most violent youth that the criminal justice system has ever encountered."[18] Butterfield documents with great attention to detail the European-American historical legacies and traditions that are manifest in contemporary practices found in inner-city communities. For example, the code of honor practiced by Whites in the American South of the 1700s dictated that "a man had to be prepared to fight to defend his honor if challenged or insulted."[19] Butterfield links this code of honor to the code of respect common in inner-city streets. A shortcoming of Butterfield's work, though brilliantly detailed with historical and social structural explanations, is his tendency from time to time to offer observations mildy reminiscent of biological determinism. In any event, biographies such as these offer insights about why some youths actually become hard; these insights are profound and enlightening.

5. Approach statistics about urban crime with skepticism. For example, the oft-quoted statistic that one out of four—some studies report one out of three—Black males is in some phase of the criminal justice system is reason for concern. However, one out of four or twenty-five percent also means seventy-five percent of black males are in no phase of the criminal justice system. And of that twenty-five percent to maybe thirty-three percent who are in some phase of the criminal justice system, the vast majority are not school-aged and the vast majority are not hardcore criminals. When presented with statistics about black and brown male criminality, be mindful of the inequities of the criminal justice system; for example, Black males are five to seven times more likely than White males to be arrested for similar crimes.[20] Most importantly, remind yourself that a *few* Black and Brown students are hard, as are students of other hues, ethnicities, and social origins, but the *vast majority* of Black and Brown students are not hard at all.

In the introduction to this book, I explained that students who are Black or Brown, urban, from low-income families and male frequently find themselves wedged between a mainstream rock and a street cultural hard place, regardless of the degree to which they personally identify with the urban gangster. Down teachers, youth workers, and mentors help street-savvy students to avoid or safely navigate this predicament. Down individuals in positions of influence do not fuel social-structural constraints or endorse myths of black inferiority or black villainy. These individuals are no panacea or cure-all, but they are part of the solution instead of agents who further the social and cultural reproduction of inequality. These individuals look at street-savvy students and do not see detention, suspension, expulsion, or crime statistics waiting to happen. Down teachers, youth workers, and mentors see students as agents of their-story, youths who make decisions and choices within the context of inner-city conditions that are beyond these youths' control. Down teachers do not blame students for conditions and forces beyond their control; instead, they further students' awareness of those things that can be controlled.

Between the rock of American mainstream representatives who frequently view urban and inner-city students as thugs and villains and the hard place of urban streets that often require these students to don hard postures to survive, the students in this study are asking for help. As observed by Michael Apple, "The lived culture of these youths speaks to a subtle 'awareness' that the culture of the school and the formal knowledge in the curriculum is not responsive to black history or experience."[21] Hence, beneath the surface of hard postures are student critiques of a mechanism of schooling, namely uncaring teachers, that facilitates educational inequality. Students implicate teachers because within schools it is the teachers with whom these students interact the most. As indicated above in my discussion of the characteristics of effective schools, this shortage of caring teachers is but one of many schooling shortcomings. Furthermore, in the wider scheme of things, teachers are simply convenient scapegoats: uncaring teachers are forged by insufficiently resourced and uncaring school districts that exist within an uncaring nation that has vilified Blacks, other peoples of color, and people from financially impoverished backgrounds for centuries.

Urban and inner-city students, like those in this study, are asking for help with navigating a world that "sees them small," a world that looks at them from a distance and sees villains and thugs. They are asking for help in a country that through historic and contemporary discrimination has confined them to urban spaces that are socially isolated. They are asking for viable advice about how to navigate urban and inner-city communities with inadequate schools and rates of crime, joblessness, and poverty that are disproportionately high. For the students of this study, requests for help often fell upon the deafened or desensitized ears of teachers, other school officials, and the representatives of other mainstream institutions. We pay little or inadequate positive attention to these students throughout their middle and junior high school years and then blame them for donning hard postures. For individuals in positions of influence, the question is clear: Will you positively influence the lives and agency of urban and inner-city students, or will you leave these students to the limiting and constraining social conditions that are beyond their control?

A Brief Review of Selected Literature
Effective Schools and Critical Theory

Several social scientists have sought to explain both the persistence of poverty in urban ghettos and the low educational achievement of minorities when compared to their White counterparts. Some, like Arthur Jensen (1972, 1973) and, more recently, Richard Herrnstein and Charles Murray (1994), claim that Blacks are inherently less intelligent than Whites. Others, like Oscar Lewis (1968), Daniel Moynihan (1965), and Kenneth Clark (1965), argue that minorities from urban ghettos are victims of a culture of poverty or tangle of pathology. Explanations such as these are deficient, to say the least. As stated in chapter 1, culture-of-poverty explanations blame the victim without linking the failure of the victim to social-structural causes.[1] Claims that Blacks are inherently less intelligent than Whites are empirically unfounded, rely heavily upon sources that can be traced to white supremacist factions of the eugenics movement,[2] and overlook a host of environmental and cultural factors— some of which are discussed in this book—that must be considered when comparing Blacks to Whites.

This book seeks cross-theoretical dialogue with four types of studies that have offered explanations for the scholastic failure of low income and/or Black students: (1) statistical analyses that argue that a child's family background is a stronger determinant of educational achievement than school factors (Coleman et al. 1966; Jencks 1972, 1979); (2) critical theories that explain the mechanisms through which schools re-create inequality instead of leveling inequality (Bowles and Gintis 1976; Bourdieu and Passeron 1977; Willis 1977; Apple 1996, 2000); (3) school climate and ecology analyses that identify the characteristics of an effective school that are stronger determinants of educational attainment than family background factors (Edmonds 1979, 1989; Comer 1980; Brookover et al. 1979); and (4) social-structural theories about the impact of social dislocation, isolation, and discrimination on Black Americans (Ogbu 1978; Glasgow 1980; Wilson, 1987, 1996). Before discussing how my study compares and contrasts to previous research, I will highlight major findings.

THE COLEMAN REPORT

Late nineteenth and early twentieth century social scientists describe schools as great equalizers of inequality. These scholars believed schools were instrumental in providing children from disadvantaged backgrounds with the requisite values, skills, and competencies for entering the American mainstream (Ward 1883; Small 1887; Dewey 1900; Cremin 1951). In contrast to this belief, the 1966 "Coleman Report" casts statistical doubt upon the emancipating ability of American public schools.

The report concluded that there was a powerful correlation between a child's family background and his/her achievement in school—that is to say, that "the relation of a child's family background to his achievement is a relationship stronger than any school factors."[3] The "Coleman Report" implied that a child born to impoverished parents was unlikely to escape the grip of poverty through schooling.

However, the school factors to which the "Coleman Report" referred were the quantifiable "non-personal resources in the school," like teacher salaries, library books per student, age of the buildings, and so on. One could summarize the major finding of the "Coleman Report" as follows:

> [T]he closest portions of the child's social environment—his family and his fellow students—affect his achievement the most, the more distant portion of his social environment—his teachers—affect it the next most, and the non-social aspects of his school environment affect it very little.[4]

CRITICAL THEORIES

Critical theories contribute to an understanding of why the non-personal aspects of schools, even when quantitatively abundant, affect student achievement very little. These theorists identify the social or societal mechanisms associated with schooling that function to re-create the inequality preexisting in the wider society. Critical theories range from the economically deterministic claims of Samuel Bowles and Herbert Gintis (1976) to the more culturally sensitive findings of Paul Willis (1977), Pierre Bourdieu and J. C. Passeron (1977), and Michael Apple (1985, 1988, 1990, 1996, 2000).

According to Bowles and Gintis, social reproduction theorists, schools are not great equalizers because schools re-create the social structural and authority relations of the capitalist workplace through a "hidden curriculum." There are several studies on tracking in schools that corroborate Bowles and Gintis's claims (Findley and Bryan 1970; Rosenbaum 1976; Oakes 1985; Hallinan 1987). Studies on tracking indicate that students who come from higher-income backgrounds attend schools (or are in tracks within schools) that emphasize open classrooms and higher-order reasoning abilities. Schools or tracks that serve working-class and lower-income students emphasize rules and conformity to authority. Hence, Bowles and Gintis would claim that schools are purposefully designed to re-create the inequalities inherent in capitalist social relations.

Pierre Bourdieu and Paul Willis, cultural reproduction theorists, have less Marxist and more culturally sensitive explanations of the mechanisms associated with schools that re-create inequality. Bourdieu argues that schools re-create inequality because they value the cultural capital of the dominant group or class(es) in society and systematically devalue the cultural goods of the non-dominant class(es).

By cultural capital, Bourdieu means the appreciations, language, knowledge, skills, mannerisms, and dispositions unique to a dominant social group.[5] As a consequence of the valuation of dominant group culture, students from upper-class backgrounds come to schools with the advantage of the "right" cultural capital and students from working-class or lower-income backgrounds come to schools with the disadvantage of inadequate cultural capital. In order to excel in school and not end up as an educational mortality statistic, students from non-dominant groups or class(es) have to acquire the appreciations, language, mannerisms, and so on, of the dominant class(es).

With respect to linguistic capital, Bourdieu argues that when working-class students survive in an educational system, this indicates that they have met "academic requirements as regards language"[6] (Bourdieu and Passeron 1977:73). Those students unable or unwilling—as demonstrated by Willis's study below—to make such cultural transitions fail in school. Hence, the majority of students who excel in school do not do so based upon some objective criterion like merit. Instead, they "survive" because schools legitimize, reinforce, and refine the very language skills, competencies, and other cultural assets these students inherit from their upper-class families. Hence schools are not great equalizers. On the contrary, schools re-create, legitimize, and perpetuate inequality through a systematic valuation of dominant group culture.

Whereas Bourdieu's research focuses upon students of upper-class origins, Paul Willis focuses upon students of working-class origins. Whereas Bourdieu contends that schools re-create inequality by devaluing working-class culture, Willis demonstrates how students' active attachment to working-class culture facilitates the process of social reproduction. In *Learning to Labor: How Working Class Kids Get Working Class Jobs*, Willis documents how British White male students from working-class backgrounds subvert teacher authority and engage in counter-school cultural activities. Willis argues that these "lads" are active participants in the re-creation of inequality. Willis's lads are anti-school because they, unlike the majority of their peers, do not espouse the school's achievement ideology and are proud to preserve their working-class heritage. These lads view the manual labor associated with traditional working-class opportunities as masculine and therefore superior to the mental labor of schooling, which they view as feminine. In *Ain't No Makin' It: Leveled Aspirations in a Low-Income Neighborhood* (1987), Jay Macleod delineates Willis's major findings regarding the counter-school cultural activities of the lads:

> In his study of a working-class school, Willis finds a major division between the students. The great bulk of the students are the "ear'oles" who conform to the roles defined for students, aspire to middle-class occupations, and comply with the rules and norms of the school. The counterschool culture of the "lads," in contrast, rejects the school's achievement ideology: these nonconformists boys subvert teacher and administrator authority, disrupt classes, mock the ear'oles (to whom they feel superior), and generally exploit any opportunity to "have a laff," usually at the expense of school officials. In short, the lads use whatever means possible to display their open opposition to the school.[7] (1987:17).

Willis's study demonstrates how students can be active and willing participants in the re-creation of inequality.

Like Bourdieu and Willis, Michael Apple sheds light on culture in schooling. However, he does so in less deterministic terms. His works *Education and Power* and *Ideology and Curriculum* illuminate the reproduction of inequality, not as a foregone conclusion but as a process that involves contradictory relationships between culture, economy, and the state, as well as resistance to domination and exploitation. Though various social mechanisms, like school curricula, do facilitate inequality, this process does not take place behind the back of social agents.[8] Apple's research reveals how the intricacies of ideology, curriculum, gender politics, and resistance in education are conceptualized and misrecognized as neutral when, in fact, they are political (Apple, 1985, 1988, 1990, 1996, 2000). Apple concludes, "There is, then, always a *politic* of official knowledge, a politic that embodies conflict over what some regard as simply neutral descriptions of the world and what others regard as elite conceptions that empower some groups while disempowering others (Apple 1995:345–346).

EFFECTIVE SCHOOLS RESEARCH

In response to the findings of the "Coleman Report," as well as Coleman's more recent claims that Catholic schools are more successful than public schools in leveling the differences between children from different socioeconomic backgrounds (Coleman and Hoffer 1987),[9] there has been a growing body of literature about "effective" schools. This body of research is briefly defined in chapter 8, so I will not elaborate it here. This effective schools research resurrects the early twentieth century faith in public schools as levelers of inequality. Instead of identifying the mechanisms associated with schooling that reproduce inequality, effective schools researchers enumerate the factors that allow schools to reduce the inequality preexisting in society.

SOCIAL-STRUCTURAL THEORIES

Social-structural theories link the persistent gap between black and white educational outcomes to macro-structural and macro-cultural forces instead of the more micro-structural or micro-cultural characteristics of schooling like those identified by the literature on effective schools. Research by William Julius Wilson (1978, 1987, 1996) suggests that there are two black Americas: one that is catching up with white America and another that is falling behind. Wilson argues that stable working and middle-class Black families are able to keep pace with the economic shifts that have reduced blue-collar jobs and increased white-collar jobs. These families benefited "disproportionately from policies that promote the rights of minority individuals by removing artificial barriers to valued positions."[10] Less stable working-class and lower-income Black families are trapped in inner cities that suffer from disproportionately high rates of social dislocation (for example, crime, joblessness, welfare recipiency, female-headed households, poverty, poor schools).

John Ogbu (1974, 1978, 1991) identifies the castelike treatment of Black Americans as the ultimate cause of the low school performance of Black children. The disproportionately high rate of school failure among Blacks is a reaction and adaptation to limited opportunities available to Blacks regardless of their educational credentials[11] (1974:12). Ogbu asserts that Black students are aware that even with the same educational credentials as their White counterparts, they will not be allowed equal occupational opportunities; hence, they do not work hard in school. Similar to Willis's "lads," Black students do not espouse the achievement ideology that hard work in school translates into social mobility. Black Americans are involuntary minorities who, unlike voluntary minorities, do not have a home country point of reference by which to gauge their progress. Unlike voluntary minorities, Black Americans have little expectation of economic, social, or political improvement. Black Americans realize that their social situation is not temporary but insurmountable and permanent. Therefore, education is not viewed as a viable option for social mobility.

THIS STUDY

The above theories offer sometimes inconsistent but not necessarily mutually exclusive explanations for the differences in school outcomes between Black and White Americans. This study neither definitively proves nor disproves any of the aforementioned theories. However, this book illuminates gray areas that these previous theories obscure or overlook. In support of the effective schools response to the "Coleman Report," this study ultimately argues that school factors like teacher expectations and experiences, and a positive school ethos, may be stronger determinants of student achievement than social origins and fellow students. Yet unlike much of the effective schools research, this study moves beyond the mere enumeration of effective characteristics to an illustration of why and how qualitative factors, like school ethos, are important.

I acknowledge that macro-level social-structural forces like economic shifts, dislocation, unequal occupational opportunities, and castelike subjugation render disadvantaged Black Americans more vulnerable to school failure. However, my findings suggests that Wilson and Ogbu paint with such broad structural strokes that they misrepresent the variation in perspectives and aspirations held by disadvantaged Black Americans. Similar to the past and more recent findings of Elijah Anderson (1976, 1994, 1999), this study reveals that a social group that looks monolithic from a panoramic macro-level perspective becomes socially stratified at the micro-level.

Some of my conclusions about the school failure of Black students are different from those of cultural reproduction theorists like Bourdieu and Willis. According to my interviews and field observations, the teachers, not the students, lack the cultural assets that would facilitate positive educational outcomes. And unlike Willis's "lads," and Ogbu's "involuntary minorities," the Black American students in my study espouse the achievement ideology of schooling. Furthermore, the counter-school cultural exploits of the students in my study are not linked to pride in a working- or lower-class heritage but to desires to maintain or acquire peer respect. But like reproduction theories, and other critical theories, my study indicates that when discrepancies exist between the cultural milieu or climate of a school and the cultural background of students, negative educational outcomes are likely to follow.

Unlike previous studies, this book explores a correlation, suggested by sociologists like Elijah Anderson (1990, 1994) and Douglas Glasgow (1980), between exposure to street culture and academic failure. For example, in *The Black Underclass: Poverty, Unemployment and Entrapment of Ghetto Youth*, Glasgow discusses the dissonance between the "school of the streets," which prepares inner-city youth for roles specific to the context of the streets, and the school of the American mainstream[12] (1980:10). Glasgow argues that some of the values most important to inner-city youth, especially males, ensue from or are forged by a street-oriented survival culture. This "survival culture is not a passive adaptation to encapsulation but a very active—at times devious, innovative, and extremely resistive—response to rejection and destruction."[13]

Although this book seeks cross-theoretical dialogue with the aforementioned theories, it has been guided by the research of Black scholars and writers including James Comer (1980), Janice E. Hale—formerly Hale-Benson—(1982, 1994), Jawanza Kunjufu (1986), Sara Lawrence-Lightfoot (1978, 1983), Spencer Holland (1987, 1989), Gloria Ladson-Billings (1994); Lisa Delpit (1995), and, most recently, Ann Ferguson (2000). These scholars have contributed to a growing body of literature that analyzes the cultural dissonance between mainstream schools and Black students.

Hale describes this dissonance in terms of Eurocentric pedagogy and curricula that are culturally inappropriate for African-American children whose learning styles are steeped in West African tradition and heritage. Kunjufu, focusing more specifically upon Black male children, describes this dissonance in terms of a school-curricular status quo that subtly and overtly resists alteration to meet the unique needs of Black boys. Holland advocates the use of Black male role models as teaching assistants in school districts where Black male failure is disproportionately high and teachers are predominantly White and female. Ladson-Billings illuminates the qualities and characteristics of teachers who facilitate academic excellence for Black students. Delpit describes this cultural dissonance in terms of well-intentioned school officials whose views of poor children and children of color are misinformed by stereotype. Delpit explains that the regard that many educators have for other peoples' children is a paternalistic, condescending one, it is a regard devoid of respect and consideration of these other peoples' world views. Ferguson analyzes how Black male students are socially constructed as "bad boys" within the disciplinary structure of schooling. She contends that within schools, "just as children [are] tracked into futures as doctors, scientists, engineers, word processors, and fast-food workers, there [are] also tracks for some children, predominantly African American and male, that [lead] to prison."[14]

I find the research of these scholars comparable to my own. Like these scholars and critical theorists like Michael Apple, I question why the perspectives of teachers, parents, and researchers of color are seldom included in debates about what was good for children of color.[15] However, this book adds one more group to the ranks of those who are traditionally excluded from educational debates: the perspectives of students. In a nutshell, this book probes previous theories, original field observations, and student interviews to gain new theoretical insight into the persistent gap between black and white educational outcomes. More specifically than previous studies, I focus upon the discrepancies between strategies for surviving inner city streets and strategies for excelling in urban schools.

Notes

FOREWORD

1. Michael W. Apple, *Official Knowledge: Democratic Education in a Conservative Age* (New York: Routledge, 2000).
2. Dance's book can be seen as part of a long line of books on youth agency and the politics of youth culture, beginning with Paul Willis, *Learning to Labour* (New York: Columbia University Press, 1981). The way in which we often pathologize youth is nicely discussed in Nancy Lesko, *Act Your Age!* (New York: Routledge, 2001).
3. Gloria Ladson-Billings, *The Dreamkeepers* (San Francisco: Jossey-Bass, 1994).
4. See, for example, Linda McNeil, *Contradictions of School Reform* (New York: Routledge, 2000) and David Gillborn and Deborah Youdell, *Rationing Education* (Philadelphia: Open University Press, 2000). I have analyzed much of this research in Michael W. Apple, *Educating the "Right" Way: Markets, Standards, God, and Inequality* (New York: Routledge, 2001).
5. Raymond Williams, *Resources of Hope* (New York: Verso, 1989).

PREFACE

1. This meeting took place on August 6–10, 1999, at the Hilton Chicago and Towers and the Hilton Palmer House Hotel in Chicago, Illinois.
2. This session was organized by Gail E. Thomas of Soka University of America and Walter R. Allen of the University of California in Los Angeles. Walter R. Allen was also the presider. The panelists included Stephan and Abigail Thernstrom, Melvin E. Thomas, Sharon Collins, and Joe R. Feagin.
3. Apple 2000:21.
4. Apple 2000:22.
5. I do not recall the exact words I used, but this quote captures the gist of what I said and the dialect in which I spoke.

INTRODUCTION

1. One supplemental, after-school program, the Paul Robeson Institute, is a collaboration between the Boston public school system and Concerned Black Men of Massachusetts. This program held classes on Saturday mornings from 9:00 A.M. to 12:00 P.M. The students at the Paul Robeson Institute (or Boston program) are all Black males who are third, fourth, fifth, sixth graders enrolled in the Boston public school system as well as seventh and eighth graders who return as alumni. These boys are predominantly from single-parent households in Roxbury, Mattapan, and Dorchester. During my first year of field observations, approximately sixty students were enrolled in the Boston program. During my second and third years of observations, the enrollment jumped to over a hundred students.

   The students in the second group are participants in an after-school program sponsored by Cambridge Community Services and the Cambridge public school system. In a few cases, friends of students in the Cambridge program were interviewed. This program held classes on Tuesdays and Thursdays from 2:30 P.M. to 4:30 P.M. The Cambridge group is composed of fifty-four students mixed by race and gender: 44% girls, 56% boys; 56% Black, 31% White, 11% Latino, 2% Asian. The majority of the students in the Cambridge program are Black and Latino males. The students in the Cambridge group are seventh, eighth, ninth, and tenth graders who come primarily from low-income households in Cambridge.

2. John Lofland, *Analyzing Social Settings: A Guide to Qualitative Observation and Analysis* (Belmont, CA: Wadsworth Publishing), 1.

3. See, for example, William Foote Whyte, *Street Corner Society: The Social Structure of an Italian Slum* (Chicago: University of Chicago Press, 1943); Elijah Anderson, *A Place on the Corner* (Chicago: University of Chicago Press, 1976); Sara Lawrence-Lightfoot, *The Good High School: Portraits of Character and Culture* (New York: Basic Books, 1983); Gary Alan Fine, *With the Boys: Little League Baseball and Preadolescent Culture* (Chicago: University of Chicago Press, 1987).

4. Pitrim A Sorokin, *Social and Cultural Mobility* (New York: Harper, 1927); Pierre Bourdieu and J. C. Passeron, *Reproduction in Education, Society, and Culture* (London: Sage Publications, 1977); Samuel Bowles and Herbert Gintis, *Schooling in Capitalist America: Educational Reform and the Contradictions of Economic Life* (New York: Basic Books, 1976); Paul Willis, *Learning to Labor: How Working Class Kids Get Working Class Jobs* (New York: Columbia University Press, 1977); Henry A. Giroux, *Theory and Resistance in Education: A Pedagogy for the Opposition* (New York: Bergin and Garvey Publishers, 1983); James Coleman, *Equality and Achievement in Education* (Boulder: Westview Press, 1990); Lisa Delpit, *Other People's Children: Cultural Conflict in the Classroom* (New York: The New Press, 1995); Ann Arnett Ferguson, *Bad Boys: Public Schools in the Making of Black Masculinity* (Ann Arbor: University of Michigan Press, 2000).

5. Bourdieu and Passeron 1977; Bowles and Gintis 1976; Giroux 1983; Willis 1977.

6. Jonathan Kozol, *Savage Inequalities: Children in America's Schools* (New York: Crown Publishers, 1991), 5.

7. Patricia Hill Collins, *Fighting Words: Black Women and the Search for Justice* (Minneapolis: University of Minnesota Press, 1998), 115–120, 278.

8. Glasgow 1981:1; Wilson 1996; Anderson 1999.

9. The students are real, but their names are pseudonyms.

10. Anderson 1994:82.

11. See, for example, Paulo Freire, *Pedagogy of the Oppressed* (New York: Continuum Publishing Company, 1970); Henry A. Giroux, *Theory and Resistance in Education: A Pedagogy for the Opposition* (New York: Bergin and Garvey Publishers, 1983); Michael Apple, *Education and Power* (Boston: Ark Paperbacks, 1985); Herbert Kohl, *"I Won't Learn From You" And Other Thoughts on Creative Maladjustment* (New York: The New Press, 1994); Philippe Bourgois, "Confronting Anthropology, Education, and Inner-City Apartheid," *American Anthropologist* 98(2)(1996), 249–265. See also Philippe Bourgois, *In Search of Respect: Selling Crack in El Barrio* (Cambridge: Cambridge University Press, 1994); and Robin D. G. Kelley, *Yo' Mama's DisFUNKtional: Fighting the Culture Wars in Urban America* (Boston: Beacon Press, 1997).

12. Portraiture is an approach to social scientific observation that embraces both art and science The science of portraiture derives from interviews, field observations, and other qualitative assessments of social actors and phenomena. The art of portraiture is not an artistic license to engage in fictional portrayals of social reality. Instead, it involves an acknowledgment that as one engages in social scientific portrayals of reality, "one's personal style, temperament, and modes of interaction are central ingredients of successful work" (Lightfoot, 1983:370). In other words, instead of pretending that s/he can obtain unbiased and purely objective data, a portraitist is "cognizant of the interventionist quality of [her/his] work and assume[s] responsibility for establishing the boundaries of interaction and exchange" (id., 372). See also Sara Lawrence-Lightfoot and Jessica Hoffman Davis, *The Art and Science of Portraiture* (San Francisco: Jossey-Bass 1997).

13. Henry A. Giroux and Peter McLaren, *Critical Pedagogy: The State and Cultural Struggle* (New York: State University of New York Press, 1989), xiii.

ONE: THERE ARE NO AGENTS HERE

1. Sucheng Chan, *Asian Americans: An Interpretive History* (New York: Twayne Publishers, 1991).
2. For the most part, I use "Black Americans" and "African Americans" interchangeably. However, "African American" is a more specific and politically correct racial-ethnic category that refers to the descendants of Africans who were enslaved and relocated to the territory presently known as the United States.
3. Joe R. Feagin and Clairece Boother Feagin, *Race and Ethnic Relations* (New Jersey: Prentice-Hall, 1996); Fergus M. Bordewich, *Killing the White Man's Indian: Reinventing Native Americans at the End of the Twentieth Century* (New York: Anchor Books, 1996); Robert F. Berkhoffer, Jr., *The Whiteman's Indian: Images of the American Indian from Columbus to the Present* (New York: Vintage, 1978); Jeanne Guillemin, *Urban Renegades: The Cultural Strategy of American Indians* (New York: Columbia University Press, 1975), 4.
4. See Richard Herrnstein, "IQ," *Atlantic Monthly* (September 1971). Reprinted in *The Bell Curve Debate: History, Documents, Opinions* (New York: Time Books, 1995); William H. Tucker, *The Science and Politics of Racial Research* (Urbana: University of Illinois Press, 1994); Charles Murray, *Losing Ground: American Social Policy, 1950–1980* (New York: Basic Books, 1984); Richard J. Herrnstein and Charles Murray, *The Bell Curve: Intelligence and Class Structure in American Life* (New York: The Free Press); Kenneth Clark, *Dark Ghetto: Dilemmas of Social Power* (New York: Harper and Row, 1965); Oscar Lewis, *A Study of Slum Cultures: Backgrounds for La Vida* (New York: Random House, 1968); Daniel Moynihan, "The Tangle of Pathology," *Social Stratification: Class, Race, and Gender in Sociological Perspective,* edited by David B. Grusky (Boulder: Westview Press, 1994); William Julius Wilson, *The Truly Disadvantaged: The Inner City, the Underclass and Public Policy* (Chicago: University of Chicago Press, 1987), 3.
5. Bordewich, 1996; H. W. Hertzberg, *The Search for an American Indian Identity* (New York: Syracuse University Press, 1971), 20–21; S. Stuckey, *Slave Culture* (1987), 42–46.
6. John Ogbu, "Minority Status and Literacy in Comparative Perspective," *Daedalus* 119(2): 141–168 (1990). See also Roldolfo Acuña, *Occupied America: A History of Chicanos*, 3rd ed. New York: HarperCollins Publishers.
7. Chan, 1991.
8. Robert F. Spencer, et al., *The Native Americans* (New York: Harper and Row, 1965); Ulf Hannerz, *Soulside: Inquiries into Ghetto Culture and Community* (New York: Columbia University Press, 1969); Lee Rainwater, ed., *Black Experience: Soul* (Transaction Books); Matthew Snipp, *The First of This Land (The Population of the United States in the 1980s: A Census Monograph Series)*; (New York: Russell Sage Foundation, 1991); Robin D. G. Kelley, *Yo' Mama's DisFUNKtional: Fighting the Culture Wars in Urban America* (Boston: Beacon Press, 1997).
9. See also, Kelly, 1997.
10. There are growing bodies of literature on Black women and the Black middle class. Scholars who focus upon the lives of Black women include Zora Neale Hurston, Joyce Ladner, bell hooks, Bonnie Thornton Dill, Sara Lawrence-Lightfoot, Patricia Hill Collins, Toni Morrison, Carol Stack, and countless others. Scholars who focus upon the Black middle class include W. E. B. DuBois, E. Franklin Frazier, William Julius Wilson, Joe R. Feagin, Bart Landry, Sara Lawrence-Lightfoot, and countless others.
11. Kelley, 1997:22.
12. J. L. Gwaltney, *Drylongso: A Self-Portrait of Black America* (New York: The New Press, 1993), xxii.
13. Chan, 1991.
14. E. Eze, *Race and the Enlightenment* (Cambridge: Blackwell Publishers, 1997).
15. Francis Galton, "Hereditary Talents and Character," *Macmillans Magazine*, 12. Reprinted in *The Bell Curve Debate: History, Documents, Opinions.* New York: Time Books, 1995).
16. Ibid. See also Steve Selden, "Eugenics and the Social Construction of Merit, Race, and Disability," *Journal of Curriculum Studies*, 32(2):235–252.

17. Steve Selden, *Inheriting Shame: The Story of Eugenics and Racism in America* (New York: Teachers College Press, 1999).
18. Eze, 1997:95.
19. In *Inheriting Shame: The Story of Eugenics and Racism in the United States*, Steve Selden explains that the term "eugenics" was coined by Francis Galton and is derived from the Greek root that means "good in birth" (New York: Teachers College Press, 1999), xix. While some academics consider research conducted by Arthur Jensen, Richard Herrnstein, and Charles Murray to be social scientific, I view this body of works as biological determinism reminiscent of the eugenics movement instead of scientifically sound research conducted by geneticists.
20. Herrnstein, September 1971.
21. Charles Murray, *Losing Ground: American Social Policy, 1950–1980* (New York: Basic Books, 1984). See especially "Part IV: Rethinking Social Policy," 196–236.
22. Murray, 1984:224–227.
23. Herrnstein and Murray, 1994.
24. R. Jacoby and N. Glauberman, eds., *The Bell Curve Debate: History, Documents, Opinions* (New York: Time Books, 1995), ix.
25. See Clark, 1965; Lewis, 1968; Moynihan, "The Tangle of Pathology."
26. Oscar Lewis, "The Culture of Poverty," *Scientific American* 215(4)(October 1966), reproduced in *The City Reader* (London: Routledge, 1996), 219.
27. Ibid., 220.
28. Moynihan, "The Tangle of Pathology," 56.
29. Ibid.
30. Instead of works by Joyce Ladner and Carol Stack, which include and focus upon Black females in inner city communities, I have reviewed works that focus primarily upon Black males because the vast majority of my student respondents are Black males.
31. E. Liebow, *Tally's Corner: A Study of Negro Streetcorner Men* (Boston: Little, Brown and Company, 1967), 209.
32. Ulf Hannerz, *Soulside: Inquiries into Ghetto Culture and Community* (New York: Columbia University Press, 1969), 37.
33. Hannerz, 1969:183.
34. Liebow, 1967:222.
35. Ibid., 32.
36. By "decency," Anderson means a standard of conduct by which the men in his study "treat other people right," are of "strong character," and are "worthwhile to be around." See Elijah Anderson, *A Place on the Corner* (Chicago: University of Chicago Press, 1970).
37. Anderson, 1970:209.
38. Elijah Anderson, *Code of the Street: Decency, Violence, and the Moral Life of the Inner City* (New York: W. W. Norton and Company, 1999), 36.
39. Douglas Massey and Nancy A. Denton, *American Apartheid: Segregation and the Making of the Underclass* (Cambridge: Harvard University Press, 1993), 171.
40. M. K. Asante, *The Afrocentric Idea* (Philadelphia: Temple University Press, 1998).
41. Ibid., 1–2.
42. Ibid.
43. Manning Marable, ed., *Dispatches from the Ebony Tower: Intellectuals Confront the African American Experience* (New York: Columbia University Press, 2000), 165.
44. See Melba Joyce Boyd, "Afrocentrics, Afro-elitists, and Afro-eccentrics: The Polarization of Black Studies since the Student Struggles of the Sixties"; Maulana Karenga, "Black Studies Revisited"; and Molefi Kete Asante, "Afrocentricy, Race, and Reason," all in Manning Marable, 2000.
45. Ibid., 205.
46. Asante, 1998:2.
47. Asante, *The Painful Demise of Eurocentrism: An Afrocentric Response to Critics* (Trenton, NJ: Africa World Press, 1992), 2. See also Asante, "Afrocentricy, Race, and Reason," in Marable, 2000:196.
48. Asante, 1998:22.

49. See Marable, 2000.
50. Francis Cress Welsing, 1991. *The Isis Papers: The Keys to the Colors* (Chicago: Third World Press, 1991).
51. Asante, 1998:5.
52. Asante, "Afrocentricy, Race, and Reason," in Marable, 2000:200.
53. Massey and Denton, 1993: 2–3.
54. R. Sennet, *Classic Essays on the Culture of Cities* (Englewood Cliffs, NJ: Prentice-Hall, 1969).
55. Sennet, 1969:126.
56. William Julius Wilson, *The Truly Disadvantaged: The Inner City, the Underclass and Public Policy* (Chicago: University of Chicago Press, 1987), 3.
57. Wilson, 1987:56.
58. Ibid., 56.
59. See also Douglas G. Glasgow, *The Black Underclass: Power, Poverty, Unemployment and Entrapment of Ghetto Youth* (New York: Vintage Books, 1980); Anderson, 1999:36.
60. W. J. Wilson, 1987:58.
61. Massey and Denton, 1993:8.
62. Ibid., 2.
63. Joe R. Feagin and Hernán Vera, *White Racism: The Basics* (New York: Routledge, 1995); Sut Jhally and Justin Lewis, *Enlightened Racism: The Cosby Show, Audiences, and the Myth of the American Dream* (Boulder: Westview Press, 1992).
64. Jhally and Lewis, 1992:95–97.
65. By "statistical discrimination," Wilson means "employers make assumptions about the inner city black workers *in general* and reach decisions based on those assumptions before they have had a chance to review systematically the qualifications of an individual applicant." See W. J. Wilson, *When Work Disappears: The World of the New Urban Poor* (New York: Alfred A. Knopf, 1996), 136–137. I term "rugged individualism" the main point Wilson makes in chapter 6 of *When Work Disappears*: "Americans remain strongly disposed to the idea that individuals are largely responsible for their economic situation" (160).
66. Massey and Denton, 1993:165–66.
67. Clark, 1965:13. Quoted in Massey and Denton, 1993:167.
68. Ogbu, 1990:146. See also John Ogbu, *Minority Education and Caste: The American System in Cross-Cultural Perspective* (New York: Academic Press, 1978).
69. Ogbu, 1990:148.
70. Ibid.
71. Signithia Fordham and John U. Ogbu, "Black Students' School Success: Coping with the "Burden of 'Acting White,'" *The Urban Review* 18(3). 1986.
72. Ibid.
73. Anderson, 1999:36.
74. Ibid., 33.
75. Ibid.
76. Ibid., 112.
77. Ibid., 36.
78. See Charles Lane, "The Tainted Sources of 'The Bell Curve,'" *The New York Review of Books* 20 (December 1, 1994): 14–19. See also Jacoby and Glauberman, 1995.
79. Boyd, "Afrocentrics, Afro-elitists, and Afro-eccentrics: The Polarization of Black Studies since the Student Struggles of the Sixties," in Marable (2000).
80. Collins, 1998.
81. Wilson, 1996:67.
82. Ibid., 55.
83. Sara Lawrence-Lightfoot, *The Good High School: Portraits of Character and Culture* (New York: Basic Books, 1983), 10.
84. Philippe Bourgois, "Confronting Anthropology, Education, and Inner-City Apartheid," *American Anthropologist* 98(2):249–265. 1996. See also Philippe Bourgois, *In Search of Respect: Selling Crack in El Barrio* (Cambridge: Cambridge University Press, 1995).

TWO: POSTURES FORGED BY SOCIAL MARGINALIZATION

1. Richard Majors and Janet Mancini Billson, *Cool Pose: The Dilemmas of Black Manhood in America* (New York: Simon and Schuster, 1992), 2.
2. Ibid., 4.
3. Ibid., 105.
4. Ibid. For earlier research on "soul," see Lee Rainwater, ed., *Black Experience: Soul,* 2nd ed. (New Brunswick, NJ: Transaction Books, 1973).
5. Erving Goffman, *The Presentation of Self in Everyday Life* (New York: Anchor Books, 1959), 2.
6. Ibid.
7. Ibid.
8. James M. Henslin, ed., *Down to Earth Sociology* (New York: The Free Press, 1991), 102.
9. "Malik" has occurred in previous works (Dance 1995; Muller, Katz, and Dance 1999) as "Raheem." I have changed his pseudonym from "Raheem" to "Malik" to prevent him from being confused with "Raheem Porter" depicted in chapter 3 within the subsubsection "Newpaper Account #2."
10. "Ms. Johnson" is a pseudonym.
11. Letter to "Ms. Johnson" dated April 10, 1993.
12. The events depicted in this narrative about Malik are based upon my recollections that were first documented in the summer of 1996. These events took place during the spring of 1993; Malik and his maternal aunt also revisit these events during my interviews with them during the spring and summer of 1996.
13. Henry A. Giroux, *Theory and Resistance in Education: A Pedagogy for the Opposition* (New York: Bergin and Garvey Publishers, 1983), 107.
14. Ibid.
15. *Webster's New Collegiate Dictionary* (G. and C. Merriam Company, 1974), p. 1151.
16. As defined in the glossary, a "crew" is a small group of neighborhood friends who hang together and look out for or protect each other.
17. In "Cities as Places Where People Live and Work: Urban Change and Neighborhood Distress," in *Interwoven Destinies: Cities and the Nation,* ed. H. G. Cisneros (New York: W. W. Norton and Company, 1993), 81–124, John Kasarda defines poverty tracts as census tracts in which at least twenty percent of the residents live below the poverty line. Extreme poverty tracts are those tracts in which at least forty percent of the residents are in poverty. Distressed neighborhoods are census tracts "that simultaneously exhibit disproportionately high levels of poverty, joblessness, female-headed families, and welfare recipiency." Finally, severely distressed neighborhoods are tracts "that have all the characteristics of distressed tracts, plus exceptionally high rates of teenaged school dropout."
18. Ibid.
19. Douglas Massey and Nancy A. Denton, *American Apartheid: Segregation and the Making of the Underclass* (Cambridge: Harvard University Press, 1993), 20.
20. The source of figures 2.1 through 2.4 is 1990 Census Data on CD–Rom, Wessex Pro/Filer, Wessex Inc., 1993.
21. Wilson uses the term "social isolation" as both an indicator and exacerbator of social dislocation. I use this term as an exacerbator of social dislocation.
22. Jonathan Kozol, *Savage Inequalities: Children in America's Schools* (New York: Crown Publishers, 1991), 5. Also, in *Poverty and Place* (New York: Russell Sage Foundation, 1997), Paul Jargowsky identifies dilapidated, vacant, or abandoned housing as an indicator of neighborhood poverty.
23. Kasarda, 1993:85; William Julius Wilson, *The Truly Disadvantaged: The Inner City, the Underclass and Public Policy* (Chicago: University of Chicago Press, 1987); Philippe Bourgois, *In Search of Respect: Selling Crack in El Barrio* (Cambridge: Cambridge University Press, 1995).
24. For more information on Cambridge, Massachusetts, see Paul Jargoski's *Poverty and Place: Ghettoes, Barrios and the American City* (New York: Russell Sage Foundation, 1997).

25. Elijah Anderson, "The Code of the Streets," *The Atlantic Monthly* August 1994 274 (2): 86.

26. Cambridge program fieldnotes, spring 1993.

27. *A Wolf in Sheep's Clothing*, "The Choice is Yours," by Black Sheep, manufactured and marketed by PolyGram Records, Inc., New York, 1991.

28. Cambridge program fieldnotes, spring 1992.

THREE: ON BEING "HARDCORE," A "HARDCORE WANNABE," OR "HARDCORE ENOUGH"

1. M. Weber, *Economy and Society* (Berkeley: University of California Press, 1978), 20.

2. Ibid., 21.

3. Newspaper account based upon the fictional events depicted in the feature film *Menace II Society*, New Line Cinema, A Hughes Brothers Film, 1993. Because the last names of the characters were not provided in the movie, the last names used here were created by the researcher.

4. Newspaper account based upon the fictional events depicted in the feature film *Juice*, Paramount Pictures, A Moritz/Heyman Production, 1992.

5. *Boston Globe*, September, p. 1. Names and locations have been changed and dates have been omitted.

6. "Ron McHale" is a pseudonym.

7. *Menace II Society*, New Line Cinema, A Hughes Brothers Film, 1993.

8. William Julius Wilson, *The Truly Disadvantaged: The Inner City, the Underclass and Public Policy* (Chicago: University of Chicago Press, 1987); Douglas Massey and Nancy A. Denton, *American Apartheid: Segregation and the Making of the Underclass* (Cambridge: Harvard University Press, 1993).

9. W. E. fieldnotes, 11/23/92.

10. Susan Roberta Katz, "Teaching in Tensions: Latino Immigrant Youth, Their Teachers and Structures of Schooling," *Teachers College Record* 100(4)(Summer 1999):812.

11. I never asked interview questions that explored why students in the Cambridge program had a tendency to harass and ridicule students of Haitian descent. But as a volunteer teacher, I did frequently observe the harassment and I frequently reprimanded the offending students.

12. This depiction of the jacket incident is summarized from the author's fieldnotes from the Cambridge after-school program.

13. Kwon and I frequented the same martial arts school in Boston, Massachusetts.

14. "Tomni" is the nickname of the author.

15. Memo to file, 9/22/93.

16. Interview with Casper; emphasis added.

17. This narrative is retold from a memorandum to file, 12/08/92.

18. Interview with Alberta, spring 1993.

19. The omission of this fourth type of student results from my focus in conducting interviews. I typically chose to interview students who were not sheltered from the streets, since my ultimate goal was to understand the impact of street culture on schooling. This fourth group is worthy of scholarly attention. Although I generally observed sheltered students during field observations, time resources did not allow me to focus upon them in particular.

20. Max Weber, *Economy and Society*, Guenther Roth and Claus Wittich, eds. (Berkeley: University of California Press, 1978), 4. As defined by Weber, an action is a social action when it "takes account of the behavior of others and is thereby oriented in its course."

21. Some scholars might argue, with respect to Max Weber's ideal-types of authority that gangsters possess traditional authority derived from the legacies passed down from infamous gangsters. I believe this to be a tenable claim. However, students in my study viewed gangsterlike posturing as a means to establishing present-day, notorious reputations that need not be linked to tradition. A gangster earns respect because of individual acts of ruthlessness or exceptional infamy (Weber, 1978). Hence, charismatic authority is the most viable sociological concept for understanding the purpose of hard posturing.

FOUR: SOCIAL CAPITAL, CULTURAL CAPITAL, AND CARING TEACHERS

1. "Ms. Bronzic" and "Malcolm" also appear in a coauthored article: C. Muller, S. Katz, and L. Dance, "Investing in Teaching and Learning: Dynamics of the Teacher-Student Relationship from Each Actor's Perspective," *Urban Education* 34(3) (September 1999). However, in this coauthored article, "Malcolm" is identified by the pseudonym "Tony." ("Malcolm," however, is also a pseudonym: "Tony" and "Malcolm" are different pseudonyms for the same respondent.)
2. All student names are pseudonyms.
3. See Schultz, 1961; Becker, 1964; Coleman and Hoffer, 1987; Farkas, 1996.
4. Before deciding upon the label "at-risk" to describe the students in my study, I considered using the labels "non-mainstream," "underprivileged," "marginalized," and "placed-at-risk." The youths in this study are students of color from impoverished urban neighborhoods and are therefore labeled by school officials as at risk of failing in, or dropping out of, school. My research findings suggest that these students are also at risk because they are not sheltered from the negative aspects of street culture. Hence, in this chapter, I will use the terms "at-risk" and "street-savvy" interchangeably.
5. Sara Lawrence-Lightfoot, *The Good High School: Portraits of Character and Culture* (New York: Basic Books, 1983), 341.
6. Ibid., 345.
7. Ibid., 5.
8. N. Noddings, *The Challenge to Care in Schools: An Alternative Approach to Education* (New York: Teachers College Press, 1992); S. Nieto, "Lessons from Students on Creating a Chance to Dream," *Harvard Educational Review* 64(4):392–426. (Winter 1994).
9. J. S. Coleman & T. Hoffer, *Public and Private High Schools: The Impact of Communities* (New York: Basic Books, 1987).
10. G. Farkas, *Human Capital or Cultural Capital: Ethnicity and Poverty Groups in an Urban School District* (New York: Aldine De Gruyter, 1996).
11. J. S. *Foundations of Social Theory* (Cambridge: Harvard University Press, 1990).
12. Coleman and Hoffer, 1987:7.
13. P. Bourdieu & J. C. Passeron, *Reproduction in Education, Society, and Culture* (London: Sage Publications, 1971).
14. Bourdieu and Passeron, 1977; Giroux, 1983; Apple, 1985.
15. Bernstein, 1973 in Karabel & Halsey, 1977; Bernstein, 1975; Bowles & Gintis, 1976; Willis, 1977; Glasgow, 1980; Heath, 1983; Coleman, 1987; Sleeter, 1991; Fine, 1991; Nieto, 1994; Delpit, 1995; Farkas, 1996.
16. The school to which this student refers has six "houses" or schools within the high school, which are smaller academic communities or home bases for students. Each house has a different academic emphasis: mechanical, academic, and fine arts; cross-grade curriculum electives; curricular emphasis on the development of study skills; traditional curricular emphasis; collaborative learning through team-teaching, heterogeneous class groupings, and integrated studies; and leadership skills (School Course Catalog, 1995–1996).
17. Coleman, 1990:333.
18. Ibid., 306.
19. See also L. Dance, *Streetwise versus Schoolwise: The Attitudes of Urban and Inner-City Youth Towards School*, dissertation, Harvard University, 1995.
20. Coleman, 1990:302.
21. In May of 1998, I returned to Boston, Massachusetts, and spent one week observing Ms. Bronzic interact with her students in various settings including the classroom, the school auditorium, and during a field trip to the House of Blues in Cambridge, Massachusetts.
22. Fieldnotes from Ms. Bronzic's class visit, June 14, 1996. Interview with Ms. Bronzic, April 30, 1996.
23. Dennison, 1969; Rist, 1970; Leacock, 1971; Hale-Benson, 1982; Sleeter, 1991; Hale, 1994; Fordham, 1996; Kohl, 1996.
24. Delpit, 1995.
25. Interview with Ms. Bronzic, p. 5, April 30, 1996.
26. Delpit, 1995:25.

27. Coleman, 1990: 310.
28. Interview with Ms. Bronzic, April 30, 1996, 4.
29. Ibid., 3–4.
30. Interview with Ms. Bronzic, April 30, 1996, 20–21.
31. Coleman, 1990:42.
32. Bill Moyer, *A World of Ideas*, Mystic Fire Direct Video, 1987.

FIVE: MALCOLM

1. Unless otherwise indicated, all personal names in this chapter are pseudonyms.
2. When I returned to Cambridge and Boston to conduct follow-up interviews, I identified ten students from my original sample of seventy who would allow me intimate access to their life stories. Three of these students were from Boston and their stories were to be included in this book. The other seven students' stories will be told in a separate book that focuses particularly upon Cambridge students. Although I made equitable effort to interview all three of the Boston students, for reasons beyond my control, Malcolm was the only student for whom I completed a full set of parallel interviews. As I completed this book, I met with Malcolm in July of 1999 and provided a draft of this chapter for his perusal.
3. During my follow-up research for this book, I had visited the Roxbury Multi-Service Center (RMSC) on at least six or so occasions. During one of these occasions, I sat outside and took notes that would allow me to paint this building and its immediate surroundings in words. Unable to find these notes while finishing my book, I contacted Richard O'Bryant, director of the John D. O'Bryant Youth Center at the RMSC. This description is based both on my recollection and my telephone conversation with Richard on April 25, 1999.
4. Interview with Richard O'Bryant, RMSC, April 18, 1996.
5. Malcolm's quotes, vignettes, and narratives in this chapter are excerpted or derived from two follow-up interviews: the first follow-up interview was conducted on April 18, 1996, at the RMSC; the second follow-up interview was conducted at Malcolm's residence on April 30, 1996. In addition to these formal interviews, both of which lasted longer than two hours, I had several informal conversations with Malcolm by phone and in person at the Paul Robeson Institute. The vignette that appears at the end of the chapter is derived from my fieldnotes from June 8, 1996, a day when I officially tagged along with Malcolm. All of the formal interviews and observations are supplemented by countless moments of informal observation and conversations that took place over a four- to five-year period.
6. See chapter 5 for a detailed description and analysis of the Paul Robeson Institute.
7. Interview with "Steve Winfield," April 27, 1996. All direct quotes from Steve are excerpted from this interview.
8. At this point it becomes very difficult for me, a sociologist full of structural explanations and other social scientific observations, to listen to Malcolm's story. I want to shed light upon all of the complex sociological reasons that have contributed to Ronald's "crazy" mental state. I agree that Mrs. Winfield has not made matters any better, but disagree that she is the sole cause of Ronald's "craziness."
9. Later, during the month of this interview, I would share this line of questioning with Sara Lawrence-Lightfoot, one of my academic mentors for this project, and she would advise me to start biographical interviews with questions about the present like, "What did you do this morning (or yesterday)?" and gradually inquire about the past. "Present events are easier to access and they offer clearer windows to past experiences," Lawrence-Lightfoot would offer as a more productive interviewing strategy.
10. Boston City Hospital is now Boston Medical Center.
11. Malcolm's mother had progressive systemic sclerosis (PSS) or scleroderma. Scleroderma is "a chronic debilitating disease that primarily affects the connective tissue." The earliest symptoms occur in the skin. These changes consist of "symmetric, painless, swelling of the hands." As the disease progresses, the skin "becomes tight and thickened." The changes caused by scleroderma do not only affect the fingers "but also the trunk, face (producing a 'purse-string' mouth), and more proximal parts of the extremities. This disease affects con-

nective tissue throughout the body. The information in this endnote on progressive systemic sclerosis (PSS) or scleroderma is excerpted (i.e., quoted and paraphrased) from *Medicine*, Mark C. Fishman, et. al., 3rd Ed. Philadelphia: J.B. Lippincott Company, 1991.

12. Mrs. Winfield was present during my second interview with Malcolm on March 30, 1996, and my first and only interview with Steve on April 27, 1996. Although I never interviewed her individually, she volunteered information on both occasions.

13. L. J. Dance, *Streetwise versus Schoolwise: The Attitudes of Urban and Inner-City Youth Towards School*, dissertation, Harvard University, 1995.

14. The quotes and vignettes in this chapter that are told from Louis' perspective are derived from an interview with "Louis Johnsson," April 1996.

15. Louis is no longer with this girlfriend. Instead, he is happily married to a woman who regards Malcolm as her son. Furthermore, Malcolm played a roll in bringing Louis and his wife together.

16. I re-created this scenario from Malcolm's words during our interview. Then, during a follow-up research visit to Cambridge in July of 1999, I allowed him to read, critique, accept, or correct the statements I had translated into thoughts to create this narrative.

17. Follow-up interview with Malcolm in July 1999.

18. In order to more vividly capture and substantiate Malcolm's present-day high school experiences, I asked him if I could tag along with him during school time. He agreed. Then, twice, I arranged to meet him at his high school and, twice, he conveniently "forgot" our appointment. I believe that Malcolm had not fully come to understand his apathy toward school, but he did understand that his grades and in-school performance did not reflect his ability. I am convinced that Malcolm did not "forget" our appointment but that he did not want me to see and document that in his high school setting, he was not living up to the expectations or standards or legacy of the Paul Robeson Institute.

19. Wilson, 1987, 1996; Massey and Denton, 1993; Kozol, 1991; Michele Fine, 1991; MacLeod, 1987; Jenny Oakes, 1985; P. Bourdieu, 1977; P. Willis, 1977.

SIX: SHADOWS, MENTORS, AND SURROGATE FATHERS

1. While it is accurate to say that the teacher-mentors are African American, some of the boys identify as African Carribbean. Hence, I use the more general racial category of black in describing the students at the institutes. Furthermore, to distinguish the teachers at the institute from public school teachers, I will interchangeably refer to them as teacher-mentors or as mentors. All names are pseudonyms. A version of this chapter appears in article form as "Shadows, Mentors, and Surrogate Fathers: Effective Schooling as Critical Pedagogy for Inner-City Boys," by L. Janelle Dance, *Sociological Focus* 34(4): 399–415, October/November 2001.

2. Interview with R. O'Bryant, 01/19/95.

3. Document from Paul Robeson Institute information packet for the 1992/1993 school year.

4. Ibid.

5. PRI fieldnotes, 10/24/92, page 3.

6. "Hotep" is a West African word for "peace." The men at the institute use this word whenever they want the boys to come to attention.

7. "Harambee" is Swahili for "let's pull together."

8. "Nguzo Saba" is Swahili for "the seven principles of Kwanzaa." Kwanzaa is an African-American holiday, celebrated from December 26—January, developed by Dr. Maulanga Karenga. The seven principles are umoja (unity), kujichagulia (self-determination), ujima (collective work and responsibility), ujamaa (cooperative economics), nia (purpose), kuumba (creativity), and imani (faith).

9. PRI Fieldnotes, 11/07/92.

10. PRI Fieldnotes, 10/24/92, p. 1.

11. Interview with Malcolm, Spring 1993.

12. PRI Fieldnotes, 10/18/93, p.4.

13. "I Am a Proud Young Black Man," written on April 7, 1990, by Keith Crawford, M.D., member of Concerned Black Men of Massachusetts, Inc.
14. Aage Sørensen, "Schools and the Distribution of Educational Opportunities," *Research in Sociology of Education* 8: 3–26; David Lee Stevenson et al., "Sequences of Opportunities for Learning," *Sociology of Education* 67 (July 1994):184–198.
15. PRI Fieldnotes, 10/3/92, p. 2.
16. Ibid.
17. PRI Fieldnotes, 10/31/92, p. 3.
18. PRI Fieldnotes, 10/24/92, p. 1.
19. PRI Fieldnotes, 10/24/93, p. 2.
20. Ibid.
21. PRI Fieldnotes, 11/14/92, p. 1.
22. Interview with Malcolm, spring 1993.
23. Interview with Ronell, 08/13/94.
24. Interview with Kogee, 08/11/94.
25. Interview with Kogee, 08/13/94.
26. Interview with Kogee and Bill, spring 1993.
27. During the Rites of Passage (graduation ceremony) of the institute in June 1994, I handed out approximately sixty surveys to parents. Eighteen surveys were returned. And although middle-class parents (family income of $40,001 or more) account for less than fifteen percent of the parents at the institute, they accounted for thirty-eight percent of the surveys returned. Working-class parents (family income of $20,001 to $40,000) accounted for forty-four percent of the surveys returned. Lower-income parents (family Income of less than $15,000) only accounted for eleven percent of the surveys returned. However, my findings about parent attitudes are the result of a combination of field observations, interviews, and surveys. Several parents provided useful feedback about the most appropriate types of questions to include in the surveys.

SEVEN: FEAR OF THE DARK

1. This event took place in the fall of 1993. I never wrote fieldnotes about this because I was off duty as a sociologist when this event took place. However, I told and retold this story frequently, as an example of how some people would jump to conclusions about street-savvy students. Just this past summer (1999), I was visiting the residence of two of my "little brothas"—both of whom were in my car that evening when that driver hit my car—and we revisited this event.
2. Pierre Bourdieu quoted in Henry A. Giroux, *Theory and Resistance: A Pedagogy for the Opposition* (New York: Bergin and Garvey, 1983), 87. Pierre Bourdieu defines "symbolic violence" as the dominant group imposition of icons or symbols or meanings that are culturally arbitrary in origin but masquerade and are experienced as legitimate. These symbols and meanings are experienced as legitimate because the dominant group in society that imposes them controls various educational mechanisms—formal and informal—that produce and reproduce these symbols and meanings. (See Pierre Bourdieu and Jean Claude Passeron, *Reproduction in Education, Society and Culture* (London: Sage Publications, 1977.)
3. Three of my mentees needed academic assistance, so I located college or graduate students who provided tutorial assistance; I assisted two of them with college applications, driving one of them to a community college to which he had applied, been accepted, and wanted to attend but did not know how to proceed.
4. Glasgow, 1980; Liebow, 1967; Morrison, 1992; Anderson, 1990, 1994, 1999; Feagin and Vera, 1995) , Wilson, 1996; and Russell, 1998.
5. See "Cruising Chevrolet History," at www.chevrolet.com/history/heritage.htm, 1999 General Motors Corporation.
6. See also Thomas Byrne Edsall and Mary D. Edsall, *Chain Reaction: The Impact of Race, Rights, and Taxes on American Politics* (New York: W. W. Norton, 1991); Winthrop Jordan,

The White Man's Burden: Historical Origins of Racism in the United States (New York: Oxford University Press, 1974); Joel Kovel, *White Racism: A Psychohistory,* rev. ed. (New York: Columbia University Press, 1984); Martín Sánchez Jankowski, *Islands in the Streets: Gangs and American Urban Society* (Berkeley: University of California Press, 1991); Patricia Williams, *The Alchemy of Race and Rights: Diary of a Law Professor* (Cambridge, MA: Harvard University Press, 1991). For an example of a similar phenomenon in Great Britain, see Stuart Hall et al., *Policing the Crisis* (New York: Holmes and Meier, 1978).

7. Joe R. Feagin, & Hernán Vera, *White Racism: The Basics* (New York: Routledge, 1995), 122.
8. Feagin and Vera, 1995: 24, 26.
9. Ibid., 26, quoted from Wilkerson, "Seeking a Racial Mix, Dubuque Finds Tension," Section 1, p. 1.
10. Ibid., 26.
11. Ibid., 84.
12. Ibid., 63, quoted from Jerry Thomas, "Mission Hill Wants Action over Searches," *Boston Globe,* February 9, 1990, Metro/Region, p.1.
13. Ibid., 124.
14. On her own behalf, Sister Souljah explained, "I was just telling the writer that . . . if a person would kill their own brother, or a baby in a drive-by, or a grandmother, what would make white people think that [he] wouldn't kill them too?" Quoted from *Newsweek,* "Rap and Dance," June 29, 1992, p. 46.
15. Feagin and Vera, 1995:126.
16. Katheryn Russell, *The Color of Crime: Racial Hoaxes, White Fear, Black Protectionism, Police Harassment, and Other Microaggressions* (New York: New York University Press, 1998), xiv, 89.
17. Feagin and Vera, 1995: 68.
18. Ibid., 1995: 68.
19. Russell, 1998:3.
20. Ibid., 72–75.
21. Ibid., 79.
22. Charles Laurence, "Yes, they might kill her . . ." *The Daily Telegraph,* January 18, 1995, p. 21.
23. Barbara Vobejda, "Smith's Kin Apologize to Blacks; Accused Mother's Tale Sparked Resentment," *The Washington Post,* November 9, 1994, p. A8.
24. Russell, 1998:71.
25. Ibid.
26. Laurence, January 18, 1995, p. 21.
27. Feagin and Vera, 1995:68.
28. Ibid., 68–69.
29. Russell, 1998:22.
30. Alex Kotlowitz, quoted from *Media Matters* (videorecording). PBS Premiere: October 1, 1999. Arnold Labaton and Daniel B. Polin, Executive Producers. © 1999, ATV Associates, Inc.
31. Ibid.
32. Richard Roeper, quoted from *Media Matters* (videorecording). PBS Premiere: October 1, 1999. Arnold Labaton and Daniel B. Polin, Executive Producers. © 1999, ATV Associates, Inc.
33. Ibid.
34. For a thoughtful discussion of media coverage and inner-city residents, see Jankowski, 1991: 284–309.
35. Ibid., 302.
36. "Interview Uhura with Nichelle Nichols," *Star Trek The Magazine,* November 1999, pp. 14–22. The fuller name Niota Uhura—niota means "star" in Swahili—resulted from conversations between Gene Roddenberry, the executive producer of *Star Trek* and Nichelle Nichols, the actress who played Lt. Uhura.
37. *Star Trek, Deep Space Nine,* "The Abandoned," Episode 52 (Production No. ST:DS9 452),

Airdate 10/31/94, © 1994 by Paramount Pictures; based upon "*Star Trek*" created by Gene Roddenberry.

38. By the way, the infant and preadolescent actors are noticeably—I dare say, noticeable to anyone with significant exposure to people of color, especially African Americans—different shades of brown.

39. I conducted this focus group in class (Sociology 699Q, Department of Sociology, University of Maryland at College Park) on October 4, 1999. Students completed brief surveys immediately following their in-class viewing of *Star Trek, Deep Space Nine*, Episode 52 (Production No. ST:DS9 452). Then the students grouped themselves in smaller groups of two to three people and discussed the episode. I suggested that, for the sake of discussion, the groups should be gender- and race-specific but I allowed students to group themselves. All but one of these smaller groups were gender-specific, three were race-specific, none were composed entirely of international students. Finally, following the small group discussion, I asked each small group to report their findings to the entire class.

40. "International student" is the official designation given to students at the University of Maryland who are not citizens of the United States. Due to the small sample of international students in my graduate seminar, in lieu of providing specific national origins, I employ this designation here to ensure these students' anonymity.

41. Quoted from a Survey/Questionnaire (SOCY 699Q) on "The Abandoned" administered in class on October 4, 1999, the Department of Sociology, University of Maryland, College Park.

42. Quoted from a Survey/Questionnaire (SOCY 699Q) on "The Abandoned" administered in class on October 4, 1999, the Department of Sociology, University of Maryland, College Park.

43. See Feagin and Vera, 1995.

44. Toni Morrison, *Playing in the Dark: Whiteness and the Literary Imagination*. (Cambridge: Harvard University Press, 1992), 5.

45. Carrie Dowling, "Smith never doubted wife's carjack tale," *USA Today*, November 16, 1994, p. 1A.

46. Feagin and Vera, 1995: 7.

47. Wilson, 1987, 1996; John Kasarda, 1993; Massey and Denton, 1993; Kozol, 1991; Oakes, 1985; and a host of others.

48. Dana Y. Takagi, *The Retreat from Race: Asian American Admissions and Racial Politics* (New Brunswick, NJ: Rutgers University Press, 1992), 13. And, to those familiar with the works of sociologist Max Weber, yes, I am making a Weberian claim that ideals or ideology and social structure go "hand in hand."

EIGHT: POLICY IMPLICATIONS FOR *INDIVIDUALS* IN POSITIONS OF INFLUENCE

1. Maxine Greene, *Releasing the Imagination: Essays on Education, the Arts, and Social Change* (San Francisco: Jossey-Bass Publishers, 1995), 10.

2. Greene, 1995: 10. The full quote reads, "Whatever the precise vantage point, seeing schooling small is preoccupied with text scores, 'time on task,' management procedures, ethnic and racial percentages, and accountability measures, while it screens out the faces and gestures of individuals of actual living persons."

3. Ibid., 10–11.

4. William Julius Wilson, *When Work Disappears: The World of the New Urban Poor* (New York: Alfred A. Knopf, 1996), 164.

5. Peter Cookson, *The Struggle for the Soul of American Education* (New Haven: Yale University Press, 1994).

6. See Ward, 1883; Dewey, 1900; Cremin, 1951.

7. J. S. Coleman and T. Hoffer, *Public and Private High Schools: The Impact of Communities* (New York: Basic Books, 1987), 3.

8. Bowles and Gintis, 1976; Cookson and Persell, 1985.

9. M. G. Fullan, *The New Meaning of Educational Change*. 2nd ed. (New York: Teachers College Press, 1991), 4.

10. J. R. Bliss, W. A. Firestone, and C. E. Richards, eds., *Rethinking Effective Schools: Research and Practice* (New Jersey: Prentice-Hall, 1991).
11. See studies by Weber, 1971; Edmonds 1979, 1989; Benjamin 1981; Comer, 1980; Moody, 1982; and Lightfoot, 1983.
12. Purkey and Smith, 1983.
13. Karweit, 1986, from Jaynes and Williams, 1989:361.
14. Jaynes and Williams, 1989: 361, emphasis added.
15. Gloria Ladson-Billings, *The Dreamkeepers: Successful Teachers of African American Children* (San Francisco: Jossey-Bass Publishers, 1994).
16. Lisa Delpit, *Other People's Children: Cultural Conflict in the Classroom* (New York: The New Press, 1995), 167.
17. Delpit, 1995:167.
18. Fox Butterfield, *All God's Children: The Bosket Family and the American Tradition of Violence* (New York: Alfred A. Knopf, 1995), 276.
19. Butterfield, 1995:10.
20. D. Hawkins, J. Laub, and J. L. Lauristsen, "Race, Ethnicity and Serious Juvenile Offending," in *Serious and Violent Juvenile Offenders: Risk Factors and Successful Interventions,* Rolf Loeber and David P. Farrington, eds. (London: Sage Publications, 1998), 37.

APPENDIX: A BRIEF REVIEW OF SELECTED LITERATURE

1. For an elaboration of the deficiencies of culture-of-poverty explanations, see William Julius Wilson, *The Truly Disadvantaged: The Inner City, the Underclass, and Public Policy* (Chicago: University of Chicago Press, 1987), 3–19.
2. See "The Tainted Sources of '*The Bell Curve*'" *The New York Review of Books* 41 (20)(December 1, 1994):14–19.
3. James Coleman, *Equality and Achievement in Education* (Boulder: Westview Press), 73.
4. Ibid., 74.
5. Bourdieu's use of the concept "cultural capital" typically connotes the cultural goods unique to the bourgeois class, for example, high culture (Bourdieu in Karabel and Halsey, 1977). But he also uses the term "cultural capital" more generally to connote cultural goods (Bourdieu and Passeron, 1977). With this latter usage of the concept "cultural capital," Bourdieu acknowledges that the dominant class could be based upon some other "cultural arbitrary" other than capitalism.
6. Bourdieu and Passeron, 1977:3.
7. Jay Macleod, "Ain't No Makin' It: Leveled Aspirations in a Low-Income Neighborhood" (Boulder, CO: Westview Press, 1987), 17.
8. See also Michael Apple, *Official Knowledge: Democratic Education in a Conservative Age* (New York: Routledge, 2000).
9. J. S. Coleman and T. Hoffer, *Public and Private High Schools: The Impact of Communities* (New York: Basic Books, 1987).
10. Wilson, 1987:147.
11. John Ogbu, *The Next Generation: An Ethnography of Education in an Urban Neighborhood* (New York: Academic Press, 1974), 12.
12. Douglas Glasgow. *The Black Underclass: Power, Poverty, Unemployment and Entrapment of Ghetto Youth* (New York: Vintage Books, 1980), 10.
13. Glasgow, 1980: 25.
14. Ann Arnett Ferguson, *Bad Boys: Public Schools in the Making of Black Masculinity*, p. 2.
15. Lisa Delpit, *Other People's Children: Cultural Conflict in the Classroom* (New York: The New Press, 1995), xvi.

Glossary of Social Scientific Terms and Concepts

When noted, the following terms are defined using three dictionaries of sociology, Oxford (OX), Harper-Collins (HC), and Blackwell (BW). These dictionary definitions have usually been reworded to render them more accessible. In other cases, the author defined terms based upon her own general knowledge of sociological concepts (LJD).

acculturation   Similar to the term "assimilation," the process by which a member of the subordinate group becomes integrated within the dominant host society. (OX)

agency   Human action. (OX) The ability of an individual to act or think independently, even though the action may be constrained or influenced by social forces, structures, or institutions. (LJD)

charismatic authority   Attributed to social theorist Max Weber, this type of authority (of three ideal-types) refers to leadership based on extraordinary personal characteristics or abilities. The other types of authority are legal-rational (authority based upon formally enacted rules, laws, or norms that have been codified) and traditional authority (based upon legacies and long-standing traditions that are not codified but have been passed down. (BW) An individual has charismatic authority when others view that individual as possessing exceptional or superhuman qualities that warrant deference and respect. (LJD)

critical theory   A body of work, which can be traced back to a group of scholars typically identified as members of the Frankfurt School; that identifies the social or societal mechanisms predisposed to re-create inequality. Critical theories elucidate these mechanisms as a means to eliminating them and alleviating inequality and injustice. (LJD)

cultural norms   A shared expectation of social behavior that implies what is considered culturally desirable and appropriate. (OX)

cultural capital   Inherited or acquired linguistic codes, dispositions, tastes, modes of thinking, norms and other social artifacts, as well as other types of social competencies deemed as legitimate by the dominant group or groups in society. (LJD) This concept, cultural capital, derives from the works of Pierre Bourdieu. Through a dominant group's ability to define the language, norms and tastes, artifacts, and the like that comprise cultural capital, this group also has the ability to establish hegemony. (HC)

dissonance   Tension produced as a result of competing or opposing thoughts, attitudes, or actions. (HC)

dyadic   (DYAD) Social interaction between two elements/persons. (HC)

economically deterministic   A critique of social theory that contends that economic systems determine social relations. (BW)

effective schools research   Research findings on schooling that reveals the qualitative characteristics of schools that matter more than family background in facilitating positive educational outcomes. (LJD)

emergent phenomena   (*Emergent properties*) Any phenomena or properties, which were previously not a part of group dynamics, that flow anew from the group and synthesize into a new form. (LJD, see also OX)

empathetic gaze   The ability of a teacher (or other individual) to see themselves, their legacies and destinies in the eyes of those they teach. The ability to relate, empathetically, to another individual. (LJD) This concept is borrowed from the works of Sara Lawrence-Lightfoot.

essentialist   One who believes in an absolute truth. (HC) Claims that definitions, properties, or ethnic attributes of an individual or social group are the result of genetic, biological, and psychological differences. (LJD)

ethnic cultural devaluation   An ethnocentric view that one culture is superior to another. In the United States mainstream, Eurocentric culture is valued and considered superior, and the cultures of U.S. ethnic minorities are devalued and considered inferior. (LJD)

ethnography   More commonly referred to as a fieldwork, this research technique includes direct observation of individuals and/or groups and the production of a comprehensive written description. (OX) This type of research attempts to understand individuals or groups on their own terms rather than on the terms of the researcher. (LJD)

ethos   A community of values or shared principles and practices that guide and inspire a social or cultural group, organization, or institution. (LJD)

formal economy   Market work, or more specifically, occupations and industries listed among official employment and market statistics. (OX) Informal economic activities that are legal and regulated by the state. (LJD)

hegemony   The ideological and cultural domination of one social group over another through control of cultural forms and major institutions. (HC)

human capital   Knowledge, skills, educational training, and other capabilities acquired by individuals that enhance economic productivity. (LJD)

ideal generalizations/categories   (IDEAL-TYPE) attributed to Max Weber; an abstract model that is used as the standard for comparison. (BW) Ideal-types are derived from empirical, social scientific observation of phenomena and they delineate essential and reliable characteristics. (LJD)

insider bias   Competencies, knowledge, or wisdom about a social or cultural group that results from being a member of that group. (LJD)

macro-cultural   Pertaining to the culture of large-scale social entities like institutions, organizations, historical events, organizations, societies, nations, and the like. (LJD)

macro-structural   Pertaining to large-scale social entities like institutions, organizations, historical events, organizations, societies, nations and the like. (LJD)

micro-cultural   Pertaining to the culture derived from small-scale social entities like small groups and face-to-face interactions. (LJD)

micro-structural   Pertaining to small-scale social entities like individuals, small groups, and face-to-face interactions. (LJD)

monolithic   Undifferentiated, massive, and lacking diversity. (LJD)

pedagogy   The science, art, or craft of teaching. (OX)

intersectional paradigm   (INTERSECTIONALITY) In the glossary of her book *Fighting Words*, Patricia Hill Collins defines intersectionality as "An analysis claiming that systems of race, economic class, gender, sexuality, ethnicity, nation, and age form mutually constructing features of social organization." (See Patricia Hill Collins, *Fighting Words: Black Women and the Search for Justice* (Minneapolis: University of Minnesota Press, 1998).

portraiture   A social scientific method, based upon ethnographically rich interviews, field observations, and other qualitative assessments of social actors and phenomena, which acknowledges and embraces the art, science, and subjectivity involved in the research process. A portraitist does not feign absolute objectivity but, instead, is "cognizant of the interventionist quality of [her/his] work and assume[s] responsibility for establishing the boundaries of interaction and exchange." (See Sara Lawrence-Lightfoot and Jessica Hoffman Davis, *The Art and Science of Portraiture* (San Francisco: Jossey Bass Publishers, 1997).

reify   (REIFICATION) Falsely regarding an abstraction as a material, concrete thing. (OX)

scientific objectivity   (OBJECTIVITY) An absence of researcher bias in interpretation. (BW)

social action   Social behavior that "takes account of the behavior of others and is thereby oriented in its course" (see Max Weber, *Economy and Society* (Berkeley: University of California Press, 1978).

social actors/agents   Anyone who performs social action. (HC)

social capital   Interpersonal, communal, organizational, or institutional relationships (social networks and group life) between and among individuals that serve to facilitate individual accomplishments or actions that would be unattainable without such relationships. (LJD) This definition is derived from the works of James Coleman.

social dislocation   According to William Julius Wilson, measures of social dislocation include disproportionately high rates of crime, joblessness, single-parent families, and welfare recipiency. See *The Truly Disadvantaged*, p. 3

social institution   An established order that comprises rule-bound and standardized behavior patterns. (HC)

social isolation   William Julius Wilson defines this concept as "the lack of contact and sustained interaction with individuals and institutions that represent mainstream society." See *The Truly Disadvantaged*, p. 60.

social organization   The process by which social structure is created and maintained within society. (HC)

social pathology   An unhealthy condition in society. (HC)

social structure   Any recurring patterns of social action, or the arrangement of different elements within a social system or society. Social structures include kinship, economic, and political institutions as well as norms, values, and social roles. (OX)

socio-structural   See social structure.

Socratic/dialectical   (SOCRATIC METHOD) Questions designed to lead to a reexamination of fundamental beliefs. (HC)

stereotype   A generalization that is unreliable, unfounded, and exaggerated. (LJD)

street culture   Range of patterned, recurrent social interactions typical to urban and inner-city streets, from hanging out with one's peers or shooting hoops to joining gangs or crews, dealing or using drugs, and engaging in other violent, gangster or mobsterlike activities. (LJD)

street-savvy students   Urban youths who are not sheltered from the criminal aspects of street culture and, therefore, have acquired a savoir-faire about navigating urban streets. (LJD)

symbolic violence   Pierre Bourdieu defines "symbolic violence" as the dominant group imposition of icons or symbols or meanings that are culturally arbitrary in origin but masquerade and are experienced as legitimate. These symbols and meanings are experienced as legitimate because the dominant group in society that imposes them controls various educational mechanisms—formal and informal—that produce and reproduce these symbols and meanings. (See Pierre Bourdieu and Jean Claude Passeron, *Reproduction in Education, Society and Culture* (London: Sage Publications, 1977).

tautology   Redundant repetition of the same statement or meaning. (OX)

References

Acuña, R. 1987. *Occupied America: A History of Chicanos.* 3rd ed. New York: HarperCollins Publishers.

Anderson, E. 1976. *A Place on the Corner.* Chicago: University of Chicago Press.

———. 1990. *Streetwise: Race, Class, and Change in an Urban Community.* Chicago: University of Chicago Press.

———. 1994. The code of the streets. *The Atlantic Monthly,* August 1994, 274 (2):80–94.

———. 1999. *The Code of the Street: Decency, Violence, and the Moral Life of the Inner City.* New York: W. W. Norton and Company.

Apple, M. 1985. *Education and Power.* Boston: Ark Paperbacks.

———. 1988. *Teachers and Texts: A Political Economy of Class and Gender Relations in Education.* New York: Routledge.

———. 1990. *Ideology and Curriculum* (2nd ed.). New York: Routledge, Chapman, and Hall.

———. 1995. "The politics of a national curriculum." In Cookson, P. W., and Scheider, B., eds., *Transforming Schools,* 345–370. New York: Garland.

———. 1996. *Cultural Politics and Education.* New York: Teachers College Press.

———. 2000. *Official Knowledge: Democratic Education in a Conservative Age.* New York: Routledge.

Asante, M. K. 1998. *The Afrocentric Idea.* Philadelphia: Temple University Press.

Becker, G. 1964. *Human Capital.* New York: National Bureau of Economic Research.

Berkhoffer, R. F., Jr. 1978. *The Whiteman's Indian: Images of the American Indian from Columbus to the Present.* New York: Vintage Books.

Bernstein, B. 1973. Social class, language, and socialisation. In Karabel, J. & Halsey, A. H., eds. 1977. *Power and Ideology in Education.* New York: Oxford University Press. pp. 473–486.

———. 1975. *Class, Codes, and Control.* London: Routledge and Kegan Paul.

Bliss, J. R., Firestone, W. A., & Richards, C. E., eds. 1991. *Rethinking Effective Schools: Research and Practice.* New Jersey: Prentice-Hall.

Bordewich, F. M. 1996. *Killing the White Man's Indian: Reinventing Native Americans at the End of the Twentieth Century.* New York: Anchor Books.

Bourdieu, P. & Passeron, J. C. 1977. *Reproduction in Education, Society, and Culture.* London: Sage Publications.

Bourdieu, P. & Wacquant, L. J. D. 1992. *An Invitation to Reflexive Sociology.* Chicago: University of Chicago Press.

Bourgois, P. 1995. *In Search of Respect: Selling Crack in El Barrio.* Cambridge: Cambridge University Press.

———. 1996. Confronting anthropology, education, and inner-city apartheid. *American Anthropologist* 98(2):249–265.

Bowles, S. & Gintis, H. 1976. *Schooling in Capitalist America: Educational Reform and the Contradictions of Economic Life.* New York: Basic Books.

Brookover, W., et al. 1979. *School Social Systems and Student Achievement: Schools Can Make a Difference.* New York: Praeger.

Butterfield, F. 1995. *All God's Children: The Bosket Family and the American Tradition of Violence.* New York: Alfred A. Knopf.

Chan, S. 1991. *Asian Americans: An Interpretive History.* New York: Twayne Publishers.

Clark, K. 1965. *Dark Ghetto: Dilemmas of Social Power.* New York: Harper and Row.

Coleman, James S. 1987. Families and schools. *Educational Researcher* 16(6):32–38.

———. 1990. *Foundations of Social Theory.* Cambridge: Harvard University Press.

———. 1990. *Equality and Achievement in Education.* Boulder: Westview Press.

Coleman, J. S. et al. 1966. *Equality of Educational Opportunity.* Washington, DC: Government Printing Office, HEW.

Coleman, J. S. & Hoffer, T. 1987. *Public and Private High Schools: The Impact of Communities.* New York: Basic Books.

Collins, P. H. 1998. *Fighting Words: Black Women and the Search for Justice.* Minneapolis: University of Minnesota Press.

Comer, J. 1980. *School Power: Implications of an Intervention Project.* New York: Free Press.

Cookson, P. 1994. The struggle for the soul of American education. New Haven: Yale University Press.

Cookson, P. W. & Schneider, B., eds. 1995. *Transforming Schools.* New York: Garland Publishing.

Cookson, P. W, and Persell, C. 1985. *Preparing for Power: America's Elite Boarding Schools.* New York: Basic Books.

Cremin, L. 1951. *The American Common School.* New York: Bureau of Publications, Teachers College, Columbia University.

Dance, L. 1995. *Streetwise versus Schoolwise: The Attitudes of Urban and Inner-City Youth Towards School.* Dissertation, Harvard University.

———. 2001. Shadows, mentors, and surrogate fathers: Effective schooling as critical pedagogy for inner-city boys. *Sociology Focus* 34(4):399–415.

Delpit, L. 1995. *Other People's Children: Cultural Conflict in the Classroom.* New York: The New Press.

Dennison, G. 1969. *The Lives of Children: The Story of the First Street School.* New York: Vintage Books.

Dewey, J. 1900. *The School and Society.* Chicago: University of Chicago Press.

Edmonds, R. 1979. Effective schools for the urban poor. *Educational Leadership* 37:15–24.

Eze, E. 1997. *Race and the Enlightenment.* Cambridge: Blackwell Publishers.

Farkas, G. 1996. *Human Capital or Cultural Capital: Ethnicity and Poverty Groups in an Urban School District.* New York: Aldine De Gruyter.

Feagin, J. R., & Feagin, C. B. 1996. *Race and Ethnic Relations.* New Jersey: Prentice-Hall.

Feagin, J. R., & Vera, H. 1995. *White Racism: The Basics.* New York: Routledge.

Ferguson, A. A. 2000. *Bad Boys: Public Schools in the Making of Black Masculinity.* Ann Arbor: University of Michigan Press.

Findley, W. G. & Bryan, M. M. 1970. "Ability Grouping: 1970–II The Impact of Ability Grouping on Social Achievement, Affective Development, Ethnic Separation, and Socioeconomic Separation." Athens: University of Georgia Center for Educational Improvement.

Fine, G. A. 1987. *With the Boys: Little League Baseball and Preadolescent Culture.* Chicago: University of Chicago Press.

Fine, M. 1991. *Framing Dropouts: Notes on the Politics of an Urban Public High School.* Albany: State University of New York Press.

Fordham, S. 1996. *Blacked Out: Dilemmas of Race, Identity, and Success at Capital High.* Chicago: University of Chicago Press.

Fordham, S., & Ogbu, J. U. 1986. Black students' school success: Coping with the burden of 'acting white.' *The Urban Review* 18(3):176–206.

Freire, P. 1970. *Pedagogy of the Oppressed.* New York: Continuum Publishing Company.

Fullan, M. G. 1991. *The New Meaning of Educational Change.* 2nd ed. New York: Teachers College Press.

Galton, F. 1865. Hereditary talents and character. *Macmillans Magazine 12.* Reprinted in *The Bell Curve Debate: History, Documents, Opinions* (New York: Time Books, 1995).

Giroux, H. 1983. *Theory and Resistance in Education: A Pedagogy for the Opposition.* New York: Bergin and Garvey Publishers.

Giroux, H. & McLaren, P. 1989. *Critical Pedagogy: The States and Cultural Struggle.* New York: State University of New York Press.

Glasgow, D. G. 1980. *The Black Underclass: Power, Poverty, Unemployment and Entrapment of Ghetto Youth.* New York: Vintage Books.

Goffman, Erving. 1959. *The Presentation of Self in Everyday Life.* New York: Anchor Books.

Greene, M. 1995. *Releasing the Imagination: Essays on Education, the Arts, and Social Change.* San Francisco: Jossey-Bass Publishers.

Guillemin, J. 1975. *Urban Renegades The Cultural Strategy of American Indians.* New York: Columbia University Press.

Gwaltney, J. L. 1993. *Drylongso: A Self-Portrait of Black America.* New York: The New Press.

Hale (Hale-Benson), J. E. 1982. *Black Children: Their Roots, Culture, and Learning Styles.* Provo, UT: Brigham Young University Press.

———. 1994. *Unbank the Fire: Visions for The Education of African-American Children.* Baltimore: Johns Hopkins University Press.

Hallinan, M. T. 1987. *Conceptualizations of School Organization and Schooling Processes.* New York: Plenum.

Hannerz, U. 1969. *Soulside: Inquiries into Ghetto Culture and Community.* New York: Columbia University Press.

Heath, S. B. 1983. *Way with Words.* Cambridge: Cambridge University Press.

Henslin, J. M. ed. 1991. *Down to Earth Sociology.* New York: The Free Press.

Herrnstein, R. 1971. IQ. *Atlantic Monthly.* September 1971. Reprinted in *The Bell Curve Debate: History, Documents, Opinions* (New York: Time Books, 1995).

Herrnstein, Richard & Murray, C. 1994. *The Bell Curve: Intelligence and Class Structure in American Life.* New York: The Free Press.

Holland, S. H. 1987. A radical approach to educating young black males. *Education Week* 24.

———. 1989. Fighting the epidemic of failure. *Teacher Magazine*, Viewpoint.

Jankowski, M. S. 1991. *Islands in the Street: Gangs and American Urban Society.* California: University of California Press.

Jargowsky, P. A. 1997. *Poverty and Place: Ghettoes, Barrios, and the American City.* New York: Russell Sage Foundation.

Jaynes, G. D. and Williams, R. M. 1989. *A Common Destiny: Blacks and American Society.* Washington, DC: National Academy Press.

Jencks, C., et al. 1972. *Inequality: A Reassessment of the Effect of Family and Schooling in America.* New York: Basic Books.

———. 1979. *Who Gets Ahead: The Determination of Economic Success in America.* New York: Basic Books.

Jenkins, R. 1992. *Pierre Bourdieu.* London: Routledge.

Jensen, A. 1972. *Genetics and Education.* London: Macmillan.

———. 1973. *Educability and Group Differences.* New York: Harper and Row.

Jhally, S. and Lewis, J. 1992. *Enlightened Racism: The Cosby Show, Audiences, and the Myth of the American Dream.* Boulder: Westview Press.

Karabel, J. & Halsey, A. H. 1977. *Power and Ideology in Education.* New York: Oxford University Press.

Kasarda, J. D. 1993. Cities as places where people live and work: Urban change and neighborhood distress. In *Interwoven Destinies: Cities and the Nation,* ed. H. G. Cisneros, 81–124. New York: W. W. Norton and Company.

Katz, S. R. 1999. Teaching in tensions: Latino immigrant youth, their teachers and structures of schooling. *Teachers College Record* 100(4):812 (Summer 1999).

Kelley, R. D. G. 1997. *Yo' Mama's DisFUNKtional: Fighting the Culture Wars in Urban America.* Boston: Beacon Press.

Kohl, H. 1994. *"I Won't Learn From You" and Other Thoughts on Creative Maladjustment.* New York: The New Press.

Kozol, J. 1991. *Savage Inequalities: Children in America's Schools.* New York: Crown Publishers.

Kunjufu, J. 1985. *Countering the Conspiracy to Destroy Black Boys.* 3 vols. Chicago: African American Images.

Ladson-Billings, G. 1994. *The Dreamkeepers: Successful Teachers of African-American Children.* San Francisco: Jossey-Bass.

Lawrence, C. R. & Matsuda, M. J. 1997. *We Won't Go Back: Making the Case for Affirmative Action.* Boston: Houghton Mifflin Company.

Leacock, E. B. 1971. *The Culture of Poverty: A Critique.* New York: Simon and Schuster.

Lewis, O. 1968. *A Study of Slum Cultures: Backgrounds for La Vida.* New York: Random House.

Liebow, E. 1967. *Tally's Corner: A Study of Negro Streetcorner Men.* Boston: Little, Brown and Company.

Lightfoot, S. L. 1978. *Worlds Apart: Relationships Between Families and School.* New York: Basic Books.

———. 1983. *The Good High School: Portraits of Character and Culture.* New York: Basic Books.

Lightfoot, S. L. and Davis, J. H. 1997. *The Art and Science of Portraiture.* San Francisco: Jossey-Bass.

Loeber, R. & Farrington, D. P., eds. 1998. *Serious and Violent Juvenile Offenders: Risk Factors and Successful Interventions.* London: Sage Publications.

Lofland, J. 1971. *Analyzing Social Settings: A Guide to Qualitative Observation and Analysis.* Belmont, CA: Wadsworth Publishing.

Majors, R. & Billson, J. M. 1992. *Cool Pose: The Dilemmas of Black Manhood in America.* New York: Simon and Schuster.

Marable, M. ed. 2000. *Dispatches from the Ebony Tower: Intellectuals Confront the African American Experience.* New York: Columbia University Press.

Massey, D. S., & Denton, N. A. 1993. *American Apartheid: Segregation and the Making of the Underclass.* Cambridge: Harvard University Press.

McLaughlin, M. W., Irby, M. A., & Langman, J. 1994. *Urban Sanctuaries.* San Francisco: Jossey-Bass.

Morrison, T. 1992. *Playing in the Dark: Whiteness and the Literary Imagination.* Cambridge: Harvard University Press.

Moyer, B. 1987. *A World of Ideas.* Mystic Fire Direct Video.

Moynihan, Daniel P. 1965. The tangle of pathology. *The Negro Family: The Case for National Action.* Washington, DC: Office of Policy, Planning and Research, U.S. Department of Labor. Reprinted in *Social Stratification: Class, Race, and Gender in Sociological Perspective,* ed. D. B. Grusky, 556. Boulder, CO: Westview Press, 1994.

Muller, C., Katz, S. R. & Dance, L. J. 1999. Investing in teaching and learning: Dynamics of the teacher-student relationship from each actor's perspective. *Urban Education* 34(3):292–337.

Murray, C. 1984. *Losing Ground: American Social Policy, 1950–1980.* New York: Basic Books.

Nieto, S. 1994. Lessons from students on creating a chance to dream. *Harvard Educational Review* 64(4) (winter 1994):392–426.

Noddings, N. 1992. *The Challenge to Care in Schools: An Alternative Approach to Education.* New York: Teachers College Press.

Oakes, J. 1985. *Keeping Track: How Schools Structure Inequality.* New Haven: Yale University Press.

Ogbu, J. U. 1974. *The Next Generation: An Ethnography of Education in an Urban Neighborhood.* New York: Academic Press.

———. 1978. *Minority Education and Caste: The American System in Cross Cultural Perspective.* New York: Academic Press.

———. 1991. *Minority Status and Schooling: A Comparative Study of Immigrant and Involuntary Minorities.* New York: Garland.

———. 1990. Minority status and literacy in comparative perspective. *Daedalus* 119(2):141–168.

Omi, M. & Winant, H. 1994. *Racial Formation in the United States: From the 1960s to the 1990s.* 2nd ed. New York: Routledge.

Rainwater, L. 1973. *Black Experiences: Soul.* 2nd ed. New Brunswick: Transaction Books.

Rist, R. 1970. Student social class and student expectations: The self-fulfilling prophecy in ghetto education. *Harvard Educational Review* 40(3):411–451.

Rosenbaum, J. 1976. *Making Inequality: The Hidden Curriculum of High School Tracking.* New York: Wiley.

Russell, K. 1998. *The Color of Crime: Racial Hoaxes, White Fear, Black Protectionism, Police Harassment, and Other Microaggressions.* New York: New York University Press.

Schultz, T. W. 1961. Investment in human capital. In *Power and Ideology in Education,* eds. J. Karabel & A. H. Halsey. New York: Oxford University Press, 313–324.

Selden, S. 1999. *Inheriting Shame: The Story of Eugenics and Racism in America.* New York: Teachers College Press.

———. 2000. Eugenics and the social construction of merit, race, and disability. *Journal of Curriculum Studies* 32(2):235–252.

Sennet, R. 1969. *Classic Essays on the Culture of Cities.* Englewood Cliffs, NJ: Prentice-Hall.

Sleeter, C. E. 1991. *Empowerment through Multicultural Education.* Albany: State University of New York Press.

Snipp, M. 1991. *American Indians: The First of This Land (The Population of the United States in the 1980s: A Census Monograph Series).* New York: Russell Sage Foundation.

Sørensen, A. 1989. Schools and the distribution of educational opportunities. *Research in Sociology of Education* 8:3–26.

Sorokin, P. A. 1927. *Schools and Cultural Mobility.* New York: Harper.

Spencer, R. F., Jennings, J. D., et al. 1965. *The Native Americans.* New York: Harper and Row.

Spindler, G. 1963. *Education and Culture: Anthropological Approaches.* New York: Holt, Rinehart and Winston.

Stanton-Salazar, R. D. 1997. A social capital framework for understanding the socialization of racial minority children and youth. *Harvard Educational Review* 67(1):1–40.

Steinberg, S. 1995. *Turning Back: The Retreat from Racial Justice in American Thought and Policy.* Boston: Beacon Press.

Stevenson, D. L., Schiller, K. S. & Schneider, B. 1994. Sequences of opportunities for learning. *Sociology of Education* 67 (July):184–198.

Stuckey, S. 1987. *Slave Culture: Nationalist Theory and the Foundations of Black America.* New York: Oxford University Press.

Takagi, D. Y. 1992. *The Retreat from Race: Asian American Admissions and Racial Politics.* New Brunswick, NJ: Rutgers University Press.

Thernstrom, S. & Thernstrom, A. 1997. *America in Black and White: One Nation, Indivisible.* New York: Simon & Schuster.

Ward, L. F. 1924. Education as the proximate means of progress. *Dynamic Sociology* 1924 edition. New York: Appleton-Century-Crofts, Vol. 2, Ch. 14 (original edition 1883).

Weber, M. 1978. *Economy and Society.* Berkeley: University of California Press.

Whyte, W. F. 1943. *Street Corner Society: The Social Structure of an Italian Slum.* Chicago: University of Chicago Press.

Williams, P. 1991. *The Alchemy of Race and Rights: Diary of a Law Professor.* Cambridge: Harvard University Press.

Willis, P. 1977. *Learning to Labor: How Working Class Kids Get Working Class Jobs.* New York: Columbia University Press.

Wilson, W. J. 1987. *The Truly Disadvantaged: The Inner City, the Underclass and Public Policy.* Chicago: University of Chicago Press.

———. 1996. *When Work Disappears: The World of the New Urban Poor.* New York: Alfred A. Knopf.

Index